THE EMPOWERED WOMAN:
HOW TO SURVIVE *AND THRIVE* IN OUR MALE-ORIENTED SOCIETY

THE
EMPOWERED
WOMAN:
HOW TO SURVIVE
AND THRIVE
IN OUR
MALE-ORIENTED
SOCIETY

Riki Robbins Jones, Ph.D.

FELL PUBLISHERS, INC.
Hollywood, Florida

The author would like to thank the following authors and publishers for their permission to reprint the following poems and quotations:

Judith Oliver's poem "Obstacles." Used by permission of the author.

Nura Jackson's quotation about empowerment. Used by permission of the author.

Jean Baker Miller, M.D.'s quotation from "What Do We Mean By Relationships," published by the Stone Center for Developmental Services and Studies of Wellesley College. Used by permission of the author.

Nancy Friday for her quotation from the article, "The Perfect Man" by Erica Jong which originally appeared in *Playboy* Magazine. Used by permission of the author.

Carl Rogers, Ph.D.'s quotation from *On Becoming a Person* published by Houghton Mifflin Publishing Company. Used by permission of the publisher.

Lonnie Barbach's quotation from *For Each Other* published by Doubleday. Used by permission of the the publisher.

Betty Friedan's quotation from *The Feminine Mystique* published by W. W. Norton & Company. Used by permission of the publisher.

Jean Tepperman's excerpt from her poem, "Going Through Changes," reprinted from *Motive* Magazine in *Sisterhood Is Powerful* edited by Robin Morgan and published by Random House.

This publication is designed to provide accurate and authoritative information in regard to the subject matter covered. It is sold with the understanding that the publisher is not engaged in rendereing legal, accounting, or other professional service. If legal advice or other expert assistance is required, the services of a competent professional person should be sought. *From a Declaration of Principles jointly adopted by a Committee of the American Bar Association and a Committee of Publishers.*

Library of Congress Cataloging-in-Publication Data

Jones, Riki.
    The empowered woman / by Riki Jones.
        p.   cm.
    ISBN 0-8119-0652-3 $19.95
    1. Women—Psychology. 2. Self-actualization (Psychology)
I. Title.
HD1206.J64   1990
155.6'33—dc20

90–3090
CIP

Manufactured in the United States of America
AGF-PA
10 9 8 7 6 5 4 3 2 1

THIS BOOK IS DEDICATED TO
PHIL
WHO UNDERSTANDS THAT
BY EMPOWERING WOMEN
WE EMPOWER THE WHOLE HUMAN RACE

ACKNOWLEDGMENTS

I am indebted to countless people who have reached out a helping hand to me, as I worked to transform this book from a dream to a reality:

My father, Oscar Robbins, who always believed that I would be an author someday;

My mother, Harriet Robbins, who passed on to me her heritage of the written word;

My husband, Phil, who encouraged and supported me from the beginning to the end of this book;

My sons, John and Mark, who gave me the time and space that I needed to be creative;

My son, Bill, who managed to tiptoe for months, so that I could write;

My dog, Mitsy, "woman's best friend," who kept me company, while I worked;

My mother-in-law, Jean Jones, whose understanding kept me going during the rough times;

My friend, Warren Farrell, Ph.D., author of *Why Men Are The Way They Are*, who inspired me to write a book that would help women understand themselves;

My colleagues, Susan Z. Rosenthal and Jan Rich, who freely shared their knowledge about personal and professional partnerships;

My publisher Donald L. Lessne, his wife Barbara Newman and his son Steven, who had confidence in me from the moment we met;

My editor, Rona Mendelsohn, who polished my prose without sacrificing either form or content;

Artists Carol Brown Goldberg and Halyna Shafransky, and poets Judith Oliver and Nura Jackson, who described empowerment with exquisite images and words;

Harvey Sussman and Bob Ballinger, whose elegant design and accurate typesetting enhanced the text;

Sandy and Patricia Lyne, who showed me how to write poetry;

Brien Benson, Ben Dean, Ph.D., Carol Farmer, Karina Golden, Bill Houser, Ken Hughes, Allan Taber and Steve and Ellen Weiss, who critiqued the manuscript with insight and sensitivity;

Kathy Reiter, who brainstormed with me during the early stages of this project;

Judy and Bill Cowin, Helmut Lorenz, Dan Maller and Dianne Mayfield, who gave me computer assistance;

Eleanor Smeal, President of the Fund for the Feminist Majority, who taught me about the contributions of feminism;

Matina S. Horner, Ph.D., former President of Harvard's Radcliffe College, who helped me distinguish between empowerment and power;

The participants in the 1989 La Jolla Program, who taught me how people empower each other;

Jean Baker Miller, M.D. and her colleagues at the Stone Center for Developmental Services and Studies of Wellesley College, who helped me realize the importance of mutuality in relationships;

Carlotta G. Miles, M.D. and Congresswoman Connie Morella, who told me their secrets of feminine empowerment;

Maxine Atwater, June Ewing, Mary Catherine Flythe, Tammie Fowles, Janice Frey, Veronica T. Jennings, Jo Johnson, Mary MacDougall, Bracken Polk, Jerilyn Ross, Pat Shakow and Beth Wainwright, 12 empowered women who introduced me to many more;

and, most of all, the women who shared their stories about how they became empowered.

CONTENTS

PREFACE

You climbed those three big steps into the yellow schoolbus
still waving good-bye
to your teary-eyed mom as the doors closed,
separating you from her.

Standing alone in front of Kennedy Elementary,
afraid and ready to run
until the bus driver took you by the hand
and led you indoors.

Strange faces and voices
circled around your head till
tears gathered in the corners of your eyes.

You couldn't memorize numbers,
but the teacher said "can't" wasn't a word.
So by recess you were able to say,
"My phone number is 723-6413."

After lunch came the green lanterns.
You were still cutting green strips,
While everyone else was cleaning up.
As your classmates loaded the buses,
you labored on . . .
Until finally a lopsided,
but finished, green lantern hung from your hand.

At the dinner table that night
your parents asked, "How was your first big day?"
"No problem," you said. "Just can't wait until tomorrow."

Inside you knew how scary it had been:
a new place, new people, and new situations
to be faced.

Remember that first day of kindergarten
as you pack for college, get married, or find a job.
Because life is filled with those "first days."

Follow your Kindergarten Teacher's Golden Rule,
"can't is not a word," and with that
obstacles become stepping stones
which will cross any stream
If you only take the chance.

Judith Oliver
"Obstacles"

A PERSONAL NOTE
FROM THE AUTHOR

The Empowered Woman is different from every other book about women you have read. I am not a conventional feminist. Nor am I a traditional woman. My beliefs fit in none of these neat categories, which, in truth, were created by men in the first place. Do I like men? Yes. But at the same time, I am aware that they, not we, have designed the world we live in.

This book is about self-realization, not accommodation. During past decades, many words have been written about how to "succeed" in a man's world. We have been told, "Make adjustments. Compromise. Do it like men do it." But men's values are not necessarily our values. As women, we have our own priorities. The time has come for us to come to terms with who we are. Why are we unique? What gifts and talents do we have? How can we create our own special discourse? How can we find and implement our own vision in a world that is mainly oriented toward men?

For this reason, this book has been written for women, not men. Although I fervently hope that men will eventually become empowered, right now women must take the lead. It is up to us to create our own reality.

My research on feminine empowerment began in 1984. I asked myself, "Is there such a thing as feminine empowerment? If so, how are women who are empowered different from those who are not? Can any woman become empowered? If so, how?"

To answer these questions, I conducted in-depth interviews with 200 women in diverse occupations from coast to coast. White, black, Hispanic and Oriental women were all included. The majority were in their 20s, 30s, 40s and 50s; senior citizens and college students were also represented. Most of the women were straight; a few were gay. Some were well-to-do; others had average incomes and a handful were "just making it." They had grade-school educations, high school diplomas, college degrees or advanced professional training.

Out of these 200 women, I have selected approximately 50 who best embody the spirit of empowerment. These women will tell you their stories. The other women I interviewed echoed their sentiments.

What you are about to read is actually my fourth complete draft. The first three were all struggles to come to terms with, and then transcend, my own sexist values. As I wrote, I gradually became conscious of the enormous, invisible influence male-oriented society had on me, which was keeping me from expressing my own inner truth. Finding my own feminine reality was like peeling an onion—removing layer after layer until I reached its core. Altogether it took me 6 years to find myself. I hope that it will take you much less time.

The Empowered Woman is not a "self-improvement" book. No one is suggesting that you spend a few hectic, futile days trying to change yourself into someone who you are not. On the contrary, I am offering you an opportunity to look at yourself in a different way and to become who you really are. Each chapter describes one of the 13 obstacles you may encounter.

For a woman, healthy development is rooted in satisfying connections with other people. Only when you are in a two-way partnership do you realize your full potential. The key to empowerment is creating mutual, autonomous and authentic relationships. This book is full of challenging questions, thoughtful exercises, fascinating dialogues and honest personal stories, so that you will experience mutuality as you read it.

"How am I going to find the time to read *The Empowered Woman?*" you may be wondering now. Carry it with you and browse through it in the privacy of your home or office, whenever you have a few extra minutes. Afterwards you can write to me at the address on the last page, to tell me about your own unique struggle for empowerment. You are also invited to attend my **Empowered Woman**™ Seminar, when it comes to your city.

I hope that my book will give you both information and inspiration. After reading it, you will know what being empowered means to you, appreciate how important your struggle is and be moved to press on. Empowerment will be an exhilarating experience, not an agony or an obsession. Expect to feel angry or sad, as you read the parts of the book that touch you deeply. After you experience these emotions, your pain, your conflicts and your confusion—which are part of learning—will start to disappear. Although *The Empowered Woman* will not give you "all the answers," it will point you in the right direction.

As the '90s begin, it is time for us women to declare who we are, what we want and where we are going. We must find and express our true identities. We must get paid what we are worth. We must create ways to care for our children, while we are fulfilling ourselves. I myself have founded a national women's educational organization, the Network of Empowered Women (NEW), so that we can support each other, as we pursue these common goals. There is so much we can learn from each other!

I do not expect that our dilemmas will be resolved in a year, or even in a decade. But we must begin to confront them today. Let us move away from men's standards, men's lifestyles and men's values and begin to discover, create and appreciate our own.

All the women you are going to read about are real people. Their names, and other significant details, have been changed to protect their privacy. Perhaps you will agree with me that true stories are more fascinating—and far more revealing—than fiction.

THE EMPOWERED WOMAN: WHO IS SHE?

The empowered woman, who is she?
A dream, a wish, a fantasy?
No, she is you and she is me
Creating our own reality!

r. r. j.

Empowerment is different from power. In our male-oriented culture, we are all told to seek power over other people. It is better to win than to compromise. Kindness, empathy and sharing are devalued. The people who express these qualities, who are usually women, are seen as deficient. While men's values of success, control and independence are praised, the womanly value of connection with others is hidden in silence.

What does it mean to have power over someone else? You use your resources, usually money or status, to make a person do something. You have power over him or her. What do you gain? Certainly not satisfaction. We have all known powerful people who constantly need more land, houses or cars to own; more members of an audience to applaud for them; or more employees or family members to dominate. The search for power over other people through gaining material possessions, fame or authority is endless.

Empowered people, on the other hand, experience satisfaction within. They may not own any real estate or have any employees to order around, but they know who they are and what they want from life. In their relationships, they make decisions by mutual discussion, not by one person telling the other what to do. Empowered people don't speak in terms of winning or losing. Instead they talk about working together for common goals.

1

This is how poet Nura Jackson describes what empowerment means to her:

In my work as a teacher, my life as a wife and mother, and my vocation as a poet, I have come to articulate my own empowerment as *connectedness*—continually seeking connection with God, or the Inner Voice, or Nature, or Being Human, or Truth, or Love. (All these terms are comfortable for me.) Empowerment, like the word "God," is more verb than noun. It seems that the state of being strong and real is a *process* of being receptive, and of channeling what enters during receptive states into manual, sensory love. I guess that a short way of saying all this is that I am an empowered woman when I *act* out of a place of stillness, toward a desire for union.

You can be powerful, but not empowered. You can buy a million shares of stock, join the most exclusive country club in town or be in charge of 25 employees, but you may not necessarily feel close to the people around you. What you have is external control, not inner connection. You may even get the notion that your family or staff is telling you what they think you want to hear, not what they really feel.

Your subordinates are probably not comfortable with you either. They do not enjoy being told what to do or feeling insignificant compared to you. Just as you are estranged from them, they are estranged from you. Your spouse, your children and your employees all wait for the time to come when they can take power. When they do, they will most likely find that something is missing, just as you did.

Power over is a cold and lonely way of life. Have you ever met a man who told you, "I don't know why my wife left me. Everything seemed fine!" Chances are your acquaintance was the dominant person in a power-over relationship. A wife playing a power-under role often puts up until she can't stand it anymore. Then she leaves. If she stays, her relationship with her husband is dissatisfying to both of them.

Empowerment together with someone else fosters dialogue. Two people striving for honest, clear communication are creating a satisfying relationship. Power-over leads to debate. Two people arguing over an issue are each striving to win; their relationship is secondary. Which would you rather have, empowerment or power? Which do you think most women would prefer? Most of us would rather not use power as it is presently conceived and used.

Yet how do we experience mutual empowerment in a power-over culture? How can we find satisfying relationships, if we are made to feel embarrassed about needing them in the first place? How slim are our chances for success, if most of the people we want to relate to give a low priority to relationships in their own lives? Creating mutually empowering relationships is extremely difficult. As a result, many of us have become unhappy and frustrated when we fail to make empowering connections with other people.

The Two Kinds of Power-Over Relationships

Have you ever noticed that, although women are more involved in relationships than men, we get less satisfaction from our relationships? Why? Because most of us play a power-under role in power-over relationships.

There are two kinds of power-over relationships. In a *controlling relationship*, you allow yourself to be dominated by another person. In *codependency*, which is simply a different kind of power-over relationship, you focus all your energy on another person. If you are a codependent woman, you are able to give to someone else, but not to receive anything from him or her.

In controlling and codependent relationships, you listen to someone else's voice, instead of your own. Your own self is swallowed up in the relationship. These are the most common subordinate roles played by women in these power-over relationships:

Woman As Fixer: She is concerned about making things right. She wants her relationships to be stable, harmonious and pleasant. Arguments and hassles frighten her.

Woman as Pleaser: She actively tries to make someone else happy. She wants to measure up to his expectations. Criticism frightens her.

Woman as Victim: She lets herself be taken advantage of, or endures pain. She desires to preserve the relationship—at all cost. Distancing frightens her.

Woman as Puppet: She allows her partner to manipulate her. She will do whatever he wants her to do. Taking action by herself frightens her.

Woman as Martyr: She gives up her own needs and aspirations for the sake of her partner. She wants her partner to prosper, even if it is at her expense. Doing something for her own benefit frightens her.

Woman as Beggar: She offers nothing of her own and is grateful for whatever crumbs her partner throws her. She expects her partner to give her just enough to sustain her, nothing more. Confronting her feelings of worthlessness frightens her.

Every woman who plays a power-under role is afraid. Of what? No matter how she describes her fears, they all boil down to this: "If I say how I really feel and do what I really want, my partner will leave me."

The irony is that a woman who spends her life as a fixer or a victim or a martyr is often the one who exits from the relationship in the end— or who is glad, in the long run, that the relationship is over.

Consider my own experience. By the age of 25, I had received a Phi Beta Kappa key from Wellesley College and a Ph.D. from Harvard University, taught over 300 college students and published half a dozen articles. Yet I still felt completely powerless in my marriage. When my physician husband announced to me that we were moving to Florida, so *he* could take a better job, I gave up my university position and followed him. Although I loved evergreens and dry, cool weather, I found myself in a city of palm trees, heat and humidity. Five years later, when he left me and our three children under the age of 5, I was devastated.

During the two years that followed, I honestly believed that there was no way to stop the incessant phone calls and letters from my husband and his lawyers, no way to find meaningful work and no way to sell my home and return to the Northeast. Night after night, I cried myself to sleep; many nights I could not go to sleep at all. I felt overcome by inertia, discouragement, despair and negativity. Like Sisyphus, each day I rolled the proverbial stone up the hill only to see it roll down again and begin my task anew. Even though we were separated, my husband still had power over me.

Men's experience in power-over relationships has been as tragic as women's. By forcing themselves into a stereotyped dominant role, men have suffered bitterly. Preoccupied with maintaining their power in relationships, they have not been able to express their true feelings and experience intimacy. Busy striving for success, they have not had the time to relax and be themselves. Their relationships have been impoverished. Men have paid a heavy price for wielding power over other people.

Recently many feminists have also embraced a power-over position, sometimes even more zealously than their male counterparts. Women who favor "being the boss" refuse to share power together with the other people in their workplace. If they take the male hierarchical approach into their personal lives, they wield power over their husbands or lovers. Eventually these women become just as frustrated and lonely as men in power-over relationships.

So how do you become empowered? Your solution is not to let go of relationships altogether. The only way to stop being a fixer, a pleaser, a victim, a puppet, a martyr or a beggar is to create relationships where you and your partner empower each other. You need to develop and maintain your own self. You need to share your deepest desires honestly with your partner. Otherwise, you will find yourself simply switching from one kind of power-under relationship to another and playing different subordinate or dominant roles.

Empowerment: Women's Greatest Treasure

As women, we are in a male-oriented society. We are accustomed to taking orders and catering to men. Or we are used to playing dominating roles and wielding power over men. All we know is relationships where people control and are controlled. What we need is to recognize our own unique way of relating.

When women are together, we tend to collaborate and cooperate. As women, we carry within us a vitally important aspect of human experience: caring for others. Our sense of self is grounded in our relationships. This does not necessarily mean that we seek to merge with another person. In empowering relationships, we maintain our integrity. We are able to act in our own best interest. We have our own strong and consistent system of values.

Women friends can empower each other. This is how I have described my relationship with my friend Paula, in my Empowerment Journal:

Friday:
"This morning, I talked to Paula. I told her how difficult it was to start writing this book and how discouraged I was feeling about its completion. She reminded me that, just one month ago, I had had the thrilling experience of meeting my publisher and discussing how excited he and I would both be when the book was out. Then she pointed out that I had already written another book, in less time than this one.

During our conversation, she enabled me to see a glorious possibility in my life, to see the best in myself and to put my feelings into this empowering perspective. . . ."

Sunday:
"Paula called me this afternoon. She told me that the night before she had met a man whom she had found very attractive, but whom she did not feel comfortable with. I asked her to visualize herself being there with someone else whose company she enjoyed and to describe to me what was happening. She said, 'We were at the same cocktail party. He and I were standing opposite each other, holding our glasses in front of us to maintain proper social distance. All of a sudden, he put down his glass and started asking me

about myself—my interests, my likes and dislikes, my hopes and my dreams. This is how I would like my relationship with a man to be!' What Paula was describing to me was a mutually empowering relationship." . . .

Wednesday:

"Guess what I received in the mail today? A paragraph from Paula describing how our friendship has empowered her. This is what she wrote:

> I see our friendship as a rare opportunity to share the burden I carry alone. I never thought that a relationship could be empowering, but this one is. Our friendship makes my life easier. I sometimes sigh when we talk, or afterwards. I feel as if I am letting go and lightening my load. I am surprised that you have the energy to care about me. Perhaps, in doing so, you are helping me to see more of my value as a human being, and what I have to offer as a friend.

Reading this paragraph enabled me to appreciate our friendship, and myself, even more."

In our friendship, Paula and I both helped each other grow in different directions. Do you have a woman friend who empowers you, as you empower her? I hope that you have several.

Unfortunately, mutual empowerment is still the exception, rather than the rule. In most of our relationships, we allow ourselves and other people to play the dominant roles of husband, boss or parent, or the subordinate roles of wife, employee or child. Why do we go along? Perhaps we do not yet appreciate our own feminine values. What is empowerment? The answer to this question lies within you.

The Spirit of Empowerment

To fully understand what empowerment is, you have to move away from a male-oriented power-over perspective and see your relationships in a new light. You are your best self when you are with men and women who empower you. People in a mutually empowering relationship relate to each other, not as "bosses" or "underlings," but as human beings with a mutually shared purpose.

Empowerment is, in essence, a spirit. You may not be able to describe it exactly, but you can recognize it when you feel it. An empowered woman has within her a profound sense of serenity, balance and wholeness. She truly knows herself. She values herself. She is an active, rather than a passive, participant in life. Although an empowered woman has close relationships with other people, she does not let them run her life. No one "starves" her; no one "stuffs" her; she feeds herself.

What happens when you become empowered? You fully express your potential—whatever it may be. You perceive your life as a work of art created by you, with the assistance of others. Nothing is done to you, against your will, by other people. You do not "sacrifice" for the sake of others. Instead, you live in harmony with your family and friends. Your relationships make you stronger; they do not destroy you.

As a woman of the '90s, you have a wide range of choices: to marry or not to marry, to have children or to remain childless, to stay at home or to pursue a career or to combine any of these options in a unique package. There are so many possibilities. Which are right? All of them. Not to desire children is neither "selfish" nor "unfeminine." Nor is it "unliberated" to put aside a career. For an empowered woman, conforming to the standards of male-oriented society (for example, "having it all") is less important than experiencing inner peace.

Becoming empowered is not easy for women. As the supposedly "weaker" half of society, we have been taught to "put up," "shut up," appease others and—most important—not to get in touch with our own wants and needs. Once we tune into our deepest selves, we are only a short step from taking action in our own behalf. To do so is a revolutionary gesture.

To become empowered is to light a candle in your deepest soul. Before you can start on the road to empowerment, you have to undertake a difficult, somewhat painful, search for a small voice deep within you. This small voice has the potential to guide you toward life goals which fit who you really are. Every woman has her own unique empowering inner voice.

Meet Dr. Jacqueline Light: An Empowered Woman

I am sitting in the office of Dr. Jacqueline Light, a black woman psychoanalyst. A large brightly-colored poster on one wall catches my eye. A silhouetted Amazon-like woman is walking across a high tightrope, strung between two trees in a jungle. Beneath her are imaginary lions, tigers and other dangerous wild animals. I am wondering, "How will she keep herself from falling off? Will she make it safely to the other side?"

Dr. Light notices me staring at the poster. "Do you like it?" she asks. "It was a gift. Every time I think of the challenges facing today's woman, I look at it."

As I listen to Dr. Light's words, I can't help thinking, "How enormous *her* challenge must have been: as a woman of color, to have become a psychoanalyst—before the '60s!" But Dr. Light's voice does not convey bitterness or frustration; on the contrary, it is full of enthusiasm and warmth. Her tone is firm—almost motherly. Dressed in a black skirt and a bright pink blouse, she appears calm, composed and completely sure of herself. Her next remark takes me by surprise:

This is a time of struggle for white women. You are changing your history—something black women have already accomplished. White women have a great deal to learn from black women, if you will only open your eyes.

"Tell me about yourself—your own life and your own struggle."

I am fortunate to have had a good relationship with my mother. She is a strong woman who is also very feminine. My mother taught me that women have to separate the different roles they play. Your home life is separate from your work life. You cannot use the same attitudes and skills in both. It is bad to be flirtatious in the office, but it is good to be flirtatious at home. It isn't necessary to nurture a cruel boss in your office, but, if you don't nurture your husband, he won't stay around. Do you know what I mean? Dr. Light raises her voice a note, as she utters these words.

"Yes, I do."

I was even luckier to have also been influenced by my grandmother. I learned a lot from her. Most important, I learned that women have to value the role that they play. Before men can value women's role, we have to value it first. Nurturing and caretaking are an essential part of being feminine. They can't be split off, separated and doled out to other people. The people who take care of your children are the people whom they love.

From my grandmother, I also learned that people respond to a positive attitude more than they respond to a negative one. My grandmother was an empowered woman who was very sure of herself; she was also a frail woman who never mentioned her ill-health. She focused on what she had, not what she didn't have. What a role model!

"You were very fortunate."

Yes, I was. I also got a chance to observe my grandmother together with my grandfather. They didn't discuss their relationship; it was all understood. My grandmother loved her husband, and he loved her. They called each other "sweetheart" for their entire lives. She took very good care of him, and he took very good care of her. In all the years they were together, I never saw him treat her with the slightest disrespect. Not even the slightest.

I was an empowered child. I was gifted, thoughtful and extremely active. Luckily, I had parents who were willing to deal with me. In the upper-class black culture, the expectations for girls are as great—or greater—than they are for boys. Upper-class black girls never get pushed back or ignored. You are treated very much as viable people, who, in the Freudian sense, can "go and do." And you are expected to "go and do" things.

My father was a real asset, because he was very interested in my intellectual development. Empowered women usually have a supportive male somewhere in the background: a father, a teacher, a professor or a mentor. My mother took tremendous delight in my being a girl who could accomplish things; my father took tremendous delight in my mind.

I always wanted to be a doctor, even when I wasn't sure what a doctor was. Since a lot of people in my family were doctors, I wanted to be like everybody else. Around the age of 3 or 4, I used to say that I was going to be a "mommy doctor," which meant both a doctor and a mommy. And that is exactly what I became! Dr. Light gives me one of her infectious laughs. She seems to be thoroughly enjoying sharing her revelation.

"Was it difficult for you, going through medical school and taking your internship and residency? Did you encounter a lot of obstacles, because you were a woman of color?"

I never perceived any difficulties. Everybody, except my husband and my mother, said, "You can't do it." But I never thought that what these people said applied to me.

Other people were awe-struck at what I was doing. But I never thought I couldn't do it. I knew other women who had done it. All of the black women whom I grew up with accomplished things. In my black society, women were achievers: they had Ph.D.'s; they were school principals, lawyers, businesswomen, dentists or doctors. They were not *only* housewives; they were *also* housewives. Their husbands didn't oppress them; they were proud of them.

"What kind of relationship have you had with your husband?"

I married an intelligent man—someone who was willing to discuss things with me. During my entire life, I always had an intellectual relationship with men: my father and my professors. My husband and I met in college, when I was pre-med.

"So, when he met you, he knew where you were heading professionally. Did you feel that your achievements would 'threaten' him?"

His mother had a career, and he expected the same of me. Whatever kind of career I wanted was fine; it didn't threaten him. It wasn't his business. I could do whatever I wanted to do. My life belonged to me. My husband didn't believe that he had—or that he should have—control over me.

"From the moment I met you, I intuited that you would not be where you are today, if you and your husband were not partners. There is no way you could have accomplished what you have—"

—without my teammate! Right. For me, marriage is not about any kind of domination by either side; it's about being part of a team. It's about finding someone who agrees with you about what the rules are. It doesn't matter what rules you make up, as long as you make them up together.

"Do you find that many men have a dominating, power-over philosophy, which they bring into their marriages?"

A lot of women do it in reverse and attempt to dominate the men about dusting and ironing. If I were a man, I wouldn't let someone tell me I had to do these tasks, if I didn't want to do them. Teamwork is two people defining their roles together and sharing responsibilities. A house can be dirty, as long as the people in it are happy!

"If a woman wants to be part of a team, can she marry someone who doesn't fully understand what she wants—"

—but is still willing to play ball, because she is in the game? Yes. When I married my husband, I expected that we would be a team. That was where I was coming from—a black value system. I would have been amazed, confused and unaccepting of anything else.

I had grown up seeing my father encourage my mother to go back and get her Master's degree. He wanted her to get it, before she wanted to. He kept saying, "You can do it! 'So and so' did it, and you're smarter than she is." When my mother got her degree, my father flew us all up to her graduation, so we could surprise her. When she put that Master's degree robe on and marched in the graduation procession, he was very proud of her. So I thought, "That's what married couples are supposed to do."

Later, when I grew up, friends of mine would tell me that their husbands had said, "No, you can't go to law school. No, you can't finish college. There is only room for one star in this family!" I would reply, "Why can't you try out for a starring role? Who has made these rules?" Dr. Light's voice is now so loud that it completely fills the room.

She pauses for a moment. Then she resumes her conversational tone. Although there is a matriarchy in the black lower class, in the black upper and middle classes, men and women are partners. Both men and women rely heavily on education to gain a foothold. It is not so much a question of a black woman being oppressed by a black man as it is two people trying to make their way in what is often a hostile environment.

Upper- and middle-class blacks don't have the "two for one" attitude of the white upper and middle classes, that is, two people work, and one person gets ahead. In the black middle and upper classes, both people work so that both people get ahead. We don't marry a man and support him through law school, so that later on he will let us stop working and take care of us, while we take care of the children. We don't subordinate ourselves to him. That's not our model.

"Yours is a more mutual model?"

Very much more mutual. Black middle- and upper-class men and women have partnerships.

The most critical ingredient in these partnerships is respect. Not just for what each person does but for who he is and how he wants to live his life.

"There is mutual respect, as opposed to one-way respect?"

Yes. Two for two, instead of "two for one." That's a real partnership!

Empowerment Is Not Success

During our interview, Dr. Light told me that considers herself an "empowered woman." What did she mean by "empowered?" That she is a successful psychoanalyst who serves on the boards of directors of several of the area's leading private schools? No.

Empowerment has nothing to do with success as defined by men. How big your house is or how much money you make are irrelevant. A congressperson or chairperson of the board is not empowered at all if he or she accepts the standards of thought and behavior imposed by male-oriented society. You may be a housewife living in a small apartment and be a very empowered woman, if you have mutually satisfying connections with other people.

Relationships Can Be Empowering

Dr. Light did not become empowered by sitting alone in a room, or acting all by herself. She realized her full potential through her relationships with her grandmother, her mother, her husband, her children and her colleagues.

Self-empowerment is an impossibility. We become empowered through our connections with other people. Imagine yourself sitting on a chair in a room—all alone. You are searching within yourself, struggling to discover your "inner power." How far can you really go by yourself? How long can you really stay by yourself? Is personal growth really a solitary pursuit?

Sooner or later, you are going to go out of the room, or other people are going to come in. They will talk to you and act towards you in ways that will make you feel differently than you felt when you were alone. You will form some relationships in which you feel empowered; you will establish others where you feel powerless. Your self will grow or diminish, depending on what happens in your relationships.

Dr. Jean Baker Miller and Dr. Janet L. Surrey, both of Wellesley College's Stone Center for Developmental Services and Studies, have pointed out that as modern women, we have a special gift: *We can become empowered through our relationships.* Rather than dominating or submitting, we can make a two-way connection. Participating in the development of other people can be a deeply satisfying experience for us. As we empower others, we can become empowered ourselves. However, we need relationships based in mutuality, that is, relationships in which each person can encourage the other to fulfill his or her potential.

Unfortunately, you and I have grown up in a system controlled by men. We have learned that power is strength and that empowerment is weakness. We have learned that it is good to separate ourselves from other people and become "independent," in order to win the respect of others.

How often have you heard these trite phrases: "Relationships tie us down and hold us back from our career goals." "Sharing and negotiating are a waste of time." Stop for a moment and examine each of them carefully:

"Relationships tie us down and hold us back from our career goals?" Mutually empowering relationships actually foster personal growth and achievement. We hold ourselves back when we argue with, and separate ourselves from, other people.

"Sharing and negotiating are a waste of time?" Living with responsive people enables us to become our best selves. Mutually empowering relationships give us self-knowledge, as we get to know others. We also gain feelings of self-worth, inner vitality, clarity of purpose, the power to act and the desire to make more empowering connections with other people.

You may recognize some of these other catch phrases of our male-oriented culture: "being your own person," "making it on your own" and "following your own destiny." No matter what words are used, the message is that you should not become too emotionally involved with anyone. Success, the ultimate goal, is achieved by competing with other people until you reach the top. Your life is devoted to becoming someone, not being someone.

The result of viewing yourself as separate from other people is a power-over view of relationships. If you see yourself as pitted against others—striving to be better than they are—you will need to dominate them.

The truth is that none of us lives in isolation; we live in relationships. Throughout our lifetime, our selves are linked with other selves. Our most crucial tasks are to understand how we can make empowering connections now, and how we can make these links grow stronger as time passes.

Can I Really Become Empowered?

Yes. Typically, an accomplished woman has had a mutually empowering relationship with at least one other person. Each has taken an active interest in the other's growth and development. As an empowered woman, you do not have to choose between loving and achieving; on the contrary, you love and achieve better when you do both at the same time. Both women in power-over relationships, and women alone, could fulfill themselves even more with the full support of a loving partner.

"No," you may be saying. "How could I work full-time, take courses toward my Master's degree at night and still have time to be married? Besides, almost every potential partner I meet tells me that he feels 'threatened' by me."

Men who tell you that they are feeling "threatened" usually mean that they are feeling unimportant or unloved. What they are experiencing has nothing to do with how you are spending your time; it has to do with the kind of relationship you have with each other. If your relationship is mutually empowering, your partner will see your accomplishments as a source of pride and strength, not as a threat. In the next chapter, Charlotte and Carl will talk about this aspect of mutuality.

In a power-over relationship, you are expected to do what the other person wants. Period. You give him what he wants, but you don't receive what you need. Eventually, you will get tired of giving, because you are not getting any of your own needs met. The other person, who is getting all his needs met, will inevitably end up feeling "threatened," once you decide to do anything at all for yourself—even if it's going to night school twice a week! No matter how much you give to him, it will never be enough.

Unlike power-over relationships, mutually empowering relationships are supportive. No one is dominated. No one is suffocated. One person does not increase his resources at the other's expense. Instead, both people enhance each other.

In a mutually empowering relationship, you find out what matters most to your partner and you give it to him or her. He or she, in turn, discovers what you like best and does it for you. One of the women I interviewed calls it "touching each other," in a metaphorical sense.

It's not that each partner demands a great deal of attention; it's that he or she needs a special kind of caring.

For example, in my marriage, I have empowered my husband by creating a warm, loving home environment which he can return to after a hard day's work. He, in turn, has empowered me by fostering my career as a writer, so that I can look forward to a promising professional future. Because of our relationship, we both feel more alive, energetic and self-confident.

Many of the women I interviewed described to me their own mutually empowering relationships. A Hispanic woman I spoke with, who is a professor at the most prestigious university in her country, comes home from work and cooks beans and rice for her husband at 10 minutes to 12. At 1:00 in the afternoon, he gains renewed strength to return to work. He in turn helps her with their teen-age children, late in the evening when she is tired. When she wakes up in the morning, she is empowered to face the next day.

Only in a mutually empowering relationship are *both* you and the other person truly satisfied. Although neither of you may initially welcome each other's deep feelings or unsettling desires, you honestly confront them, in order to feel close to each other. What men and women want most in their relationships is to be accepted as they really are. A woman who wants to become empowered together with another person will never be lonely!

If you are in a power-over relationship, you will inevitably "rock the boat," if you decide to speak up for empowerment. This is not your fault. Power-over relationships are inherently unstable, since the person playing the power-under role is not getting his or her needs met. If the other person refuses to pay attention to what you are saying, the relationship may dissolve; if he or she listens to you, it may become stronger than ever before. You take this chance. By "rocking the boat," you may overturn the relationship—or you may move it into a safe harbor.

You neglect your own needs for honesty, acceptance and closeness at your own peril. To move out of your power-under role, you must value yourself enough that you expect to be treated as an equal. You must also learn what it feels like to be side-by-side with a partner.

Empowerment Exercises

The exercises which follow, and the others at the end of each chapter, have been designed to help you become empowered. Several types of exercises have been included, because different ones work for different women. Try each exercise once and then repeat the ones that help you turn the obstacles in *your* life into stepping stones.

1. Compare Power with Empowerment: Think of the men and women in your life who regularly tell you what to do. How do you feel about these people? Are your relationships with them fulfilling? Now consider those individuals whom you mainly dominate. What are your feelings toward them? Do you experience satisfaction in any of these relationships?

Now ask yourself, "Is there anyone in my life whom I do not control and who does not control me? If so, who is this person? Do we give each other support, comfort and renewed strength to face difficulties? If not, would I like to have a mutually empowering relationship like this?"

2. Take Charge of Your Life Right Now: After you put down this book, what will you do during the rest of the day? What will you say? Decide now to say or do something in an important relationship that will reflect who you really are. Perhaps it will be breaking out of your role, doing something that "wives don't do" or "women don't do" or "someone who is 'feminine' doesn't do." It may be expressing how you really feel (not how you are "supposed to" feel) or doing what you truly want to do (not what you think you "should" do). Remember, you can start becoming an empowered woman today!

DISCOVER THE THREE SECRETS OF EMPOWERMENT: MUTUALITY, AUTONOMY AND AUTHENTICITY

2

> *"Relationships grounded in mutuality do not lead to an increase in the activities of one individual, alone, but to the empowerment of all the people involved."*
>
> Jean Baker Miller, M.D.
> *"What Do We Mean by Relationships?"*

Where do you experience empowerment? In a *mutual* relationship where both of you maintain your *autonomy* and act *authentically*. The three secrets of empowerment are:

1. Mutuality: Two for Two, Not "Two for One"
2. Autonomy: Acting Instead of Reacting
3. Authenticity: Being Who You Are

Let's consider these secrets one at a time.

Mutuality: Two for Two, Not "Two for One"

Listen to the word, "mutuality." You can almost hear the word "two" in it. Actually mutuality comes from a Latin word which means exchanged or reciprocal. It suggests a back-and-forth relationship, where you and your partner empower each other. You give something; you get something. You are empowered together with your partner.

The opposite of mutuality is power-over. In a power-over relationship, the focus is only on one of you, not on both of you. In a mutual relationship, you are a member of a team. The relationship is for you, as well as the other person. There is room for both of you in the relationship.

Mutuality is sharing. You and your partner participate in activities—from a splendid evening at the theater to a mundane morning vacuuming rugs—together. This does not mean that you are a pair of Siamese twins. Both of you cook meals, exercise and go for walks together often, but not always. When each of you goes off alone, you enrich each other's experiences by sharing your own.

If your relationship is mutual, you care—and are cared for. Both of you nurture each other, share each other's lives and grow in the relationship. You work together to achieve goals: yours, your partner's and the ones you share in common. What you give up is far outweighed by the benefits you receive.

Each member of a partnership has a dual role: to work for his or her own benefit and also to promote the well-being of his or her partner. Both people must be able to deal with the complex demands of this dual role. Both partners must also be willing to modify their own lifeplans, if the partnership is to survive over the long term. Charlotte and Carl, a charming, well-spoken black couple in their late 40s whom I interviewed, have overcome both of these obstacles. When I asked Charlotte, "Did you and Carl develop a friendship before you got married?" she replied:

Actually, the week before our first date, I got the flu. I was in awful shape; I couldn't even wash my hair. When Carl came to pick me up, he had stitches in his foot. Here we were, both of us, in no condition to go to a dance. But we went anyway. This was the beginning of a strong friendship between us.

Two years later, we got married, after I had finished my second year of college. Carl was commissioned to go overseas.

Our conversation continued: "Charlotte, when you got married, did you tell Carl that you intended to complete your education and have a career?"

Charlotte: I think he was just as determined to have an educated, successful wife as I was to become well-educated and successful. Carl had a certain pride in me. He was the one who called up to find out where the nearest college was, after we came back from Germany!

Carl: There was no question that Charlotte should go as far as she wanted to go. In my own family, I was the first college graduate. Charlotte had 2 years of college, so it was clear that she should finish, as well. That way, we would both be able to take advantage of the better job opportunities that were open to college graduates.

"Carl, how did you feel about her working outside the home?"

Carl: Although Charlotte participated in the military wives' club, she wanted to have her own profession. She was committed to doing what she chose to do, but she was committed to helping me, too. If she needed to have a luncheon for the wives, she had one. If she needed to take off an evening from her studies to accompany me to a military event, she went.

Charlotte knew that there were certain things she could do to hurt my career, and there were certain things that she could do to enhance it. She chose to do the latter—and pursue her own profession at the same time.

Charlotte: Perhaps I put a bit too much emphasis on Carl's career, especially at the beginning. I always took pride in being a soldier's wife.

Still, in the eyes of the military, I was a bit of a renegade; I was frowned upon in some circles. But I was respected, especially after I got my degree and started teaching.

"You never based your relationship on other people's expectations?"

Charlotte and Carl in unison: "Never. We made up our own rules together."

"It sounds as if each of you were supporting each other, in your respective career goals."

Carl: No question about it, especially in view of the backgrounds we came from. My parents had given me an education, which had cost them all the money they had. Charlotte's family had sent her to college for 2 years. There was no additional money forthcoming from them. Whatever we wanted to have in the future, we would have to earn the money for it ourselves. Together we built a working relationship.

"Has it continued to this day?"

Carl: Yes. Since we have left the military, Charlotte has worked much harder on establishing her own identity. After she finished college, she did postgraduate work and then became a high school counselor. I supported her, through it all.

I used to type all of Charlotte's papers, even write a few of them. She didn't type, and I did. Sometimes she would wait to the last minute, and I would be up typing until 3:00 in the morning! But I did it.

"You weren't 'threatened' by Charlotte's having a Master's degree, when you did not?"

Carl: I really didn't need to go back to school to earn a good salary, but Charlotte did. I knew that if she was to succeed in the field of education, she needed to get her Master's. She was smart, so I encouraged her. When she did get her degree, I was really happy and proud.

Once we both had degrees we felt equal. We became a team. Actually, we were more a corporation than we were husband and wife. Because we didn't have very much, we learned to manage our money. We talked about what we wanted to do, set goals and then put our plans into motion. Then we would reach another plateau. That's how we made progress—systematically. We never thought that there were any limits to what we could do.

"How did you work things out, once you had children?"

Carl: "Charlotte wanted kids, but I didn't."

"By agreeing to have children, did you feel that you were sacrificing—getting into something that you didn't want?"

Carl: I have always thought that marriage is teamwork. If one partner wanted something, and the other person didn't, then we should discuss it and reach a compromise. So that's how we handled it. Instead of having 10 kids, we had two! He laughs.

A mutual partnership is comfortable, fulfilling and lasting. There is room for both of you to be yourselves—and to grow. You give, and you receive. When you need your partner, he or she is there for you, particularly during times of stress and sorrow. Each of you takes the time to understand and appreciate each other's lives.

Power-over relationships are tense, frustrating and destined to fail. How can you get to know yourself well, if you are always listening to your partner's voice? How can you be who you really are, if you are always doing what your partner wants you to do? How can your partner get to know the real you, if you don't know her?

Is your most important relationship a mutual one? Or is it a power-over one? To find out, consider these statements, one at a time:

My relationship is probably a power-over, rather than a mutual one, if:

1. Our friends are mainly *his* friends.
2. We usually go out to places *he* enjoys.
3. We generally have sex when and how *he* desires it.
4. If we have children, they are being raised the way *he* wants.
5. I have adopted *his* religious faith—or *his* political views.
6. I am not free to choose the career I want.
7. I do most of the household chores.
8. His mother stayed home, and his father went to work.
9. His father dominated his mother.
10. He has strong beliefs about men's and women's "proper" roles.

The more of these statements that apply to you, the greater the likelihood that the other person in the relationship has power over you.

Another way you can tell how much mutuality there is in your relationship is to ask yourself, "Does the other person cooperate with me in the daily tasks of life?" If not, then the relationship is probably not mutual.

A woman I interviewed told me about a "two-for-one" relationship she used to have:

My former husband was a lot of trouble. When I would ask him to go to the store, he would always come home with the wrong groceries! He'd complain about being stuck in traffic and how much time he had wasted. So I would say to myself, "He's no help. It's easier to get the groceries myself." When I would ask him to assist me with other tasks, he would usually forget—which would be twice as much trouble for me.

I wasn't growing; my energy was slipping. I could talk to Ray, but when I needed him to take action, he didn't. Whenever I wanted to do something or go somewhere, he always had an "overdue proposal." He said that he couldn't do what I asked, because he was burdened with worries. At first, I thought that, with all my energy, I could unburden him, and we could both have more pep and energy. But I finally realized that Ray would always have "overdue proposals."

A third way you can recognize mutuality in your relationship is by examining what you talk about. Are your conversations about both of your concerns, or do they focus mainly on one of you? If both of you talk mainly about him, your relationship is probably a power-over one. If the main subject of discussion is you, your relationship is not mutual either.

Another woman I interviewed shared her experience with this kind of relationship:

When I used to get very upset, my first husband, Andy, would send me to a psychiatrist. He would not go with me to group therapy. The whole time we were married, he would always talk about "my" problems. That's how we related. We never talked about "our" problems.

We would always talk about how I couldn't get along with my parents, although Andy had enormous difficulties getting along with his own. They divorced when he was very young, and he was forced to mediate between them. My first husband's way of dealing with his problem was to shift the focus over to me.

When I told Andy I wanted a divorce, he said, "No." I think I was really valuable to him. In order not to look at his problems, he would keep talking about mine. If I left, he would lose his smokescreen! Finally, we agreed to separate.

It is really different with my second husband, Earl. He has been a real help to me, not just someone I have to take care of. I can really talk with him. When Earl and I were engaged, we would take a 1-hour walk every evening on the oceanfront. We would discuss the littlest things—what happened to us during the day—and our future plans. We would spend so much time and take so much care to go into the smallest detail with each other.

I never did talk like that with Andy. With Andy, we talked about "me," as opposed to "us." And I put up with it; I don't know why. My relationship with Earl has been totally different from anything I have ever known before. Until we met, I was unable to experience this kind of relating. I didn't know that it was supposed to be good for me, too!

Mutuality alone will not empower you. Sometimes you want to do what you want to do; you want to be left alone; and you get tired of sharing and cooperating. For a relationship to be empowering, you must also have autonomy.

Autonomy: Acting, Instead of Reacting

Autonomy comes from a Greek word which means self-ruling. An autonomous person is not controlled by anyone else. In an autonomous relationship, you rule yourself.

In our male-oriented society, autonomy is often confused with independence. Independence, which many men consider an ideal state, is standing alone—not relying on anyone. Independent people do not need relationships. Is this realistic? Stop and think. How many truly "independent" people do *you* know?

Autonomous men and women do not want to spend their lives alone. But they do want to be their own persons. They seek mutually empowering relationships, in which they are free to disagree, express anger and distance themselves. When there is conflict, these relationships don't dissolve; they grow stronger, as both partners confront their differences and work to resolve them.

Before you can become autonomous, you must have a self. You can honestly say, "This is who I am. This is what I want. This is what I don't want." How do you express your autonomy in a relationship? By setting limits. Rather than surrendering yourself entirely to your partner, you keep your own self intact. You say to him or her, "This is what I will do in my own behalf. This is what I will do in your behalf. This is what I will not do. This is what I will do for both of us."

You are autonomous in a relationship by being pro-active. Rather than waiting for your partner to act—and then reacting—you act on your own. If there is a problem to be solved, you get the necessary information and solve it, after consulting with your partner. You do not just sit back and expect your partner to take the lead. In your conversations together, you bring up new ideas, instead of only responding to what your partner says. If there is a particular subject you want to talk about, you bring it up. You are active on behalf of yourself.

According to Dr. Jacqueline Light, a pro-active woman does not sit back and let her marriage drift. She takes definite steps to establish and preserve mutuality:

Make time for your marriage. The daily demands of your job, your children, the household, your friends and your family can be overwhelming. But you must build a solid partnership with your husband.

When you give birth to a child, you have to keep your finger not only on your own pulse but also on the pulse of the marriage. Most of the time, women forget their husbands. They get swept up in what is for them a biological miracle. After all, what is happening feels like a miracle!

Some fathers are not tuned in to having children either. Later on, after they have more self-confidence and money, they may remarry a younger woman, in order to "do it right." They want to enjoy having children, if they didn't enjoy it the first time.

"Do you think that women, whose husbands leave them for younger ones, are victims?"

If you ever allow your husband to write your marriage job description, you become a victim. You have to write your own marriage job description—one that works for both you and your husband. And many a women who was left behind didn't write hers.

Typically, she supported him emotionally, and perhaps financially, during the early years. She did not grow, but instead waited for him to graduate, so he could support her. He went to work and he grew, while she stayed home and took care of the children. Or she took a job, just to have something to do. She may have taken him for granted; she may have taken herself for granted; she may have taken the marriage for granted. She may not have paid much attention to his ego—or hers. She probably didn't know who he was seeing every day, even who he was having lunch with.

I think that often a woman doesn't "tune in" to the difficulties of being a man. She assumes that all men want to assume financial and emotional responsibility for their wives and children. The truth is, they don't. It is a dreadful burden to feel that you are responsible for all of these people in your family all of the time. Many men are not that strong. Sometimes they can't express their feelings loudly enough, and sometimes she can't hear them. Or he knows that she doesn't want to hear him. Then, one day, he says to her, "I've had enough of this. I can't handle this. I don't want this anymore."

"There is no way a man can take a sabbatical."

"So he just leaves."

"It all comes down to the quality of the relationship you have with your spouse. In many cases, the two people are not accustomed to being part of a team, really listening to each other and being involved in each other's lives."

"Exactly."

"Many women are now creating their own marriage job descriptions. Ironically, men seem to like it better."

Yes. But there are still no guarantees. A happy marriage is like a moving target. You have to move with the times. Women's roles and expectations may change every decade. You may remain married through 3, 4, 5 or 6 decades. During one of these decades, someone in his office may catch his eye. Getting to know her may seem to be an attractive experience at the time. And he may be going through a period where he needs someone to talk to—and he doesn't think about talking to you.

You have to ask questions, talk with him, "be there" for him. Go to his office. See what his life is like, when he is not with you. Let him come to your office, too. . . .

"If you are in a partnership, you will share your lives naturally."

You want to find out about the kind of life he's living, and he wants to know about yours. Both of you want to help each other out.

According to Dr. Light, you can do a great deal to create a mutually satisfying marriage by being pro-active. If you are pro-active, you do not always do exactly what your partner asks. If you decide to do something for yourself, you let him or her handle his own feelings. You are not devastated by his or her anger.

For example, your husband has invited you to meet him at a restaurant at 8:00 in the evening. Just as you are about to leave, the phone rings. It is Claire, an old friend whom you haven't heard from in a long time. You both want to talk to each other right now. At this moment, you tune out your husband's voice and listen to your own.

On the way to the restaurant, you might feel pleased that you finally set a limit as to how much you were willing to give to your husband. At the same time, you might also feel guilty for disregarding his wishes. If he were to reprimand you for being late, you could say, "Please don't be angry with me. I did what I thought was right." Then you could tell him about Claire's telephone call. After you shared your feelings honestly, he might continue to react angrily. You could receive what he says, consider it and decide later on whether or not to act differently in the future.

I do not mean that autonomous people avoid pleasing their partners. We often choose to please another person, because we enjoy it. Many empowered women I interviewed told me that they looked for opportunities to do things for their husbands and their children, because they found self-fulfillment in sharing. They expressed their true selves by pleasing others.

In a mutually empowering relationship, you and your partner are both your own persons. No matter how close you are to each other, each of you retains your identity in the relationship. Each of you is in touch with your own needs and wants. Neither of you is controlled by the other—when expressing your feelings or when making choices.

When something bothers you, you talk it over with each other freely. You are willing to listen to your partner's criticism, but not necessarily to be guided by it. Each of you has the same liberty: to decide what you need, but not to decide what your partner needs. By making your own choices, both of you empower yourselves and each other.

Both of you love and believe in each other enough to "ride the big waves" together—without either of you falling out of the boat. When you do what you need to do, you have confidence that you can deal with your partner's feelings, whatever they may be. You also trust that your partner is strong enough to handle his or her own reactions—and still stay in the relationship.

Two autonomous people are empowered together with each other; they do not control, or let themselves be controlled by, their partner. Vera experienced this kind of transformation, when she decided to become autonomous:

"Sometimes it takes a confrontation with death to get in touch with yourself," Vera remarks, as she leads me into her comfortable two-story frame house. The energetic bounce in her walk is unmistakable. As we introduce ourselves, I notice her strong, clear voice, full of enthusiasm. We sit down at her dining room table, and she continues to talk:

I got married to my husband strictly because it was the thing to do. I really didn't have a clear career goal. I was 22 years old and I had gotten this Master's degree in chemistry. I didn't really conceive of a lifelong career; nobody had ever encouraged me to go ahead and get a Ph.D. While I was in graduate school, I had met this extremely good-looking, bright and eligible chemist, 4 years older than I was, and he courted me. He was from a good family, and he was courteous and pleasant. It seemed like a good match.

I cared for Burt, but I was never intensely happy with him. I never had experienced love in grammar school, in high school or at any other time. I liked Burt a little more than I liked anybody else. So I asked myself, "Is this love?" I had read books and magazines about love and heard women say, "You'll get married, and you'll live together. True love grows." I thought, "This is what they are talking about." After all, it was much better than what my mom had. So I decided, "This is the best I can do." I married Burt. Vera shrugs her shoulders.

We had a pleasant life, but I never experienced any intense desire for sex or any joy in my profession. He became distressed if I was too ambitious. Burt was from the South and, when we really got to know each other, I found that he had a very strong belief that a married woman had to depend on her husband. Unless I truly needed him, what else would our marriage be based on? Anything I did to strengthen myself was a threat to our relationship. I had an interesting job doing chemical testing for film crews; he came to see me once or twice, but he was really ill at ease. "It just makes me feel funny to see you bossing those people around," he told me later. Yes, I was having a great time, but it was interfering with my marriage. So I quit the job.

Then we adopted Darlene. It was what you did in those days; you had children. I didn't have an intense desire for one, but it was the *McCalls* Magazine Package; having children was what you were supposed to do after you got married. This was what promised a woman happiness! Only after I had a husband and a child, and found that I still wasn't completely satisfied, could I see what was missing. But first, I had to do what I was "supposed to do." Vera gets up from her chair and opens the dining room window blinds.

When Darlene was about 2 years old, I got very sick. I developed a disease called scleroderma, which is pretty rare. It's an autoimmune disease that just destroys parts of your body. At the time I felt very ugly—and very scared. I soon learned that this particular disease could either be disfiguring or it could be fatal. If you get it through your whole system, your internal organs get scarred, and you die. As Vera says these words, she trembles.

So here I was 30 years old, in the hospital, and not knowing whether I'd be severely disfigured or dead. What I did know was that I was extremely unhappy. Up to now, I just hadn't faced up to it. While I was lying in that hospital bed, I kept asking myself, "What am I doing with my life? What am I living for?" I couldn't find any answers. I wasn't very excited about my existence; I could have died, and I wouldn't have even cared. As a matter of fact, I really didn't care about anything. Lying in that hospital bed facing death really woke me up.

A week later, the doctor said to me, "I think you're going to be okay; you don't have the disease in your internal organs. After the illness runs its course, you can have plastic surgery." I was numb. The waters had parted and I was able to pass through. I realized that I had been losing my whole life anyway, by the way I was living it. Forging forward would be easy now.

Once I got out of the hospital, I was driven toward living my own life much more completely. I started taking much better care of myself: exercising, eating health foods and getting more rest. I was amazed to discover how much energy I had! When my husband told me he was going to spend a sabbatical year as a guest lecturer at a university in New York State, I said, "Hey, if we're going to New York, why don't I do something, too?" So I got myself a job teaching freshman chemistry at a nearby college. Believe it or not, I started speaking up in bed, too. Our sex life started to improve dramatically, once I started telling Burt what I liked. My pleasure became just as important as his.

When Darlene and I spent time together, we began doing things we both liked to do, instead of always going shopping, just to please her. We went to the zoo and on nature trails—activities I had enjoyed as a child. If Darlene asked me for something I didn't want her to have, I just said "No!" I wasn't afraid of my daughter anymore.

What was different about me now? I wasn't just focusing on preserving my relationships with my husband and daughter at any cost. I started to experience passion in my own life and to seek what I desired. Finally, I started doing what was best for me. Vera smiles broadly. And I don't plan to stop!

After her illness, Vera became autonomous in her relationship with her husband. For her, it was a struggle. Why do many women find it hard to become autonomous? Because we do not yet fully appreciate our own value as human beings. We need to give own personal growth a higher priority. Every time we say to another person, "This is who I am" or "This is who I am not" or "This is what I want" or "This is what I don't want," we are creating an empowering relationship.

Are you autonomous in your relationship with your partner? To find out, answer these hypothetical questions:

1. My partner does not like one of my woman friends. Would I continue to see her?
2. There is an art exhibit which I want to attend, but my partner does not want to go. Would I go by myself?
3. Although I enjoy my job, my partner does not approve of it. Would I find another one?
4. There is a set of pots and pans on sale. I want them, but my partner thinks they are an extravagance. Would I buy them anyway?
5. My partner expresses a prejudice against a certain ethnic group. I strongly disagree. Would I speak up?

6. I prefer one political candidate; my partner prefers another. Would I vote for my choice?
7. My partner and I have different religions. Would I adopt his?
8. My partner does not like my hairstyle, but I do. Would I change it?
9. I feel uncomfortable in "frilly" clothes, but my partner likes them? Would I buy and wear "frills?"
10. Although I am high-strung, my partner tells me that he likes calm, peaceful women. Would I hold my emotions in check, even if it caused me pain?

If you are autonomous in your relationship, you will answer "yes" to questions 1, 2, 4, 5 and 6 and "no" to questions 3, 7, 8, 9 and 10.

Codependent and controlled women are not autonomous. Rather than looking at herself in a mirror, a codependent woman looks away, at someone else. She is so wrapped up in this other person that she does not take the time to discover her own self. Since she does not know who she is and what she wants, she cannot take action in her own behalf. A woman controlled by another person who has power over her is not her own boss either. She is a marionette whose strings are being pulled by a puppeteer. She is taking orders from him, rather than listening to her own voice. She may not even know what her inner voice is saying.

Authenticity: Being Who You Really Are

Authenticity is derived from a Latin word which means "create." The words "author" and "authority" are derived from the same Latin word. An author creates a book; an authority creates expertise on a particular subject; and an authentic person creates himself or herself, exactly as he or she is.

What is the opposite of authenticity? Acting or pretending. Someone who is not authentic is not being real. He or she is pretending to be someone he or she is not.

An authentic person creates himself by being himself. If you are authentic, you are in touch with how you feel, and able to express it to others. In an authentic relationship, you and your partner are real with each other. Even when it is painful, you are honest about your emotions.

Authenticity is not usually valued in our male-oriented society. We are taught to "win," "save face" and "not show weakness." Women's empowerment does not come from buying into the male-oriented model. It comes from being ourselves.

To empower yourself in a relationship, you share your true feelings—and your vulnerability. Kelley, an empowered woman stockbroker, puts it like this:

Relationship empowerment is accepting that you aren't perfect and that other people aren't either. We all play "games of pride" with each other. One person says, "I'm better," and the other person feels put down and replies, "I don't like you." Then they both wonder why they don't like each other. The best part of knowing people is understanding their weaknesses—and accepting them. If we would only say to each other instead, "I really care about you. I truly admire you. Being with you was a truly happy time for me," we would all be very empowered in our relationships.

You will never get what you want from life by yourself. So you have to start from a place of vulnerability and be able to ask for help. You have say, "I need this; I need that; please help me." If other people don't know what you need from them, they'll never give it to you and then you'll never get what you want!

Although being authentic enhances your relationships in the long run, it can cause upsets in the short run. Vera's daughter, Darlene, now 23 years old, gave me this example from her experience:

Last year, I started straightening out my relationships with my relatives. I yelled at my grandmother, something I had never done before. I told her, "This is the way I want our relationship to be. I can't stand the way it is now." I picked fights with my mom, my stepfather and my dad, so that I could get all our anger out in the open. Needless to say, I was not a particularly pleasant person to be around. But now it's all out; it's gone. My family and I haven't had a harsh word since. And I am a much calmer person.

Nora, a dynamic television marketing executive whom I interviewed, was authentic in her relationships, even though her husband was not. As she told me:

I married my husband, whom I "thought" was an engineer, while I was working in New York. It took me six years to find out that he was an agent for the CIA.

After we were married a few years, my husband started working at home. He had an office at one end of the house, which he kept locked when no one was there. One day I accidentally came home from work in the middle of the day. I walked into my husband's office to say "Hello" to his secretary. She jumped up from her desk and shouted, "Mrs. Waldman, you can't come in here!"

Now things had been happening all along that had made me wonder. My husband had been going into our savings and taking money out. He had also been receiving large cash payments from an unknown source. After this incident, I confronted him. "What are you doing with all the money, Manny?" I asked. "I can't tell you," he replied. So I said, "I want a divorce." He disappeared, with all the money, right after my son's second birthday party. That was the last time the children and I saw him for 6 years. All he left behind him was a load of bills.

How did I deal with my husband's disappearance? I realized that my husband had a problem relating to other people, but it was his problem. I always told our kids the truth. And I stayed very close with my family and friends. I never held anything back from anyone, no matter how embarrassing it was.

After her husband left, Nora became empowered in her relationships by telling the truth about herself. She was not alone in her revelation. Alexandra, who endured a much more brutal trauma, came to the identical conclusion.

Four years ago, I read about Alexandra in the local newspaper. Her story was grisly—and unforgettable. Now, upon meeting her for the first time, I am amazed that, after her harrowing experience, she is so calm. In spite of all the publicity she has received, Alexandra is a sincere and modest woman. What is extraordinary about her is her sensitivity—to her own feelings and those of others.

As Alexandra ushers me into her office, I notice how gracefully she walks, almost like a dancer. I cannot stop myself from looking into her deep hazel eyes. They emit so many messages: warmth, understanding and, above all, inner strength. Alexandra takes a deep breath and begins to speak.

Self-knowledge has always been the driving force in my life. I have always known that there is an incredible capacity within me, but I have not known how to get in touch with it and share it with others. When I was 20 years old, I decided to start psychotherapy. I have also attended many personal growth seminars and done a lot of volunteer work. It has always been important to me to have a clear picture of my "self."

Before the trauma, I never slowed down enough to face myself. It was only after the trauma that I looked within. By connecting with a deeper part of myself, I found the true source of my inner power—being authentic. I started being real with people, instead of trying to hide parts of my own self from them.

My therapist had once said to me, "Alexandra, maybe you're a little bit proud." "Me?" I replied. "I'm not a proud person!" Now I understand what she meant. To myself and others, I appeared to be nice, kind, good and loving. But I was protecting myself with a shell. Underneath that, there was a lot of pain and fear and anger—"not-so-niceness." I only wanted to accept the goodness in life and the goodness in me. Part of healing has been accepting all my feelings, including my fear and anger.

There had been signs that something was wrong within me, but I had ignored them. When I had been traveling through Europe, several strangers had made sexual advances toward me. I cowered, instead of fighting back. I didn't give in, but I didn't express my true feelings to them either. After I had returned to the States, my sister and I had been held up at gunpoint. I treated this incident casually; I did not allow myself to fully experience my fear. I said to myself, "The robbery happened; it's over; now get on with your life." It wasn't until I almost died that I had to say to myself, "Alexandra, You can't live like this anymore. You have to face yourself. You have to be real."

At 10:00 in the evening, I had gone to the supermarket to buy orange juice, to break a fast I had started 5 days before. For 120 hours, I hadn't eaten or drunk anything at all, except for a little lemonade laced with honey. I was very much into my higher self—in a place of omnipotence.

As I walked out of the store, I saw a pickup truck parked right next to my car. Its door was right next to mine. I could see that there was a man inside. My inner voice said, "Something's not okay here. Maybe you should go back to the store and ask someone to walk you to your car." Then this same voice hesitated. "Oh, they'll probably say, 'Why are you bothering me?' or something stupid like that. Besides, Alexandra, how many times in your life have you bulldozed your way through this kind of scenario and gotten out fine? Just get in your car quickly, lock the door and drive off."

Instead, when I opened my car door, the man jumped out of his pickup truck. He held a long jagged-edge knife to my throat, forced me into my car and made me drive to a motel. After he raped me twice in the motel room, he handcuffed me, gagged me, drove me to a bridge and threw me off. I fell 40 feet down into the freezing water, but I managed to kick my way to the shore. Then I crawled up 40 feet of rocks and walked 2 1/2 hours in my ice-covered clothes until I found help.

How did I get through these 5 terrifying hours? My fear was so great that I couldn't acknowledge it at the time, so I had to create a world apart from my emotions. No matter what happened, I always looked for a way out. I let my mind take over. I had an ongoing dialogue with Alexandra. After he raped me, I kept saying to myself, "He has your body, but not your soul . . ." When I was struggling for survival in the icy water, I kept saying to myself, "Kick, Alexandra, kick, kick, kick . . . ." While I was looking for help in the middle of the night, I kept saying to myself, "Keep walking, Alexandra, one foot in front of the other. Keep walking or you'll freeze to death right here on this road. . ." I find myself shivering as she says these words.

Never once did I doubt that I would escape. I always felt, "It's possible for me to get out of here." My ignorance was bliss, because the police told me later, that my chances of coming out alive were very, very slim! While I was kidnapped, there were moments when I slipped into a dream-like state, but I never actually went to sleep, because I was afraid of what this man might do to me. I prayed that I would live—I prayed a lot that night! Alexandra pauses for a moment and closes her eyes, as if she were saying a silent prayer of thanks.

Once I realized I had survived, being authentic was very important to me. When I was in the hospital, I made a decision that everyone had to know what had happened to me—my boss, my friends and the people in my spiritual community. I didn't realize it was a news event—that everyone would find out anyway. I just knew that I couldn't face other people pretending to be someone I wasn't. When people asked me how I was, I was not going to say, "Fine, thank you" or "Terrific!"

After a trauma like mine, so many people say, "I just want to go back to the way I was." But you just can't. You're not the way you were. You can't erase what happened. The best you can do is to make it part of your life, not the center of it.

I will never forget what happened to me the night of February 7, 1985. For at least 2 years you couldn't meet me on the street without my telling you about it. That was what defined me—what made me who I was. Part of my healing was allowing myself to fully experience what had happened, not to "shove it under the rug." Now I don't talk much about the trauma. I don't think about it every day, although for a long time I did.

I used to hold on very tightly to my privacy. Yes, I always had lots of friends, and lots of people in my life, but I was very much into doing it alone, doing it "my way"—being the independent '80s woman! I wasn't going to let myself and other people know how I really felt; I wasn't going to allow myself to be helped; I wasn't going to allow myself to be seen. I was going to bulldoze my way through life.

If I had met you before the trauma, I would put on a stoic face and listen to all your problems. I wouldn't let you know that anything bad had ever happened to me. After the trauma, I finally reached out. Going through the embarrassment of the trial was the most empowering event of my life. I realized that people still loved me after they saw me at what I thought was my "worst." After that, where else could I go but up?

Now I believe more than ever in honest relationships. Not that you can nave many of them; you have to choose. If you have one or two, that's enough. If you have more, that's great. Every woman needs relationships where she can totally be herself.

I pick up my tape recorder, say "Goodbye" and walk out of

Alexandra's office. A few hours later, I find myself thinking, "If I had met Alexandra before her trauma, our relationship might not have been mutually empowering at all. Since she would not have shared her problems openly, I would have thought that she was somehow superior to me. I would have tried to impress her, instead of being honest about myself. Because she shared her real self during our interview, I felt free to open up and share mine."

In our male-oriented culture, we do not learn to be authentic. We learn to cultivate the "right image." A person who plays a dominant role in a power-over relationship is always striving to appear better than the other person. To admit imperfections or mistakes, or to say "I'm sorry" or "I was wrong," would endanger the other person's illusions.

Alexandra followed a different path. She empowered herself in her authentic relationships with me, her family, her friends and her spiritual community. As she realized, when you stop pretending to be perfect and start being yourself, you may lose your power-over relationships with other people. What you gain instead is empowerment together with them.

Codependent and controlled women are not authentic. A codependent woman focuses outward on someone else, rather than inward on herself. Since she does not know her real feelings, how can she possibly share them? A controlled woman obeys someone else. Even if she knows what she is experiencing, she prefers to tell the other person what he wants to hear. She is afraid to speak her mind, because she might "disturb the peace" in the short run. What she gets is superficial, fragile harmony. She does not realize that, by listening to her own voice and sharing what it says, she will create a lasting, intimate relationship in the long run.

Are you honest in an intimate relationship? Answer each of these questions silently:

1. When my partner unintentionally says something that hurts me, do I tell him or her how I feel?
2. When I am angry at my partner, do I hide my feelings?
3. When my partner asks me my opinion, am I usually truthful?
4. Am I afraid to openly disagree with my partner ?
5. If I felt uncomfortable in front of certain mutual friends, would I share my feelings?
6. If I didn't like a gift my partner gave me, would I pretend that I did?

7. If something embarrassing had happened that was bothering me, would I tell my partner?
8. If my partner did something I strongly disapproved of, would I let him or her know?

If you answer "no" to questions 2, 4 and 6, and "yes" to all the rest, you are truly authentic with a person you love.

A New Approach to Your Relationships

What can you learn from Alexandra, Vera, Charlotte and Dr. Jacqueline Light? During the last 20 years, millions of copies of dozens of self-help books have been bought by women dissatisfied with their relationships. None of these books has confronted the basic reason for their dissatisfaction: *Most women play a power-under role in power-over relationships.* Now you know that empowering relationships are the only ones that work. Mutuality, autonomy and authenticity are the three secrets of empowerment. If this book inspires you to listen to your own voice and give up your power-under role once and for all, it may be the last "relationship book" you will ever buy.

Techniques for Listening to Your Inner Voice

Focusing and journal writing are two excellent techniques for listening to your own voice. In focusing, a technique developed by University of Chicago psychologist Dr. Eugene T. Gendlin, you sit quietly and tune into your own physical sensations. As you tune in to whatever pain, tension or pleasure you are experiencing, you begin to understand messages your body is sending you. Then you find a word or a phrase to describe how you feel. You use the word or phrase to keep on probing—to look at your concern from every angle. For example, when I began to focus, I realized that the center of my tension was in my lower back. I felt as if something heavy was pressing down on me. The word "burden" kept coming up for me. Later on, I realized that my back had been hurting because my load was too heavy. I had taken on too many responsibilities.

Keeping a journal can also help you tune into your feelings. As you write, you become aware of the words and phrases you use to describe your experiences. For example, while I was experiencing lower back pain, I kept writing the word "paralyzed." I began to understand that I was feeling overwhelmed, even incapable of taking action, by heavy responsibilities I had at the time. When used together, focusing and journal writing can give you incredible insights into your own self.

Empowerment Exercises

1. *Keep an Empowerment Journal:* Get a notebook to record your empowering experiences. If you prefer to speak, rather than to write, you may prefer to use a tape recorder. Begin by describing the most empowering moments of your life: for example, your graduation from college, your first job, your wedding or the birth of a child. Were these accidental events, or were they fulfillments of your deepest desires? What role, if any, did you play in making each one come to pass? Then recall, one at a time, your empowering relationships. Take time to think how you have created them. Have you nurtured a parent through illness, been loyal to a spouse with financial troubles, raised a difficult child or arranged a reunion with a dear, but estranged, friend? Have you been empowered for a long time, but simply not aware of it?

2. *My Scrapbook of Empowering Experiences:* Every time you have an empowering experience in a mutual relationship, write it down in your Empowerment Journal or talk about it into a tape recorder. Since I am a writer, guess which alternative I have chosen? Here are a couple of mine:

a. "Yesterday I went to my medical doctor. After he examined me, he took me into his office and explained exactly what was wrong. He even took the time to show me diagrams of the human spine, so that I would fully understand my condition. When he prescribed medication, he told me clearly what it would do for me and how often and how long I should take it. Afterwards I went to the public library and looked up the medication in the *Physicians Desk Reference*, to get additional details about it. Knowledge can be empowering."

b. "Today I went to my chiropractor. For over an hour, he listened to me talk about my problem. I felt that he really understood what I was saying and genuinely cared about helping me get better. Afterwards, he showed me how to massage myself at certain pressure points, how to sit and stand in proper alignment and how to do some helpful exercises. One of the exercises seemed impossible to me, and I said to him, 'I can't do it.' He said, 'Attempt the exercise. Get the approximate position, even if you can't reach it completely. Begin the movement, even if you can't do it all.' These were inspiring words. By teaching me to heal myself, he empowered me."

3. *Focus on Mutuality, Autonomy and Authenticity:* Sit down in a quiet place, close your eyes and relax.

a. Repeat this sentence silently, *"I share and grow in my relationships."*

1) What comes up for you? Do you find yourself thinking of any particular relationship?

2) How does your body feel? Are you relaxed? Are you experiencing tension anywhere?

3) Can you think of a word or phrase that describes your physical sensations?

4) Keep on searching until you can find a word or phrase that fits just right. Then say it to yourself over and over again.

5) What else does this word or phrase bring up for you? Follow your thoughts wherever they lead.

6) Now pause and reflect. Have you learned anything about yourself?

b. Repeat this sentence silently, *"I am my own boss."* Ask yourself the same questions.

c. Repeat this sentence silently, *"I am my real self with other people."* Ask yourself the same questions.

4. *Create an Empowering Relationship:* Although empowerment takes place inside you, it begins when you share yourself with other people who are caring and supportive. You are the person who knows best whom you might open up to: a therapist, a relative, a close friend or someone you have recently met are all possibilities. What is important is that you decide to reach out. What first, small step will you take? A phone call? A visit? Although you may not be able to commit yourself to a long-term relationship, you can make a decision to telephone someone and talk for an hour or to go to a Women's Empowerment (WE) Community meeting. You will learn what a WE Community is in Chapter 13.

Now that you understand what it means to become empowered together with someone else, would you like to create a satisfying mutual partnership? "Yes," perhaps you may say, "but how can I do this? I am in a power-over relationship with my husband or lover." Or perhaps you may say, "I do not have an intimate relationship now, and I cannot find a suitable partner." Let's find out now how to turn these obstacles into stepping stones.

CREATE A MUTUAL PARTNERSHIP

3

One plus one equals much more than two.
You plus me plus what you expand in me,
Me plus you plus what I expand in you.
We nourish each other like green plants and soil.
Alone we stand tall;
Together we are mountains.

r. r. j.

"I want to leave my husband." It was my friend Melanie on the phone. "Why?" I asked her. "I don't know why," she replied tearfully. "All I know is that my marriage doesn't feel right to me. It hasn't felt right for a long time." "Let's talk again tomorrow," I told her. "In the meantime, Melanie, don't do anything rash."

Somewhat bewildered, I hung up the telephone. Although Melanie had been married for over 15 years, she still did not feel satisfied in her relationship with her husband. Yet I was blissfully happy in mine, although I had gotten married just 3 years ago. Why did my present marriage feel right to me now? Why had my two previous marriages both felt wrong to me? And why did Melanie's feel wrong to her now?

Your Relationships Should Feel Right

In my interviews, I have noticed again and again how important it is for women to feel genuinely connected to other people. Yet for many of us, this has not been the case. Traditionally, we have nurtured husbands, children and other family members. No one has really nurtured us. While we have fostered the growth of others, our relationships have not been mutual. We have related to people who

37

have power over us, but not to people who are empowered together with us. Although we have spent our lives giving to our families and employers, we have often felt isolated from them.

What we need most are mutually empowering relationships with other people. Yet what most of us actually experience in our relationships, particularly with husbands and lovers, is disconnection. Our feelings can be disturbing—sometimes even terrifying. They stunt our psychological growth and often cause us to become depressed or addicted. Yet, because it is so important to us to stay in relationships, we strive to preserve them, even the isolating ones. As we try to stay connected, we often endure both physical pain and psychological destruction.

Annette is such a woman. Married to a man who abused her emotionally and physically, she stayed with him for 12 years. Finally she managed to extricate herself from this power-over relationship and become empowered. Late one evening, she told me how she did it.

Annette: "I Don't Have to Be Married."

It has taken me over 2 hours to find Annette's townhouse. Now, at 9:30 in the evening, she comes out of her house to meet me. She is walking briskly—like a woman who knows exactly where she is going. "I'm sorry to be late," I begin. "Come right in," Annette replies quickly. I trust you'll find your trip worthwhile.

Her living room is small, but elegantly furnished. We sit next to each other: I on a white and navy blue Chinese rug, and she in a black highbacked chair. Annette starts off speaking slowly, but soon torrents of words rush out of her mouth.

When I was growing up, women did not have the luxury to decide whether or not they would get married. I never knew a woman who did not have a husband. I did even not know a woman who was divorced, except for someone who lived upstairs. My father told us never to go near her apartment. I thought, "This woman must be really evil, if she is divorced!"

What I learned from my mother was, "Your goal in life is to get married and stay married at any cost. It is your job to make sure that your marriage works." This was a very strong and very frightening message: There is no life for a woman outside of a relationship with a man who calls all the shots. You have to humor him, cajole him and "keep" him, because, without him, your life will be over. Annette tosses her auburn curly hair, briefly glances at the ceiling and then looks down at her feet.

When I did marry, I didn't make a good choice. And when I saw that my marriage was going bad, I didn't have the good sense to get out of it. Once I distanced myself from my marriage, I started asking myself, "Why would I stay in a relationship that was so destructive to me?" It was because it had been hammered into my head that a woman's job was to be married and have children. As a result, I had a state of mind that allowed me to be abused.

In our family, my father and grandfather were considered the intelligent ones. I was considered unusual, because I was a bright woman. Because I liked school, I went on to college. My parents thought I had made a foolish decision. Although they didn't say it in so many words, they implied, "Why should you bother going to college, when you are just going to get married anyway?" Annette seems almost to be asking herself this question. Her voice is very soft; I detect a trace of a Southern accent.

Unfortunately, I didn't have the sense to pick a good husband. I never loved Jeff; it was a rebound relationship. I had cared for someone else a great deal, but he didn't want to get married. I got angry and told this other man that I didn't want to see him anymore. Then my girlfriend fixed me up with Jeff, a young, good-looking soldier. After we had gone together for about a year and a half, Jeff asked me to marry him. I accepted.

After Jeff and I got married, I finished college. I was feeling very unhappy, so I studied psychology and social psychology to find out why. After I graduated, I went to work as a probation officer. I was very dissatisfied with my job. I started asking myself, "Why do I want to deal with all these hostile people? They're not going to change, and I don't need the money." So I got pregnant. That was my career move!

My marriage with Jeff hadn't been going very well, but I thought,"Having a baby will make us happy." I had read in women's magazines that a baby was not the answer to a troubled marriage, but I said to myself, "We're different." It turned out that we were not different at all. As soon as I had our daughter, Jeff started to use her to fight with me. When Glenda was 2 years old, she marched up to me, looked me straight in the eye and said, "I don't have to listen to you, because Daddy says that I can do anything I want." Then she stuck her nose up in the air, marched right up to Jeff, sat on his lap and snickered at me.

I kept saying to myself, "Look, you have this bad marriage, this obnoxious child, no career and no future. Where is your life going? What are you going to do?" After a couple of months, I went into a deep depression. For about 2 weeks, I lay in bed thinking, "I don't care if I wake up. I don't even have the energy to get out of this bed."

Then something happened inside me. I started thinking, "The reason I'm feeling so unhappy is my marriage. I am only in my 20s. Why do I have to live the rest of my life in this nightmare? I don't know what's ahead, but I'm not going to let my marriage destroy me. Even if I have to abandon everything I own, I will get a divorce. My will to live is at stake."

Somehow I pulled myself together. I told Jeff that I wanted to take Glenda to my parents' home in Atlanta for a while. We stayed for 3 months. I never told my parents what was going on, because I was sure that they wouldn't understand. They would just blame me.

I had been raised to think, "If something is wrong, it's my fault. If my parents let me down, it's my fault. If the teacher mistreats me, it's my fault. If my husband is cruel, it's my fault." So I said to myself, "If everything is your fault, then this is your fault, too. Don't expect your parents to give you sympathy; they're going to say, 'It's your fault. Go back and work it out. You made your bed, lie in it.'"

When I returned to Jeff, our relationship got better for a while. Then I got pregnant again. I thought a second baby would make everything better—for sure. But instead Jeff really went off the deep end. Jeff saw our newborn son, Derek, as a rival and became very cruel to the baby. From this point on, the marriage became intolerable. I told Jeff that I wanted to go back to Atlanta, so that both of the children could be near their grandparents. The truth was that I just had to get away from him. I left; Jeff followed me. We went back together again, and then we split up. This went on until Derek was almost 4. Our marriage was getting even worse.

Now I was really scared. Not only did I have my old fear, "What will I do if I'm not married?" but there was a new fear, as well. "What in the world will I, a mother of two small children, do without a husband?" My will to live was disappearing again. I knew I had to do something.

Finally I said to myself, "I don't know if I'm right or wrong; I don't care if anyone understands; I have a right to live. I know that I'm going to do something to obliterate how horrible I feel, and it's going to be self-destructive. And, if I start drinking or taking drugs, I'm not going to be any good to my kids."

Once a week, I started going to marriage counseling by myself. (Jeff went with me once and told the counselor that we had no problems!) Fortunately, I really felt comfortable with this marriage counselor. I said to him, "I need help. I don't know if I'm crazy, or if my husband is crazy, but our relationship is really bad. If there's something wrong with me, tell me; I want to get better. I'm willing to take a chance and tell you the truth—things I've never shared with anyone. There's no one else I can talk to."

So I told the marriage counselor what was really going on in my marriage. And he looked at me and said, "There's nothing wrong with you. Your husband has a very bad problem." This marriage counselor had absolutely no idea what a burden he took off of my shoulders.

Annette's voice suddenly hardens; her words cut me like broken glass. Jeff always blamed me for causing his abuse. He would say, "I've never acted this way with anyone else; this is your fault." So I would say to myself, "He must be so hateful and cruel to me because I deserve it. I must be bad." Jeff used to pick up on that. All he would have to say to me is, "You're not being nice; you're being bad." Then he would start mistreating me.

Now here was a doctor telling me that there was nothing wrong with me at all. I said to myself, "No, I will not put up with my husband's brutality anymore." From that time on, I stood right up to Jeff. He later told a friend of mine that my whole personality changed, after I went into counseling. And it did. He was right. I never endured his mistreatment again.

After about a year and a half of counseling, I found the courage to make the decision to leave Jeff. I told my parents that if I didn't get out of my marriage, I was going to have a nervous breakdown. They lent me some money. But I couldn't tell Jeff what I was going to do, because I was afraid he would hurt me—attack me, harm the children or destroy the furniture. Deep inside, I felt he was unstable. And he did do a lot of scary, scary things.

Jeff came after me with vengeance, after I took the children and left. He wrote me a letter that said, "I'm going to make things so miserable for you that I'm going to break you. You're going to come back to me. And, when you come back, then we're going to talk." What he really meant was, "When you come back, I'm going to kick the living daylights out of you." He was serious. Jeff couldn't believe that I had any backbone, because I had never stood up to him. Annette does not raise her voice at all. I am amazed that she is speaking so matter-of-factly about her traumatic experiences.

Mine was not just a struggle to get out of a bad marriage, but a statement of my own will to live. So much of my identity had been in my marriage; I was terrified to live by myself. Now, for the first time, I had to pull away from my parents, my husband and my children and stand up to all of them. My two main goals were to earn enough money to support myself and my kids and to sort out in my mind the bad attitudes that had kept me in my marriage for so long.

Jeff and I got involved in litigation. Attorneys were expensive, and I didn't understand very much about divorce law. So I enrolled in a paralegal training program. During these 2 years, I spent so much time in the law library that I could talk intelligently to any attorney I was thinking of hiring—tell him what had to be done and what would be a fair fee. I could even draw up my own legal papers. This is how determined I was to understand what was happening to me in court.

After I graduated as a paralegal, I got a job in a well-known law firm.

Since then, I have quadrupled my annual income. I've had two homes and four cars. I'm working on a six-figure savings account. I've had my own stockbroker, bought my own life insurance, faced my children's illnesses and endured major surgery. Having made the decision to take my mother off life-support systems, when she was terminally ill, I've learned to accept natural death. I'm not afraid of anything anymore—except maybe acute physical pain.

The divorce has been difficult for my children. But, looking back, I realize that I did the right thing. I had a husband who hated women, abused me and refused to enter therapy. The relationship was suffocating my will to live. I only wish that more women had reached out to me during this terrible time.

A young woman holding a crying baby passes through the living room and goes up the nearby stairs. Annette gives me a half-smile. "That's my daughter, Glenda, and my granddaughter, Melissa. They both came to live with me right after Melissa was born. I'm doing the best I can for both of them." I nod my head. Annette continues:

About 2 years ago, I joined a women's support group to meet women at the same stage of life as I was. Most of the women were newly separated. There was one woman in the group who had a terrible need to feel that she was loved. It was so pathetic. She would talk about a so-called romance she had with one man, and keep saying, "I just know he loves me; he doesn't call, but I know he loves me . . . I just know." After a while I finally said to her, "Why are you so pathetically attached to this man, who does not care about you? Why does his acceptance and approval mean more to you than your love for yourself? Why do you care if he loves you? Why don't you love your-self? The issue is not him; the issue is you."

Most of the members of my support group were women who had been left behind by someone else; they weren't the ones who broke away. These were women who wanted to hold to a relationship, even if it was destroying them. Even if they were unhappy, they wouldn't say "Goodbye." And that's a different kind of woman from one who says, "This relationship doesn't make any sense; I don't want it." That's what I did. I'm proud of myself!

Forcefully shaking her head up and down, Annette lets me know that she really means what she has just said.

It is easy to see that Annette had been in a relationship where she did not feel connected. Yet she desperately wanted to stay married. "I must be crazy," Annette said to herself early on in the relationship. "My parents, my sister, and my friends all think that Jeff is a wonderful man. They must be right. I should stop being so emotional and try harder to be a better wife." Like many women, Annette decided that she was the reason for her isolation. If she was so upset with Jeff, she must be a wicked, worthless person. If she was so bad, any actions she took would only make her marriage worse. She felt helpless to do anything about her marriage.

The turning point for Annette was when she decided to stop destroying herself and seek help. Fortunately, she found a therapist with whom she could share what she had been experiencing in her marriage—and discuss how she actually felt about it. Six months of regular weekly visits gave her time to explore her own reality. When he told her, "You are not crazy; you are being horribly abused," her world turned upside down. Someone cared about her depression, her anger and her fear. Someone understood. She was sane after all.

Annette could not have become empowered alone. She needed someone else, or perhaps several other people, to listen attentively to her. In order to begin to heal, she needed to find a supportive place in which her true voice could emerge. She had to be with someone else who would allow her to continue to talk until she became fully aware of all that was inside of her. The therapist's silent—and sometimes not so silent—presence enabled her to explore her deepest places. *A single thread of genuine human connection had restored Annette's mental health.*

When Annette started expressing her real feelings to Jeff, he was dumbfounded. "You've become a completely different person," was his response. Jeff could only accept Annette as a "pleaser." After she tore up her script and broke out of her power-under role, he became cruel and rejecting.

Later on, after Annette left Jeff, she became even more empowered in the women's support group she joined. Although she didn't always like the conversation, she was able to connect with women who had problems like hers in a mutual, autonomous and authentic way.

Anger Can Be Either Empowering or Destructive

The first step in Annette's empowerment was when she allowed herself to get angry at her husband. Although Jeff did not accept Annette's anger, she was being authentic with him for the first time in their marriage.

Women's anger is a resource. Anger is an emotion that is an essential part of the movement of relationships. It is a symptom that something is wrong; something "hurts." Human growth results from this kind of exchange:

- We accept each other's anger.
- We are moved.
- We take action; the relationship moves along.

Anger expressed in this way is empowering. Exchanging real anger has a critical function in the growth and building of relationships. In an empowering relationship, your anger is received. The other person acknowledges it, understands the cause and strives to remedy it.

Growth does not take place when anger is expressed in destructive ways. In our male-oriented society, men are encouraged to be violent. To take power over someone else, they attempt to prevail by force.

Actually, acts of violence are substitutes for expressions of real feelings. Angry people are vulnerable, because they are hurting. By acting destructively, they can avoid facing their own pain. Perhaps this is why people in power-over relationships often get "stuck" in cycles of violence. Neither one can deal with his or her own authentic feelings. Real anger, expressed and accepted, would empower both people in the relationship.

In our own special ways, most of us strive to make positive connections. Yet our biggest questions still remain unanswered. Exactly how do we create the kind of empowering relationships we need? Is it possible to transform a relationship where our husband or lover has power over us into one where empowerment is shared? At what point should we decide to abandon a relationship in which we feel isolated and search for a mutually empowering one?

I decided to begin my search for the answers to these questions by visiting Quincy, who, I had heard, had experienced satisfaction in her relationship with her late husband.

Quincy: Our Marriage Was a Partnership

Quincy's living room looks like a large playroom. On one side is a toy chest, an old piano, a chest of drawers and some bookshelves crowded with schoolbooks and comics. The gray sofa, faded and torn, is surrounded by a hi fi from the '70s and a black-and-white television set. A small boy and a large dog are wrestling on a small brown rug nearby. "Let's go into the dining room. Would you like to share my dinner?" Quincy asks. "I know it's 9:00 in the evening, but this is the first time I've had a moment to sit down."

"Thanks, I've already eaten. But I'll share your orange juice. Tell me a little about yourself, Quincy," I begin. There is a very long pause.

Two years ago, I became a widow at the age of 39. I married Joe when he was a law student . He was completely blind; I have perfect vision. As I helped Joe finish his law degree, write two books and set up his own consulting business, I had many exciting adventures. Sharing Joe's life was ecstasy, because he was warm, caring and fun to be with.

Somehow, in the middle of it all, I managed to get my M.B.A., which I am extremely grateful for now. You see, Joe left me with three young children, almost no money and a pile of unpaid bills. "Financial nowhere." I'm not yet on the other side of my loss . Like an injured bird, I'm still in the healing process. Every day seems like an eternity."

Quincy pauses for a moment. "Would you like to know about my relationship with Joe?"

"Yes," I answer quickly.

Our marriage was a partnership. During the 16 years we were together, Joe turned all our money over to me and trusted me to take care of it. He never signed our checks, or even our tax return. When he would write something, I would edit it. We had a complete understanding about almost everything.

In our relationship, it never mattered who did this and who did that. When Joe finished his book, it was my idea to dedicate it to his family. Even though I had done most of the research and the writing, I didn't need the credit. Our relationship was enough credit.

What I did for Joe was never a sacrifice. It just got tiring, like raising kids. Even when I got sick, there was no one to relieve me. But having so many responsibilities was a very small price to pay for the meaning of having a union like this, which was so enormous that it dwarfed everything else. It was so rewarding that I never thought of doing anything else. It seemed to me that sitting on a corporate board or being on television was far less crucial than being so intimately involved in someone's life.

My sense of self developed in my relationship with Joe. No matter how sick he was, things never seemed so bad, because we were "in it" together. In my marriage, I found a purpose for my life that I could never have found myself.

My husband never stood in the way of anything I wanted to do. When I went back to school, he paid my tuition. Now this doesn't mean that everything was always perfect. Sometimes I didn't tell him the absolute truth, because I didn't want to hurt him. When he was sick at home and I was getting my M.B.A., I would come home exhilarated. I loved business school—I adored it. But I would say to him, "How I wish I could have been with you today," because I knew how much my words would mean to him.

But, most of the time, I would just say whatever I thought. I'm not saying that I was always completely honest, but I never held anything back that really needed to be said. Thinking back, I probably should have been more honest about my feelings—how tired and confined I often felt. Maybe I should have said, "I wish you could pick out your clothes or drive the car. There is no respite for me." But how could I get angry at him for being blind and sick? It wasn't his fault.

Underneath it all, there was a deep and abiding bond between the two of us. From time to time, there would be periods in our relationship, where we would get involved in other things—he, with his career, and I, with the children. Each of us would feel excluded from each other's life for a while. But our emotional distance was always temporary.

Joe and I were each other's friend. I always felt that he cared about me and wanted to listen to me. As his health worsened, we spent more and more time together. When he had a stroke, we had to go away for 3 months, so that he could recover. We had such wonderful times! The children remember us sitting outside on the porch just talking and talking and talking. We never seemed to run out of things to say to each other.

When Joe died I said to myself, "At least it's over. Now I can go on to the next phase of my life." Little did I know what it would take to pull myself through. I am glad I didn't know how absolutely horrible I would feel and how long it was going to take me to go through all the stages of grief. And I've had a lot of help! Anyone who loses a treasured partner feels an astounding range of painful emotions. It's been 3 years since Joe passed away, and I'm not done yet.

Part of me is tempted to spend the rest of my life remembering Joe. I know that many happily married widows continue to relive the past. They say, "My marriage was the greatest thing that ever happened to me." But my common sense tells me that this part of my life is done. I have to go forward—somehow.

"Your marriage was a mutually empowering relationship, wasn't it?" I ask her. "Yes, it was. For 16 years, we both helped each other realize our potential. I got everything I wanted: three children, an M. B. A. and an exciting life. Our partnership was my passport to adventure." For a moment we both hold our breath. Quincy continues:

Now I have a full-time job. I put on my suit and go to work every day. Then I come home and pay the bills. The children feel unhappy, even a bit devastated. I sometimes feel guilty that I'm not there when they come home from school. . . that I can't provide them with the things other parents can. . . that I'm tired when I come home. . . and that I can't be with them sometimes. Quincy sighs. But I am doing what I have to do to support us financially—and to preserve my own identity. She laughs dryly. No, I'm not looking to get married again right away; I don't need a man to validate me. My marriage was a special opportunity to fulfill myself. I'll wait until another one comes my way.

Quincy stands up. "I guess I'd better go to sleep now. Tomorrow I have to wake up at 5:30 in the morning to get the children off to school." After she watches me pack up my tape recorder, we retrace our steps through her living room.

"Goodbye," Quincy says. "Thanks a lot." The front door closes behind me. Suddenly I realize that I have tears in my eyes. Why am I so moved? I think for a moment. Then I realize why. To give so much of yourself to a marriage, the way Quincy did, is indeed an act of courage.

A Different Kind of Team

Esther, an attractive, outspoken black woman in her 50s, paints a different picture of the partnership she has with her husband:

My husband and I will be married 36 years. He's made my life so easy! My husband is one of the nicest men you could ever meet. He has always put his family first. When his children call "Dad," he always answers. Anything that needs to be done, he does it. He's always been there for our children and for me, no matter what. He cares for me. We understand each other. I've been very blessed.

My husband likes to listen—very closely. He'll ask you questions about all the details. How can I explain how he is? He is the type of person who will pay attention to what I tell him and then say to me, "Esther, I see it a different way." When I told him that I was going to be interviewed for this book, he said to me, "Oh, that's nice, Esther. Tell me more about it."

In the days when our children were growing up, my husband's main job was to work. But if I had to go out, he would take care of the kids. I liked that. I never felt that it was unfair that he worked and I was home, because what he did was all for us. He was always thinking about his family. He and my children have always come first for me, too. I'm from the old school.

Nowadays my son, daughters, sons-in-law and daughters-in-law all have jobs. It takes two to pay the mortgage and the other bills, now. But my son and sons-in-law can cook, iron and wash. They bathe their babies and change their babies. Everyone does equal work.

I once said to my son, after he got a promotion, "Sammy, you know that I chose to have a family and not go to college." His reply was, "Momma, it is because of you that we have all that we have." He meant it. You know, he's right. I have backed my children and my husband in everything they have ever done. They have accomplished what they have accomplished because I have been right there behind them. We are all part of a team.

When we first started out, my husband worked and I didn't. We pinched our pennies—went on family outings with other families. We went to the zoo or had cookouts in the park. Maybe that's why our kids are so family-oriented. They're always over here at my house.

In my son's neighborhood, they recently had an event called "family day." My daughter-in-law called me up and said, "Hey, Momma. Can you make that macaroni that I like?" So I made her two big pans. She took one and kept the other for herself! She laughs. Anything my husband and children need me to do—or anything I want them to do—we don't hesitate to ask.

Although Esther stayed home and took care of the children and her husband worked outside the home, they were still partners. They were both working together toward common goals. What each of them did was for the benefit of their marriage and their children. It is not how the work is divided up—who does what—that makes a partnership; it is the spirit of mutuality.

No One Ever Said It Was Going to Be Easy!

Congresswoman Patricia Wynn's marriage is a model to many women. Her husband has supported her, with his words and actions, since she first decided to go into politics. Yet, when she spoke to me in her district office, Congresswoman Wynn made it clear that she had experienced no "miracles." When she first went out to work as a teacher, her husband was not enthusiastic about her having a paying job. He rarely helped out at home. How did her husband change, as time passed?

The friendship you have in marriage constantly evolves. My husband and I are now best friends. It wasn't always this way. We met at college and then moved to the Washington, D. C. area. He was going to law school; I had a job. After our first child was born, we still needed money for him to finish law school. So when our first son was a year and a half, I went into teaching. I continued teaching part-time for a while; then I stayed home and had my second and third children. After that, I got involved in the community and got my Master's degree. When all our children were in school, I decided to teach full-time.

Part of my husband's attitude has to do with the generation we were born in. When he was in law school, he had to go through a transition in order to accept financial assistance from me. Afterwards when I went back to work, he experienced another adjustment, because he always regarded himself as the breadwinner. His attitude was, "This is the male role." By the way, I think that this role assignment is happening less with the next generation. My sons and daughters do not believe that "women should do this" and "men should do that." The husbands do not seem intimidated because their wives are pursuing their professions.

For many years, I was very happy taking care of my family, being involved in education and working in the community. My springboard to politics was when I became involved in the cause of equality for women. As I testified before legislative committees, I decided that I wanted to be "on the other side."

My husband supported my running for elective office, although he had actually entered politics before I did. This year he is going to get the "Good Guy's Award" from the National Women's Political Caucus. Hal has received many professional awards on his own, but he is very excited about this one. We like to tease him about how he is trying to straighten out the Congressional Wives Club and make it the Congressional Spouses Club, so that people will look harder at husbands and their role. He's also taken over all the cooking and enjoys it very much; we buy him cookbooks as gifts. In short, my husband has become an excellent partner and confidante.

What I'm saying is that it didn't come easy. It didn't just happen; it was slow. Let me tell you a story. A friend of mine saw my husband in the supermarket last weekend. She said to him, "I am impressed. Do you do this often?" He replied, "Why are you impressed? You're here, too." She quipped, "Yes, but you have coupons in your hand."

My husband and I have experienced a real role reversal; I used to do the shopping, except I never saved coupons! It took a lot of maturity—and patience—to stand by, while my husband grew. Thank goodness, my husband had a great deal of confidence in himself. Men who have a sense of who they are, are not intimidated by the success of women. It is a tribute to my husband, as well as to my children and my extended family, that I am a congresswoman.

Mutuality: You Give a Lot, and You Receive a Lot

Denise and Dan got married 20 years ago, before they emigrated from Australia to the United States. Because both of them had top-level careers, it was not easy for either of them to deviate from their professional paths for the sake of the partnership. Seated next to each other on a loveseat in their high ceilinged living room, they were eager to share their story:

Denise: Dan and I have been together 22 years. Until the eighth, I was reluctant to say what I felt about certain issues.

"Did you know each other very well before you got married?"

Denise: We dated for a year before we became engaged. We got married 6 months later, after we graduated. We used to sit and talk for hours about our future plans. It was clear to both of us that we wanted to travel and to get advanced degrees.

Dan: When we got married, we had certain ground rules. The most important one was that we would take turns making career choices. At this point, we had no idea how far we were going. So first we went to Iowa, where I wanted to go, because the most prominent agricultural economist in the country was teaching there.

Denise: Iowa was the last place in the world I wanted to go. Lots of places, but not Iowa! From day one, I reminded him that it was my turn to make the next choice. This time we both had to get assistantships at whatever university we went to. Fortunately, we both ended up attending the University of Michigan.

Dan: After we got our Ph.D.'s, we kept on taking turns every few years, as each career choice would come up. After a couple of more turns, we decided that we would come to Baltimore, just for a year.

When we had been here just a few months, Denise started saying that 1 year was definitely not enough for her. She needed at least 2. But I had come very reluctantly, without a permanent job. I really wanted to return to the small university town out West, where we had previously been—or else to a similar place. So when Denise told me she wanted to stay here, in a big Northeastern city, there was a major crisis.

I also resented the long hours that Denise was spending in the lab. She would work from 6:00 in the morning to 11:00 at night, 6 days a week.

These were issues that were important to us—and difficult to share. Both of us had items on our agenda that hadn't been talked about—and had to be dealt with.

Denise: There was a lot building up inside us, especially because we had two different careers that were moving in two different directions. When we tried to solve our problems on our own, it was very nearly the end of everything.

"Did you think your marriage would break up at this point?"

Denise: He actually intended to leave! That evening he met someone on the street who knew me. She asked him, "How is your wife, Denise—that wonderful person?" Her kind remarks may have encouraged him to return home!"

Dan: The only reason I came back that night was that I couldn't find any other place to live. They both laugh. Soon afterwards I received a very good job offer from another university in the West. I said to Denise, "Either we will separate, or you will relocate with me." Finally, Denise convinced me to interview here in Baltimore. I was offered a well-paying position with the government. I accepted it. So we would continue to live in a big city, where Denise wanted to be.

At this point, we entered marriage counseling. It was more or less a Band-Aid treatment. But then we attended a relationships seminar. Its effect on our marriage was dramatic.

After we finished the seminar, Denise and I went on vacation. I made the decision that we were going to have a fabulous time. I was going to be agreeable and do whatever Denise wanted. Until then, when we had gone on trips she would want one thing and I would want another. We would wind up endlessly fighting.

What I discovered was that the more I gave to Denise, the more she was willing to give to me. This was a revelation!

Denise: Now we still had different positions, but we were reconciling them. Dan was saying, "Denise, you're right," and I found myself saying, "No, it's my fault." We had made new rules for our relationship.

After the relationships seminar, neither of us was willing to make a compromise so large that it felt like self-sacrifice. For the first time, we questioned our rule of taking turns making career decisions. No longer could either one of us call the shots. We started making joint decisions. If one of us had become a "winner" and the other, a "loser," it would have been very damaging. We redefined what winning meant, so that we could both win. It was a whole different way of thinking for us. Everything was thrown open to reconsideration.

Dan: Now I started to say to Denise, "Why don't you change jobs? I hardly ever see you. Your work in the lab is not bringing you—or us—the happiness we deserve. Why don't you consider a scientific job outside of a lab? Why don't we have some children?"

My suggestion was incredibly threatening to her, because she had programmed herself to be a laboratory scientist ever since high school. To give up her scientific career was like stepping into an enormous black hole.

"Denise, how did you feel when you were confronted with this decision?"

Denise: I knew it would have to happen, sooner or later. My career in the lab wasn't working out. It wasn't good for our marriage—and it wasn't making me happy. I was spending evenings and weekends there and not getting the results I wanted. Yet I could not imagine what working in an office would be like. I decided to ask a few people. One of them offered me a job, which I later accepted.

"You moved to a position that was more comfortable for you."

Denise: Yes, in the long run. But for quite a while, I felt that, because of our marriage, I had lost opportunities to accomplish what I had hoped to accomplish. Later on I realized that, although I had given up a lot, I had not sacrificed for my husband. I had simply grown in a different direction.

Dan: I also had to make major changes in my life plan. A big city is not my favorite place to live. The only reason I was willing to stay was that we could both find jobs here. Furthermore, from the time I was a little boy, I had been programmed to be a university professor. Working for the government was a difficult adjustment for me.

Denise: The career issue brought our differences to a head. We really did reach rock bottom. We couldn't continue the way we were; it was too destructive. Until we took the relationships seminar, neither of us had thought about an alternative career path. I had never realized that what I contributed to the partnership would benefit me as well.

When I realized that our marriage was breaking up, I knew there was no way my career could make up for it. I felt that the ultimate disaster would be divorce. Although my career was intensely important to me, my marriage was even more important. Perhaps Dan did not feel this way; but I did. Now that we have children, I cannot imagine life without them—or without Dan.

Denise and Dan valued their marriage sufficiently that each of them was willing to bend, in order to stay together. While they still had a two-career marriage, their paths were slightly different from those that they had planned. In the relationships seminar they attended, they learned to pay attention to each other's needs. Denise became a scientific administrator, instead of a laboratory scientist, so that she could spend more time with Dan and raise their children. Dan became an employee of a prestigious government agency, rather than a college professor, so he could live in a big city with job opportunities for both him and Denise. What they lost was their rigid ideas about how relationships and careers "should be." What they gained was a partnership marriage and two beloved sons.

How Did I Create a Mutual Partnership?

A friend of mine posed this question to me recently: "Why did a highly educated woman like you give up a promising career and devote 20 years of your life to raising kids? What did you get out of it?"

I have also been asked frequently, "How did you manage to happily remarry, during the middle of your life, in a major metropolitan area with a 'man shortage?'" The answers to both these questions lie in my unconscious search for empowering relationships.

During my teens and early 20s, I used to flee from other people. My solace was my books. I would lock myself in my room with them and read for days at a time. When I would leave my own room, I would head straight for a cubicle at the library. At college, I had a roommate; we managed to live together for only 1 semester. Two years after I graduated, I married a medical student. Our "every-other-night, every-other-weekend" encounters were often distant. The main thing we agreed about was that we both adored *him*! Our marriage ended in divorce. Another relationship disappointment for me.

Did I understand what a satisfying relationship was like? No. All I knew was that almost every relationship I had ever had in my life had felt bad and that I wanted to have some in which I felt good. Perhaps the other people in my relationships had enjoyed them, but I had not. Later on, I realized that this was because I was always playing a power-under role. I had never experienced mutuality.

My relationships with my children were the first mutually empowering ones I ever had. I figured that my chances of success were excellent. Since this was their first close relationship, they had no bad habits to break. I made friends with my children; I shared myself with them; I grew with them. We talked about our satisfactions and our disappointments; nothing was hidden. Each of us was his own person. We had tremendous quarrels, but very strong bonds. When our family seemed to be falling apart, actually it was at its strongest. We were a community.

When I met Phil, my present husband, I had already spent 15 years in three mutually empowering relationships. In my heart and soul, I could not settle for less.

Fortunately, I had intuitively selected a man who also desired mutuality. I acted the same way with him as I had with my children. I told him everything that was on my mind, in the most nonthreatening way I could. At first Phil tried to ignore me, but he found that I expected him to listen to me, just as my children had. When I revealed my honest feelings to him, he often became confused, irritated and angry. We screamed at each other, hid from each other and reunited with each other. As I accepted his bad feelings and he accepted mine, they disappeared. All that was left was love.

After we got married we kept on talking to each other and listening to each other. Two more years went by before we both felt completely comfortable together. Finally I had a mutual partnership with another adult.

If I was able to create a mutual partnership, you can do it, too. Ask yourself these questions:

1. What kinds of gifts do I have as a woman for building empowering relationships? Which of my contributions do I value the most? The least?

2. What are my greatest weaknesses in forming relationships?

3. What would I like a romantic partner to know about me, so that he could understand me?

4. What do I value most in a romantic partner?

5. How can I create a mutual partnership, where I am neither subordinate nor dominant?

Believe it or not, you have a unique capacity for forming empowering relationships, just because you are a woman.

Women's Unique Relationship Strengths

Your relationship strengths are the essence of your femininity. As a woman, you have your own special expertise for creating a mutual partnership. What you need to do is to value your assets in relationships, rather than dismiss them as "unimportant."

These are the eight relationship strengths women have. Which ones do you have in abundance?

1. *Most important, we seek relationships.* Aware of our connectedness from the time we are little girls, we are interested in relating to other people. Most of us want to have a boyfriend, get married and have children. Almost every one of us has experienced a deep desire for friendships with other women. We join support groups to create a place for ourselves to be angry, fearful and envious together. Then we use these intense emotions to empower ourselves.

2. *Having experienced the pain of being dominated in relationships, we appreciate the value of being empowered together with a partner.* We understand that a person who controls is equally as isolated as one who is being repressed. We renounce aggressive power struggles. Our goal is to create peaceful, egalitarian relationships.

3. *We have a deep-rooted intuitive presence.* One of our unique strengths is knowing how to focus on the present moment and really "be with" someone else. We are able to honor another person's perspective by seeing the world through his eyes.

4. *We are sensitive to feelings.* Being aware of our feelings is natural for us; it is not a difficult task, as it is for many men. "My passion is in the caboose, the last car in a long train of rational thoughts." This statement, made by one man I know, does not apply to most women. We are able to get in touch with our emotions and then put them into words. Rather than being "stuck" in logic, as many men are, women sense a connection between intellect and feelings. We are comfortable with a wide range of emotions: love, fear and anger. We understand

that anger is compatible with love and that expressing and receiving angry feelings helps us stay connected.

5. *We are able to be vulnerable—to admit our errors and imperfections.* A retired woman I interviewed told me, "I always thought my husband knew everything, because he never said, 'I don't know.'" Unlike most men, we can say, "I'm sorry" or "I don't know" without being afraid that we will endanger our superior position. With this perspective, we are able to accept other people's weaknesses, especially men's. Women do not expect to be in charge all the time and always to get what we want. We enjoy the give-and-take of a mutual relationship.

6. *We are comfortable talking about a relationship.* This can be a weakness if it is carried too far. As one of the women I interviewed put it, "Sometimes I think the main thing that holds my relationship together is discussing the problems it has."

7. *We understand how shared work can be a powerful bond between two people.* We enjoy working together with someone else, talking about our work and listening to our partner talk about his. We are also learning that a woman can participate in two worlds: she can be grounded in a healthy relationship and also go out and get her Ph.D.

8. *We persist in connecting with other people.* We hold on tenaciously to a relationship that is important to us and "hang in there," even when the problems seem insurmountable at the time. We even care enough about relationships to buy thousands of books about relationships!

Women's Weaknesses in Relationships

Conversely, these are our weaknesses:

1. *Our biggest difficulty is our need for relationships, whether they are with a man, other woman friends or children.* Somehow we have absorbed the cultural belief that we are somehow defective without a family. We accept it and even "play into" it. We deal with our fear of all men by staying in a relationship with one of them. We are always trying to please other people, seek approval, fit in and sacrifice to keep relationships going—even at our own expense.

2. *Another weakness, related to our deep desire for connection, is that we often have to learn to let go, as well as to hold tight* . . . to stop seeing an old friend with whom we no longer feel connected . . . to freely allow our children to leave home and lead their own lives . . . to say goodbye to a lover or a husband who wants to move on.

3. *We tend to think that we know how to "do relationships" and that men do not.* Our desire to teach others about relationships often gets in the way of our listening closely and sharing ourselves. Women's expecta-

tions for a romantic relationship can be much too high. Sometimes we are embarrassed to admit when we are satisfied with a partner who may not meet the "standards" of other women.

4. *We are too verbal. Sometimes we literally talk a relationship to death.* We are continually monitoring what is going on in the relationship and asking to negotiate about it more often than our partner would like.

5. *We want so much to be listened to in relationships that we become excessively angry when we are not.* It is impossible for anyone to make up for 30 or 40 years of not being heard in one night—or even in a year's worth of nights.

Men will give up their power over us only if they are convinced that they are gaining something much more precious instead. We need to know our own value—and to be aware of our own assets—in order to persuade men to connect in a mutually empowering way.

Wendy: "I Want a Partnership."

Are you seeking a partner right now? Or is the relationship you have a power-over one? Like many women, you may not have yet experienced a mutually empowering partnership. Perhaps you are wondering, "What will it feel like? How will I participate? How will the other person participate? What kind of person shall I look for?"

Wendy, a high school language teacher, has answers to these questions. She tells me her story over a cup of tea. In her black turtleneck sweater, red and black plaid skirt and black tights, Wendy looks well-organized and sure of herself. We talk in her luxurious new home with spacious tiled floors and cedar beams stretched across high ceilings.

"You may have noticed the 'for sale' sign outside," Wendy begins. "After 10 years of marriage, I am now going through a divorce." Wendy puts her head back for a moment to stop the tears that begin to flow.

The year before our 10th anniversary, there had been a lot going on. For the past 5 years, my husband, Charles and I had tried to have a child. Then Charles found out that he was sterile. When he told me, I said, "It's okay. I love you. It doesn't matter if we never have children." But I don't think he believed me. Two months later, he told me he was going to a big trade conference. I got hysterical. "You can't go," I told him. "It will be the end of us." I'm very intuitive; I go with my feelings and gut reactions. But he went anyway. When he came home, I knew immediately that our marriage had ended. Charles told me that he had met someone there and wanted to move out and live with her. For a minute, Wendy puts her head in her hands. Then she sits up very straight and tosses her shiny, brown hair.

I was furious. "You don't throw away 10 years for a weekend affair! These things happen; we can work it out." All he said was, "I don't love you. I never loved you. I'm not committed to this relationship anymore."

Initially, I was numb. Since the first day of our marriage, I had been emotionally dependent on Charles. He was my entire life. He always did a lot of traveling. While he was gone 2,3,4 weeks at a time, all I did was think of him. Now he was going away forever.

Nothing mattered to me, not even my life. I started thinking suicidal thoughts. The day before my birthday, the day before our 11th wedding anniversary, on Halloween Eve, I decided to kill myself. But something stopped me from going all the way. I asked myself, "What are you doing? Why are you punishing yourself for him?" I guess it shocked me that I would destroy myself because of some other person. Why should anyone have this power over me?

I put away the sleeping pills and decided to do something—anything. I organized a women's support group, which at least got me out of the house twice a week. Then I became connected to one of the women in it. Not physically, but emotionally. I realized that I would care if something happened to her, and that she would care if something happened to me.

I said to myself, "Yes, you can do things by yourself. Just because you're single doesn't mean you can't still enjoy life." I started seeing a therapist, and I was willing to let him help me help myself. My most important decision was to sell this beautiful, large house and buy a condominium, so that I could make the mortgage payments all by myself and not depend on anyone else to assist me. The place I'm moving to may not be as elegant, but at least it will be mine! Wendy looks across the table and stares at me. Her green eyes have an unquenchable fire in them.

I did what I had to do. Before Charles walked out, I had reached a point where I was very complacent. I lived a charmed life. Everything I wanted was given to me. Then, for the first time, I was in a position where I had to rely on myself. I could not fall back on a husband or a boyfriend or anyone else. A trauma happened and I was given choices. It was up to me to set myself free.

Now I have developed a sense of self. I realize that I am responsible for the quality of my life. It is up to me to find out what I want. Since I deserve the best, I will get the best. If I want something, I ask for it outright. "I want a pizza. I want to get married." . . . Wendy laughs heartily. There is so much warmth in her voice. I tell him, "This is the way I feel. You don't have to like it, but you have to deal with it." If a person says "No," I then have to decide whether or not it is a critical issue. If it is, I have to be prepared to get out of the relationship.

A married friend of mine who has stayed home with her children for the past 12 years surprised me the other day, when she said to me, "I need to do something for myself. Dave might not always be there." It made me realize that she had finally reached the point in her marriage where she realized that she had to look out for her own interests, because her marriage might not work out. Luckily it has, but she still has no guarantees.

Marriage is not an end point. You can't say, "We're married now, so that's it." That's death right there. Marriage is a living organism that develops with a lot of care and work. If someone were to say to me, "Wendy, you're a very attractive, desirable woman. What would you like your next relationship to be like?" I would reply, "I want a partnership." Both of us should be able:

- *To get past the myths.* For example, "There is only one right person for you." There are many right people; you just have to find the one who you like to be with at these moments in time. Or, "When you meet the man you're going to marry, you just know immediately." Sometimes you don't. The relationship just grows.
- *To exchange roles.* We each can be the seeker as well as the sought. I don't always have to be passive, and you don't always have to be active. Each of us can take turns asking each other for money, planning an evening out, and initiating quiet time together, cuddling or sex.
- *To be autonomous, as well as to share.* "Let me be autonomous. I want to be able to keep the interests I have. I would not want to spend 100 percent of my time with you." We each have to have our own interests. You have to give me a lot of space, because there are lots of things I need to do on my own. You're not going to say, "You can't do this or that."
- *To express our anger constructively.* This is very important to me—to get past the taboo that women aren't supposed to show anger. I don't want just to yell and scream, but to be able to fight fairly, so that I am not hurting or attacking the other person. I want to share my true feelings and to receive the other person's as well.

Somehow, as I gaze at Wendy, I can imagine her having a mutual partnership just like this!

The relationship that Wendy wants now is one where she can be autonomous. As an empowered woman, she wants to maintain her sense of self in all her relationships not only with her spouse but also with her friends, co-workers and students.

Although Wendy was not autonomous in her first marriage, she became her own person after her husband left her. She learned how to let go of Charles and become psychologically and financially independent. In the women's support group she joined, she became accustomed to talking honestly and openly with the other members of the group. She even formed a mutually empowering relationship with one of them. Now Wendy is ready for a partnership.

It is easiest to create a mutual partnership—with a "new" man. Who might he be? While there are no hard and fast rules, the "new" man is usually someone who is warm, caring and comfortable expressing his feelings, just as you are. Author Nancy Friday describes an ideal "new" man this way.

The perfect man sees the best in you—sees it constantly—not just when you occasionally are that way but also when you waver, when you forget yourself, act like less than you are. In time, you become more like his vision of you—which is the person you have always wanted to be.

What kind of partner is a "new" man looking for? Typically, he seeks an empowered woman. Recently I said to an unmarried retired executive, "Tell me about the qualities you seek in a partner." This was his reply:

I want a woman who:
Is a whole person, with her own ideas and interests;
Lives her own life, not mine vicariously;
Fulfills her potential, instead of ignoring it;
Enjoys taking risks and having adventures;
Above all, I want a woman with a dream.

Do these words describe you?

Gender Stereotypes Can Poison a Partnership

People in a mutual partnership shed their gender stereotypes. Vera's mother, a well-known labor union organizer who later became a teacher, describes her experience:

I would have accomplished the same things, if I had been a man. From the very beginning, my husband always supported me. I always felt that, first and foremost, I was a human being to him.

Although we should recognize and appreciate gender differences, we experience true mutuality when we see each other as human beings, not as men or women. How angry I feel when I hear someone say, "Just like a woman!" Men have told me that they feel the same way, when a woman calls them a "male chauvinist."

We need to avoid generalizing about the opposite sex by making statements like "Women do this," and "Men do that." Stereotypes of our own sex and the opposite one both blind us to reality. They keep us from seeing a person as he or she is and creating a relationship that fosters mutual growth.

Who Does the Housework?

When you are in a partnership with someone else, you are active, not passive. Both of you are constantly growing and changing. Neither of you is defined or limited by sex roles.

Discarding sex roles is particularly important. When I asked Carl, "Did you help Charlotte out in taking care of the children?" he replied emphatically, "Yes." All the men in mutual partnerships whom I interviewed told me they played an active role in raising their children. Child care was not strictly a woman's job.

In a genuine mutual partnership, there are no "women's jobs" or "men's jobs." Each person contributes in his or her own way to the needs of the partnership. You divide up tasks by deciding together what each of you likes to do—and can do best. Both of you are working together to achieve goals: yours, your partner's and the ones you share in common.

If you refuse to allow your partner to share what has traditionally been "women's work," you end up assuming power over him. Carl told me about his and Charlotte's experience:

"After you got married, how did you handle the housework?"

Carl: My mother had taught me how to sew, wash, iron and cook. When we were first married, I used to get home about 4:30 in the afternoon. Charlotte didn't arrive until 6:00. So I would go in the kitchen and experiment with casseroles. But Charlotte ran me out of the kitchen immediately. She said, "That's my job; I can cook."

Yes, Charlotte did cook very well. But I stopped cooking—and I haven't returned to the kitchen yet. In later years, she would ask me, "Why don't you go back into the kitchen?" And I would say, "No, that's your job!" A lot of women still think in these terms, "This is my job, and that is your job."

"Wasn't this a woman's 'power play'—like a man's saying, 'It's my job to make money?'"

Carl: "Exactly."

Denise and Dan handled this issue differently from Charlotte and Carl:

Denise: Early in our marriage, we would arrive home for dinner about the same time. We were good friends, so we would stand at the counter together and cook dinner. I said to my mother, "It is so painful for me to watch Dan peeling a potato. You cannot imagine how slow he is. I don't believe he has ever peeled a vegetable in his life; he doesn't even know how to hold the knife." My mother told me, "It's not a big deal to peel a potato. Give him a chance. If he doesn't learn now, he'll never learn!"

Today I think about what would have happened if I had sat Dan down with a newspaper and declared that I was going to be "Supercook." A few years later, he would have felt frustrated—and I would have gotten angry. I'm not sure how we would have gotten out of our rigid positions. We certainly would not be able to share the household tasks the way we do now. I would have lost a valuable opportunity.

Dan: You wanted to take over the cooking, in order to gain control in the relationship. "See, I'm the one who knows how to peel the potatoes. I can do all of my work at the office—and more." Power-over—with a potato peeler!

Women, as well as men, are capable of assuming power over their marriage partner. The woman who says, "I know how to peel a potato and you don't" is taking control of the relationship just like the man who says, "I know how to make a living and you don't." Each of them is trying to render his or her partner helpless by making himself or herself "indispensable."

What happens if your partner does not want to do any housework? If you insist that he does, you will be dominating him in your own way.

It is up to your partner to decide how he wants to participate in running the household. If he wants to help, you can share the work-load. If not, perhaps your older children can help, you can hire a paid employee or you can live in a dirty house and eat fast food for dinner.

Be Your Own Person

If you are used to "going along" with other people, "being nice" or "fitting in," a partnership can be a revolutionary experience. In a mutual partnership, each of you is your own person. You do not completely depend on each other for approval. You do not remain "stuck" in conflict nor do you constantly distance yourself from your partner. Within togetherness, you create separateness.

Katharine and Kyle, a college-age couple, described to me how they both maintain their autonomy within their relationship:

Kyle: We have always given each other a lot of space. If anything, I have given her too much. At the beginning of our relationship, she hung around with a lot of other guys, but I always stayed out of her way.

Katharine: Kyle never asked me to give up my normal social life. If he had, I would have refused. He didn't like some of my buddies, and I didn't like a couple of his. But we didn't stop seeing these people.

If Katharine had been very upset about someone Kyle was seeing, she would have told him about her feelings.

Autonomous people share their important desires. Yet for many women, asking for something is difficult. Perhaps this is because we do not really value ourselves. We are afraid that, if the other person says, "No," we will feel even more worthless. The flip side of our fear is that we find it hard to decline other people's requests, however unreasonable they may be to us. If we say, "No," we end up feeling guilty—and even more worthless! To create a mutual partnership, we have to say to ourselves over and over again, "Don't be afraid to ask. Don't be afraid to say 'No.'" Then we have to translate our thoughts into actions.

To be in a mutual partnership, you must value yourself. Then you can tell your partner about both your needs *and* your limits. You can ask for what you want and decline what you don't want. You will receive "no" answers, but you also will give them.

Autonomy is a crucial ingredient in a satisfying mutual partnership. People who feel strangled in a relationship eventually get out—one way or the other.

Trust Your Inner Voice

Have you ever had this dialogue with someone else?

You: What's the matter?

The Other Person: Nothing.

You: Oh, come on. I know something's the matter. I can tell by the expression on your face and the tone of your voice.

The Other Person: Well, you're wrong. I just told you, THERE IS NOTHING THE MATTER. You're just imagining things. Leave me alone!

If the other person said that you were wrong 100 times, would you believe him or her? Or would you still trust yourself? The essence of empowerment is believing your own voice, no matter what anyone else says. If you were to ignore the nagging feeling within you, you would be creating a power-over relationship. You would be allowing your partner to tell you what you feel and to decide what is real for both of you.

You would also be giving your partner permission to deny his or her angry, fearful or jealous feelings and push them deeper inside. Although ignoring unpleasant emotions is easier in the short run, openness and honesty strengthen a relationship in the long run. Even if you do not like what your partner says, confront it. Then deal with it and get past it, rather than having it remain hidden and slowly poison your relationship.

If your partner is not very talkative, you have to pay attention to his or her moods and reach out to him or her, when you perceive that he or she is upset. During our interview, Katharine and Kyle gave me this example from their experience:

Kyle: Katharine likes to talk more than I do. She is more open about sharing what is on her mind. But, if I am upset, I let her know.

Katharine: Kyle doesn't usually say, "Katharine, I have a problem." But I can tell when he has something on his mind. I just keep asking him, "What's the matter?" Eventually he always tells me.

Two people in a mutual partnership know themselves and can be themselves together. No, you will not like many of the messages your inner voice whispers to you. Perhaps it will tell you, "I am furious about the way my husband is treating me." Then what do you do? If you listen to, trust and act upon this feeling, your partner may end up calling you a "witch" by the end of the evening. But at least you won't have the aches and pains of being in a relationship where you are playing the role of pleaser or martyr or victim.

Be Authentic

In a mutually empowering relationship, you acknowledge your humanness—both your strengths and your weaknesses. You share yourself with another being who is human, too.

For a partnership to be successful, you and your partner must both be honest. When there is a conflict, the two of you need to be aware of what is bothering you and be able to discuss it openly. Each of you must be able to listen, as well as to talk.

Charlotte and Carl describe their marriage this way:

Charlotte: I am the kind of person who always confronts an issue. I have to talk about it.

Carl: I agree. We have always been able to put it "out there." Coming to a resolution has been much more difficult, of course. It is obvious if I have a problem, and it is obvious if Charlotte has a problem. We always express our feelings to each other. Then there is a discussion. Sometimes the issue is not always resolved right away But at least we are talking about it.

As an empowered woman, you will share your true feelings, whenever possible. You will be open with your partner, and with others as well. You will allow other people to be authentic, even if they are sometimes unpleasant, or even brutal. If you genuinely like someone, you will not be afraid to show it. Some men and women will be put off, but others will respond to your sincere acceptance of them.

Finding a Man is Not "The Answer"

As an empowered woman, you like men. But you do not live life vicariously through them. A man enriches your life; he does not define it. You seek a loving friend, not a male "status symbol" to support you. You take the time to discover your own values before you get involved with a partner. You refuse to remain in a close relationship, if it is a power-over one. As Wendy put it:

You can be happy without a man in your life. You are still a complete human being. Finding a man is not "the answer," especially if he puts you down.

If you have been playing a power-under role in your previous relationship with men, you do not want to become "over-independent" either. When you insist, "I don't need anyone," you are parroting a false message of male-oriented society. Just because one of your relationships has been frustrating does not mean that all of them will be. It *is* possible for you to become partners with someone else.

Once you don't feel that you have to be a wife to be "okay," you are able to take a good, hard look at anyone who you are thinking of marrying. A man's professional or financial success does not blind you to the real issue, "What kind of a human being is he?" You reject men who cannot share themselves and refuse to obsess yourself with any one of them.

Look Before You Leap!

Are you contemplating a permanent relationship, but have not yet made a final decision? Before you "leap," consider the following:

The person I have chosen is an excellent candidate for a mutual partnership if:

1. He is less than 5 years older than I am.
2. We have about the same amount of education.
3. Neither of us is much wealthier than the other.
4. He is committed to making the relationship work for both of us.
5. He is accustomed to doing jobs usually performed by the opposite sex.
6. He has attended at least one relationships seminar.
7. He has respect for women—and for the women's movement.
8. He treats his mother well.
9. His parents' marriage was a mutual partnership.

---

10. He is not concerned with traditional male and female roles.
The more "yes" answers you give, the greater the relationship's potential for mutuality.

Be flexible. Please don't expect your partner to meet all these standards right now. As the two of you become each other's teachers, your partner may grow in new and delightful directions.

How to Be a "Good Picker"

In order to create a mutual partnership, there have to be two willing participants. One is not enough.

If you value yourself, you will respect and like yourself. Ideally, you would like to have other people around who also feel the same way about you. But this is not always the case. Although you may give yourself respect, your romantic partner, your supervisor at work or some of your friends may not. You may want to become empowered, but keep on getting into relationships with men and women who don't.

This was my own experience. After my first marriage dissolved, I remarried quickly on the rebound. My second marriage lasted less than 3 years. Divorced twice, I was horrified at myself. I felt like a fallen woman; sometimes I imagined that I was wearing two big red "D's" that everyone could see. Finally I made an appointment with a therapist to find out why I had experienced this double disaster. After 6 months of twice-a-week sessions, I realized that there was nothing wrong with me. The problem was that I had selected men who were attractive, well-educated, well-off and exciting, but uninterested in becoming partners with me. What I had experienced was two power-over relationships.

If you already value and respect yourself, the key to creating an empowering relationship is to be a "good picker." If you are self-confident, you will feel able to master the outside world. You will decide to select a partner who allows you to be yourself, makes decisions together with you and listens to what is on your mind.

Julia, a pretty, self-employed businesswoman in her mid-30s, told me:

I am seeking a husband who wants to be in a marriage—and is willing to work on it. Ideally, this should be one of his highest priorities. After the initial attraction, it takes two to make a partnership.

Both of us have to want the same kind of relationship. If he is into being "the boss" and I want to build together what the two of us want, it won't work. I get turned off very quickly, when I feel as if someone is trying to control me. If we have a problem, let's discuss it.

I think that how you handle money is symbolic of what is happening in the relationship. In a partnership, you share everything—including money. One person doesn't decide how all the dollars are spent. It doesn't matter how much each person brought into the relationship or how much each one is earning now. What matters is how much you have together.

Choose an autonomous individual with whom you have an excellent chance of forming an empowering connection. Avoid dominating people who will form power-over relationships and put you in the power-under role. Remember, it takes two to create a mutual partnership. You cannot share power with someone who does not want to. Give yourself a head start in your search for mutuality. Pick your partner very carefully.

What about Romance?

Romantic relationships are usually power-over ones, at least at the beginning. Men and women both strive to present a good image. Each tells the other what he wants to hear, rather than the whole truth. To maintain their superiority, men use women as "sex objects," and women use men as "success objects," as Dr. Warren Farrell points out in *Why Men Are the Way They Are*. This is why it is often easier to become partners with a man or a woman with whom you have a nonsexual relationship.

An empowering romantic relationship evolves. Often it starts out with one person having power over the other. Slowly both people become empowered together with each other.

There are three stages in the transition from power over, to empowerment together with, someone else. The first stage is getting to know each other. You and the other person find out the necessary information to decide whether or not you are compatible. The second stage is a contest for control. Who will dominate? Since both of you are products of male-oriented society, power struggles are almost inevitable. The third stage is when you go beyond control and become empowered together. Little by little, each of you finds the strength, wisdom and maturity to give up your dominant and subordinate positions and become loving friends instead.

How Does a Mutual Partnership Feel?

How will you know if you have finally created a mutual partnership? There are two signs. First, you are able to be yourself in the relationship. Second, no matter how deeply involved you and your partner are, you are still autonomous. You experience life by yourself and with him, but not through him. You have your own private space and your own private time. And always, you are free to have friendships with other men.

By answering these questions silently to yourself, you can evaluate your current relationship:

I have a mutual partnership if:

1. Neither of us dominates the other.
2. I am "me" in the partnership; I don't pretend or act.
3. Since our aim is to "get the job done," we disregard traditional sex roles.
4. I neither seek to control my partner nor to allow him to control me.
5. When I give to my partner, it is from my abundance; I do not "sacrifice" for him.
6. I do not expect my partner always to take care of me; often I take care of him.
7. When we are angry, we express our feelings promptly and constructively.
8. I set clear limits about what treatment I will not accept from my partner.
9. If my partner repeatedly violates these limits, I am prepared to leave.
10. I have chosen my partner because I care for him, not because he is good-looking, wealthy or socially acceptable.

The more "yes" answers you give, the greater the likelihood that you have created a mutual partnership.

Empowerment Exercises

1. *"How Mutual Is My Romantic Relationship?"* Think of the most precious romantic relationship you now have. Close your eyes and visualize this person sitting next to you. Greet him. Experience what it is like when you are together. Which subjects do you both enjoy talking about? Which friends do you both like to be with? What are your shared interests? What tasks do you perform together? What common joys and sorrows do you have? What are your mutual values? Is there a joint contribution that the two of you would like to make to the world during your lifetimes? Now say, "Goodbye" to this person and

experience being alone. Now pull together all your feelings about this relationship. Is it a mutual partnership, or does one of you dominate? How much do the two of you really share?

2. *"How Can I Move from Conflict to Sharing?"* Now concentrate on an important relationship you have which is full of conflict, argument and pain. Visualize that person sitting across from you: look closely first at his face and then at yours. Do you feel that you want to be right, superior or more powerful than him? Do feelings of competition—a desire to win—pervade your relationship? How could you free yourself from your "win-lose" positions and move toward sharing your feelings together honestly and openly?

3. *Journal Writing: Diary of a Mutual Partnership:* If you are already in a mutual partnership, jot down in your Empowerment Journal its most memorable incidents. In love, sex, work and play, how have each of you empowered each other? When has the relationship been truly mutual? How have you and your partner managed to be your own persons? When have both of you been most real with each other? If you have additional time, you will benefit from also writing a few sentences about how the relationship has empowered you and your partner, at the end of each day. If you read back what you have written at the end of the year, you can get a valuable perspective on the relationship's strengths and weaknesses. It is up to you to decide whether or not to share what you have written with your partner.

4. *Visualize the Relationship You Want:* What kind of relationship would you like that you do not have now? First visualize the qualities you would like in the relationship. Then think of at least two people you have wanted to have relationships with in the past. Picture each of them in your mind. Do you think that each of these people would be comfortable in the kind of relationship you want? Just for a moment, imagine throwing all your socially approved standards to the winds and selecting a person who would fit into your ideal relationship, instead of vice versa.

Whether you are in a mutual partnership, or are working to create one, you must know how an empowered woman communicates. Do you? Or is your communication with your partner unsatisfying? This obstacle will become a stepping stone in the next chapter.

LEARN HOW AN EMPOWERED WOMAN COMMUNICATES

"Real communication occurs . . .when we listen with understanding. What does this mean? It means to see the expressed idea and attitude from the other person's point of view, to sense how it feels to him."

Carl Rogers, Ph.D.
On Becoming a Person

As women, how can we move from conflict to connection? We want to break down the walls between us and our partners, even if it means confronting them, initiating painful discussions or even walking out as a dire last warning. Yet so often our attempts to share our feelings end in empty arguments. We and our partners wind up as adversaries, each one of us holding tightly onto our position.

I meet Shana in Virginia Beach at a seminar for women. Immediately I can tell by the expression on her face that something is wrong. I ask her gently if she wants to talk. She tells me that, when she left for the seminar, her husband, Max, was lying in a hospital intensive care unit. He had just had his third heart attack in less than a year.

Shana tells me, "I am waiting for a call from the hospital to tell me if Max will be released or kept in the intensive care unit for a while longer." For 3 days we wait together in suspense. On the fourth, the news is good: Max is out of the hospital. He is on his way to Virginia Beach to join Shana at the seminar.

The next morning, I am delighted to see Shana arm in arm with a smiling, gray-haired man. He looks a little pale. We talk together.

Shana bursts out, "My feelings are bruised and swollen. I long to be comforted." Then she turns to me. "Am I entitled to get what I need?" she asks. Max seems vaguely aware of the fears inside of him. "If I get in touch with what I feel, I may lose control," he muses.

Shana finally gathers her courage to tell Max she needs to talk. He is on the defensive; he does not want to be pushed. They sit down on the floor facing each other. Shana begins, "I'm always the caretaker. When are you going to heal my feelings?" Max takes his defensive position: "Here I am on the firing line again; why can't you just leave me alone?" Shana and Max are at an impasse. They have the following conversation in my presence:

Max: I look at you and all I can see is your red eyes full of tears. How are you feeling?

Shana: Sad and scared. But I am with you.

Max: I feel that whatever I say or do will not be enough for you. What words can I speak, what actions can I take, so that you will be satisfied?

Shana: I don't want to be the only one who is dealing with the fear that you might die.

Max. You're not. I am dealing with it every day. I am more scared than you are, because I am the one who will die.

Shana: But you won't have to deal with the mess that's left.

Max: When I was in the hospital, critically ill, there was absolutely nothing I could do for you. I remember that you were there all the time by my side, taking care of me and dealing with my family. You were always in control. I remember that there was a lot of sadness centering around my children, who weren't able to handle my illness. I couldn't be available to help you deal with their problems. I want you to know, Shana, that I value both how you took care of me and how you took care of yourself during that difficult time.

The struggle within me is that I want to deny it all; I want to shut down. It is much easier for me to say, "Yesterday is yesterday, and today is today; let's get on with it." But I know that's not what you want. And I also realize that what has happened to me is controlling our lives. Every morning I have to deal with your unspoken fear that you may lose me.

Shana: I experience a loss of connection with you when I think that our relationship is about to end. I want you to share how you feel about what is happening to us—not all the time, but when it comes up for you. When you deal with the difficult stuff, I would like you to think out loud. Can we make an agreement when, where and how we could do this? Otherwise, I will keep bringing this subject up and you will get more and more annoyed.

Max: I need a time limit, so I won't feel that our talk will go on and on and on. For me, 30 minutes of discussion seem like 4 hours. But for you 30 minutes may not be nearly enough. Is there any chance that we can work around this period of time?"

Shana: Yes, I'm willing to accept a time limit that is comfortable for you.

Max: Then I agree to talk with you. How many 30-minute periods do you need and how many days a week do you need them?

Shana: Right now, I don't really know. How about starting with one talk tomorrow morning at 8:00, after we wake up, and then we'll decide after that.

In this conversation, Shana did not "win." Nor did she "lose." Shana did not dominate Max, and Max did not gain power over Shana. They moved toward mutual agreement, because Shana made her husband her ally, rather than her adversary. After sharing how she felt, Shana listened empathetically to what Max had to say. When she responded, she honored what he had shared, particularly his need for a time limit in their discussions.

How Does An Empowered Woman Communicate?

If you are an empowered woman, you are your own person, instead of being a pleaser, a martyr or a beggar who is dependent on someone else for approval. In your relationships, you talk honestly, rather than fight or run away. You tell your partner how you really feel, and you listen to his or her honest words. Empowering communication is natural for you.

The hallmark of an empowering relationship is mutuality. Like everything else, your communication is two for two, instead of "two for one." No one is concerned with being the "boss," "winning" an argument, being "right" or even changing the subject to one he or she prefers. Instead, two or more people are simply making a connection with each other. Speaker and listener have a special way of sharing which enables the conversation to move along freely.

Empowering communication is no accident. You make it happen by listening as well as talking, telling the truth about yourself and playing an active role in directing the conversation. To make a conversation mutual, authentic and autonomous, cultivate these 12 skills:

1. *Make a deep and genuine connection with the other person.* Do your best to look directly into the eyes of a person who is talking, or listening, to you. If you experience emotions while you are connecting, stop and describe what is inside you. For example, "I feel as if you really understand what I am saying," or "I feel as if you are utterly bored with what I am telling you." Then pause and allow the other person to react.

2. *Get in touch with the other person's perspective.* How does he or she

see reality? To let a speaker know that you have been moved by his or her experience, you might say, "I understand how you feel," or "If I were you, I would have felt that way, too," or "I can appreciate how it must have been for you," or "There must have been a reason why you did these things; you were not crazy."

You are under no obligation to agree with what the speaker is saying. To say, "I agree with you" or "I feel the same way" or "I would have done the same thing," is not only unnecessary but also inappropriate. You are not judging someone else's feelings by your own values; rather, you are doing your best to understand another person's unique experience from his or her distinct point of view.

3. *Fully receive the speaker's words.* If you are listening, you need to get yourself involved with what you are hearing. There is a vast difference between just physically being with another person and truly being with that person emotionally. Listen carefully to what is being said. Even if you do not like the message you are hearing, allow yourself to fully receive it.

4. *When you are speaking, share your own personal experiences rather than talking in generalities.* "I felt so hurt last night, when my husband told me to 'shut up' and closed the door to his office in my face" is clearer than, "Men never listen to women; they are always putting us down."

5. *Describe your real feelings in the "here and now."* Don't hide or mask them. "I feel furious when I think about how my husband, Arthur, shuts me off," is more real than, "I am used to being ignored when my husband is busy with his work; it really doesn't matter to me anymore."

6. *Avoid the temptation to hold back what comes up for you.* When a past experience comes to your mind, describe it. Suppose the other person responds, "I remember how my father used to tell me, 'Don't bother me; I'm busy now.' I felt as if he didn't love me." Think how something that once happened to you relates to what the speaker is saying. You might search your memory and come up with, "When my father would fight with my mother, slam the door and leave the house, I used to feel exactly the same way."

7. *Share; don't compete.* You cannot create an empowering relationship with someone you are competing with. Get your ego out of the way. If you are trying to be smarter, funnier or wiser than the person you are listening to, you will end up focusing attention on yourself, not on him or her. Your experience is your own; it is not to be compared with anyone else's. What the speaker says is about him or her, not about you.

8. *Welcome a silence, whenever it occurs.* It gives you a chance to rest, to think about how you are feeling now and to decide what to share

next. Silence is a form of communication. Speakers and listeners need time to process what they have heard, get in touch with how they felt about it and frame an appropriate response. Be patient; like good coffee, a conversation needs to brew.

9. *Allow the other person to assist you in keeping the dialogue going.* Don't stop the conversation if you start feeling anxious. When you reach this point, you might say something like, "I'm getting more and more upset, as we continue to talk about how you distance yourself from me. Right now I feel like walking out." Let your listener support you.

When the conversation becomes much too intense for you, say so. Your feelings are like a thermometer measuring how hot it is in a room. If you become extremely uncomfortable, chances are that you have touched an alarm button. In all likelihood, the speaker is also experiencing pain from what is being shared.

10. *Avoid arguments.* If the conversation turns into an argument, end it. Plan a time to resume it, after you have both cooled down. If all of your "conversations" turn into arguments, then most likely you are facing a die-hard conventional power struggle—which will never heal you.

11. *Appreciate your own special strengths as a woman.* These are the essence of your femininity. Because you have a keen desire to connect with other people, you are interested in what makes them tick.

12. *Focus on feelings, rather than logic.* Honestly shared feelings defy rational analysis. In an empowering relationship, you learn to tolerate paradoxes and ambiguities; you understand that the flow of the relationship isn't always clear. As the conversation moves on, leave yourself open to asking new questions and embracing solutions that you may never have thought of before.

An Example of Empowering Communication

In a mutually empowering relationship, you share your true feelings and listen very carefully to what your partner is saying. Sharing your true feelings means taking the time to get in touch with what is inside of you. Listening very carefully means being there for your partner; it does not necessarily mean agreeing with everything he or she says. It is up to you to take the first steps in opening the lines of communication with your partner.

For example, one night, out of the blue, your male partner says to you, "Lately when you're with me, you're always so tense. Sometimes it bothers me so much I want to get away from you." It is very important that you stop talking and receive what your partner is saying. Tell him that you hear him. Let him know that you have been moved by what he just said. Make "I" statements: "I understand that;" "I appreciate that."

Get past your initial reaction, which is probably to make "you" statements. You may be inclined to either discredit him ("You don't know what you're talking about!"), argue ("You're imagining it; I'm actually quite relaxed"), or defend yourself ("Yes, but that's because I've got an important project that's due at the end of the month"). All of these "you" responses make him feel that his message is being judged, rather than received. Your self-righteousness may make you feel less vulnerable, but it may make it impossible for him to continue to express what he is really feeling.

Describe what he has said and then move the focus back to you. After you have acknowledged his experience, help him understand yours—how it is the same and how it is different. "I heard you say that lately I seem so tense that you sometimes don't want to be with me. What you are saying reminds me of how I used to feel about my best friend, Ella, when she was studying for exams or going out on job interviews. I used to dread picking up the phone to dial her number."

Then wait for his response. He has told you his experience; you have shared yours; and now he needs to put them together in his mind. This is no easy task. What you both are doing is understanding your differences, so that you can get past "I" and "you" to "we." There may be a long silence. Wait for his response. You are not playing "verbal ping-pong." By slowing the conversation down, you give him time to think about what he is going to say.

Avoid saying, "Tell me what you are feeling now." To many men, this approach is a directive to "do something." Many men fear women 's competence in expressing feelings, just as women fear men's dominance in the workplace. As one man put it, "When someone says, 'Tell me how you feel,' to me, it sounds like I'm about to take an oral examination about my emotions. It is as if I were at work and my supervisor has asked me to report back to him about a task he has assigned to me."

What works better is, "I'd really appreciate your sharing with me what you heard me say, whatever it is. If you didn't understand what I said, feel free to say so and I'll repeat it again." Then wait for his response. Finally, he says, "No, you're not quite the way Ella was; she used to talk a blue streak when she got uptight. Yours is a more silent tension. What bothers me is that it's getting harder and harder for me to enjoy myself with you, the way I used to when we first met. We haven't gone out together to have fun in 5 weeks."

When you hear your partner's words, you may feel tears coming to your eyes. This is a sign that you are truly listening to him. If you are touched or moved by what he says, express it. When he feels that you are truly with him in what he is experiencing, empowering communication will begin.

It may take several exchanges before you finally understand each other's feelings. For a while, you may feel as if you are throwing stones into a faraway pool; only rarely do you get a ripple. After a long silence, you say, "Yes, I remember how you used to tell me that what you liked best about being with me is how we could be silly together. You're right; we haven't had any good laughs in over a month. I guess this project deadline is really getting to me."

Suddenly you see a gleam of understanding in your partner's eyes. Perhaps he says to you, "I feel that you've heard me." Or perhaps his glow tells you all you need to know. Now you are ready to think out loud together and creatively resolve your differences. You say, "It's going to be very hard for me to take a lot of time to relax until I get the project done. But I can spend at least one evening this week unwinding. I need a break. This Friday night is Halloween. How about we dress up in our Walt Disney costumes and go out trick-or-treating, just like we used to do? I'll be Bugs Bunny, and you can be Donald Duck!"

Perhaps the resolution of your differences may not be quite so simple. You may say, "I understand your feelings, but I don't really see myself as acting more uptight than usual." Or he may say, "I don't know if having a few laughs 1 night a week is will make me feel differently about being with you." Or one or both of you may need some time alone to think about what has been said, so you can resume the discussion later on. The most creative solutions often emerge after each person has spent a few hours alone.

Getting out of an Impasse

Often we reach an impasse with our partners. We start a discussion, only to find ourselves in an argument. Instead of sharing our feelings, we are shouting at each other. You are "right," and he is "wrong." He is "winning," and you are "losing." To create empowering communication, what strategies can we use to move from argument to connection? How can we get out of an impasse?

About 6 months after I married my husband, Phil, we reached our own first impasse. Cleo, a young single woman, whom he had known for about 5 years before our marriage, continued to ask him to go out. Phil insisted that he and Cleo were "good friends," that he enjoyed going out to cultural events with her and that he had a "right" to do this. I was equally adamant not only that this was inappropriate behavior for a married man but also that Cleo seemed to me to be "more than just a friend."

Our arguments grew louder and more fruitless. In desperation, I sought help from the minister who had married us. After one session in his office, I was empowered to have this dialogue with Phil:

Riki: Phil, I am clear that there is no way I can control you or make you do anything that you do not want to do.

Phil: Obviously. If I want to see Cleo, I am going to see her.

Riki: This line of talk is not helpful. Let's move in a different direction. Phil, I am talking about me, not about you. You have done nothing wrong. You are a not a bad person; you are a wonderful person—that's why I married you. I understand that you enjoy being with her and that you value her friendship. What I need to tell you is how I feel when Cleo calls you and when you go out for the evening. The pain and the anger are more than I can bear. You know sometimes I have cried for hours. For me, it has been the only way I know to ease my excruciating pain.

Phil: It has been terrible for me when you have had these "crying spells." Sometimes I wonder how long I can stand them.

Riki: Phil, I am not telling you to stop being friends with Cleo. I am asking you to make something else more important than your seeing Cleo: my feelings and our marriage. I have tried every way I know to heal my pain: I have talked for hours with supportive women friends, gone with you to our minister and prayed every night for strength to understand your need. Right now, I am "stuck." I cannot overcome these incredibly deep feelings within me.

Phil: I love you, Riki, and I want to preserve our marriage. At the same time, what you are saying makes absolutely no sense to me. Cleo is an old friend who wants to see me from time to time. I cannot think of a single logical reason why I should not see her.

Riki: I agree with you. My feelings are not logical. But they are very strong and I hurt a lot. So I end up hurting you. I can't control you, Phil. I don't want to control you. What I am doing is asking you to respect my feelings—and to preserve our relationship. Which is more important to you—being friends with Cleo or being happily married?

Phil: "Do I have to make a choice?" He laughs. Then he is silent for what seems to me like eternity, but is actually only about 2 minutes. "When you put it this way, the situation looks different to me. Perhaps I'll keep away from her for a while."

It was no accident that this conversation ended in mutual agreement. After Phil's initial remark, "If I want to see Cleo, I am going to see her," I immediately saw the danger of renewed conflict. If we were to make any progress, I had to stop and shift the direction of the conversation from control to mutual intention. Like many people caught in an defensive posture, Phil perceived that I was pushing him to do something. As a matter of pride, he was not going to be coerced. He was going to get his way and "win."

As soon as I told him that I was only talking about my feelings, not what he was doing, Phil no longer felt attacked. He could comfortably discuss my behavior and then consider how he was being affected by it. It was very important that we both understood that, although my feelings were not rational, they were very painful and very real to both of us.

Once we reached mutuality, we could expand our discussion to include our most important shared goal, the preservation of our marriage. As we talked, Phil realized how important our union was to him. The tone of our conversation changed, as we pondered how we could continue to work together toward this common purpose. We both became aware how my reactions to his encounters with Cleo were poisoning our marriage. After we expressed our mutual intention to stay together, Phil decided that he would distance himself from Cleo.

Like so many relationship stories, this one did not end here. About 6 months later, I went off to La Jolla, California, by myself for a 16-day seminar at the Center for Studies of the Person. During those days, I met several men whose company I enjoyed. After an evening with one of them, I suddenly woke up about 3:00 in the morning. I had a very important thought. No matter how much I had enjoyed this man's company, I was sure that there was nothing he could have said or done that would have threatened my marriage in any way. My relationship with Phil was so deep and so strong that any other encounter was trivial by comparison.

Suddenly I realized that this was true for Phil as well. As I trusted myself, so I could trust him. Yes, he might see Cleo aeain, bud somehow it didn't matter anymore. As soon as I saw Phil again, I told him about my revelation. He received what I had to say, without judgments or recriminations. Phil and I had moved from an impasse to mutuality.

"Womantalk" Is Empowering Communication

As women, we have within us all the tools we need for empowering communication. A man once told me, "Women talk very deeply about very inconsequential things." If two men were to start a conversation like women do, one of them might begin by remarking, "I like the shape of your beard." Sounds odd, doesn't it? Yet it is commonplace for one woman to start a conversation in the ladies' room by re-marking, "Your hair looks nice."

Women's discussions are personal, intimate and caring. They don't only concern what we do for a living, the latest political scandals or who won yesterday's major league baseball games. They are about people, relationships and feelings. "Womantalk" is nurturing, rather than isolating. Even our silences are productive. They are spaces where we feel close to each other, without the need for words.

Gossip is not "womantalk." While "womantalk" means sharing and caring, gossip means isolating and hurting someone else. Two people gossip about a third person who is not present to speak the truth. Their remarks are often inaccurate and sometimes destructive. Gossip is neither honest nor empowering. "Womantalk" is both.

How to Cut off Communication Before It Starts

Although women have the potential for empowering communica-tion, most of us do not stay in dialogue with a partner long enough to get what we want. Consciously or unconsciously, we end the conver-sation by:

1. *Aggressively quizzing him.* "Did you hear me?" "Do you under-stand what I am saying?" He feels like a 6-year-old boy, and you look to him like his mother or his first-grade teacher.

2. *Changing the subject, or allowing him to change the subject, when the discussion gets slow or painful.* "Isn't it time for dinner?" or "The phone is ringing; don't you think one of us should answer it?"

3. *Talking only about your own feelings, instead of asking him questions and listening carefully to his responses.* "I'm furious about what hap-pened last night. How could you have treated me like that? Don't you have any respect for my feelings?" . . .

4. *Acting as if you know how he feels, rather than asking him to tell you.* "I'm sure you think you've done nothing wrong. You've probably got some good explanation, as usual." Or, "You never seem to care about how I feel. You don't even realize how upset I am right now!" Since men fear women's dominance in the area of feelings, these kinds of statements will usually lead to an immediate end to the discussion.

5. *Putting him down.* Often men feel that they are being scolded, be-littled, or judged when they talk with women. Phrases like, "There is much good in you," or "You have so many fine qualities," are strangely absent from these conversations.

Every person needs a "safe place" where he or she can be heard. An empowered woman creates one for her partner.

Inviting Men to Open Up

Somehow it is easier to feel a common purpose with someone of your own sex. In women's support groups and empowerment communities, we shed our defensive armor as we realize that we are allies, with the same perspective and the same problems. Men who have attended men's groups also come to life, as they mutually share similar feelings. Especially in the women's groups, there is less accusing, blaming, dominating, being "right" and taking sides, although sometimes feminists can become argumentative in the presence of traditional women.

To move from opposition to cooperation in a male-female relationship means to create these same feelings of mutuality with a person of the opposite sex. Although both of you will inevitably start off in defensive positions, you, as an empowered woman, will take the initiative in creating a climate of mutuality.

The first step is to establish mutual trust, so that both of you feel free to reveal your emotions and vulnerabilities. Men who have been accused of "not being in touch with their feelings" have told me that often they are "in touch," but they are unwilling to share their private feelings and vulnerabilities openly with a woman. Typically a man feels this way because he fears that:

- A woman may make fun of what he says.
- A woman may use what he says against him later.
- A woman may tell other people about what he has said.

Once you have shown a man that you will truly respect the feelings he shares with you, you are ready to move your discussions toward a common purpose.

When a man opens up, he wants to feel that you will welcome what he says. He will not continue to share his feelings, if you:

1. *Talk on and on and on and on.* If torrents of words are pouring out of your mouth, you cannot possibly listen to someone else, or even to yourself. At best you are dull; at worst, you are intimidating. If you cannot convince him to agree with you, he may "give in," just to have some peace and quiet.

2. *Become consumed with self-righteous anger.* Anger, combined with self-righteousness, gives you a feeling of power over others. Underneath the anger is usually pain. Regardless of the subject, the message is, "I am right; other people are wrong." Whether or not you are "right," you are not communicating. Instead of sharing, you are blaming. No one wants to listen to another person who makes him or her

feel "wrong." Because self-righteous anger evokes guilt, it is sometimes used to control other people.

3. *Argue.* Arguing polarizes communication. Two people take opposite sides, instead of seeing each other's point of view. You may win
points in a debate, or a victory in the courtroom, but you will not gain
a loving friend. An argument often ends with shouting, name-calling
and other bullying tactics. Although you cannot avoid arguments
completely, you can do your best to minimize them.

Women who communicate in a power-over style intimidate others,
including men. An empowered woman knows that a dialogue re-
solves differences far better than a monologue or an argument.

Is This What You Want?

Julia, the self-employed businesswoman in her 30s, told me during
our interview what she was looking for in a relationship:

Most of all, I would like a partner who is sensitive to the feelings of other
people. He should be willing to listen to me. Lots of times a problem which
seems to be very big gets smaller once you tell the other person about it,
even if it doesn't change. By revealing something, it gets to be less important.

I am also looking for a partner who is aware of what is going on inside of
him and is not afraid to share it. For example, he might say, "At this moment,
I feel as if I'm 3 years old and nobody loves me. My feelings are not rational;
you can't change them. All you can do is hold me and tell me that it's okay to
feel this way right now." I would be very receptive to this kind of message.

To sum up, I am attracted to someone with whom I can discuss relationships. He doesn't have to understand how computers work, just how people
work. If he is interested in talking about our relationship, then he probably
wants a good one.

Julia realized that empowering communication takes place between two people who can share their honest feelings and accept the
truth from each other.

Empowering Communication Can Heal You

If you are "stuck" in many painful connections with other people,
you need to create a healing, understanding relationship with at least
one person who will:

1. *Really listen to you.* He or she will fully receive what you are saying—understand your feelings and your point of view.

2. *Validate your experience.* He or she will allow you to realize that

whatever is going on in your life really did happen, and that you are not "crazy."

3. *Appreciate your goodness.* He or she will let you know that he admires your fine qualities and that you are not a "bad" person for feeling as you do.

4. *Share the importance of relationships.* He or she will allow you to acknowledge that, up to now, the old connections did have value for you and that you had to do whatever you did in these relationships.

5. *Acknowledge your growth.* He or she will understand how angry, afraid and sad you were when the connections became painful, and help you realize that you can now begin to heal.

6. *Empower you to act.* He or she will enable you to be your true self within the old connections or else to move beyond the old connections to establish new ones.

Once you have one relationship where you experience genuine communication, you will be empowered to have others. You will know what it feels like to have someone really listen to you.

What Does It Mean to Really Listen?

A genuine, caring and sensitive listener becomes a companion in another person's inner world. After a person speaks, the listener lets the speaker know that he or she has been heard. Perhaps the listener may complete an unfinished sentence, sum up what the speaker has said or gently suggest how the speaker may be feeling. When the listener does not understand exactly what the speaker is saying, the listener can speak. By sharing an experience of his or her own that has come to mind, the listener can bring their two worlds together.

A real listener accepts all the speaker's negative feelings—fear, despair and worthlessness—without making judgments about them. Neither advice nor help is offered; just silent support. It is possible for a good listener to literally forget himself or herself completely, as he or she becomes absorbed in what the other person is saying.

The speaker feels, "My listener completely understands what it is like to be me. I am no longer alone; someone else is truly with me." Only in this kind of conversation can people get truly close to each other.

Often empowering communication is more than just really listening. It means genuinely caring about the person who is talking to you. Sometimes you need to show your concern with actions, as well as words. If the other person is resisting, you may need to do something dramatic, to break through his or her protective shield. Vera reached out to her daughter Darlene, now 23 years old, by getting her attention first. Then Vera enabled Darlene to deal with a problem she could not solve alone.

Vera and Darlene: "I'm Trying to Go Off Drugs."

Vera and I are seated in her office with the door closed. This is our second interview. She has been discussing her job for half an hour in a staccato, matter-of-fact tone of voice. To change the subject, I ask, "By the way, how is your daughter, Darlene?" Now Vera suddenly starts to talk quickly and passionately. . . .

About a month ago, I found out that my daughter, Darlene, had become heavily dependent on drugs. Darlene has always been worried about her weight. Apparently, she had heard that a certain kind of amphetamine called "crystal" would lead to weight loss. The dealers who were selling her the drug told her that it wouldn't "hook" her, but it did.

Darlene did lose weight, but she became cranky and irritable. But, because she was on this drug, she couldn't tell that she was being unpleasant; she was sure that she was being calm and reasonable. When I did tell her how terribly she was behaving, she wouldn't believe me.

When Darlene came home in June, it seemed as if it was going to be another miserable summer for me. Last June, July and August, she had spent all her time sitting in front of the television set and eating. I realize now that this was her way of dulling her pain. I did not know that she was on drugs.

This time, Darlene immediately informed me that she had been telling all her friends, "There's no point in spending time with me anymore; I am a sinking ship." The first day she was home, she slept until 7:00 in the evening. I was shocked.

The following morning at 9:00, I called the local hospital and got her an appointment with a psychiatrist and an internist—both the same day. If you've ever dealt with a hospital clinic, you know this was not easy. When she came back from her appointments, she told me that she had an infection in her nose. I should have immediately suspected drug use. But she did not tell me what her conversation with the psychiatrist was about, and I did not ask her.

"But you had expressed genuine concern."

Yes. I had also made a dental appointment for her the next day. In the early afternoon, she called me at work and told me that she couldn't get to the dentist by herself. So during my lunch hour, I drove 30 miles to pick her up at home, took her to the dentist, dropped her off and then drove back to work. I really went out of my way to reach out to her.

The dentist told Darlene that she was grinding her teeth, which would eventually lead to serious gum problems. He asked her, "Are you under stress?" "No," she replied. Then she turned to me and said, "It's all right, Mom; don't worry about me." But I think she finally realized that she had to do something about her addiction.

The following day, Darlene was supposed to drive up to Ocean City, Maryland, to see her dad, but I realized that she wasn't going to be able to make the trip by herself. So I drove her 400 miles to the beach, dropped her off at her dad's house, stayed overnight with a friend and then drove her home. When we got back, I was exhausted.

"This was a very dramatic expression of your caring."

Yes, I really went way out of my way. Luckily, I was not very busy at work, so I could take 2 days off.

"After you arrived home, did you continue to reach out to her?"

Yes, but in a nagging way. It was all I could manage.

One night, I found Darlene hunched over the television set with a bowl of cereal on her lap. Although it was a beautiful evening, the living room curtains were tightly shut and the television was blaring. Her appearance just shouted, "Don't bother me. I'm not going to do anything enjoyable on this nice summer evening."

I casually ventured, "I'd like to go out shopping later. Maybe we can go together. . . ." Darlene did not reply. So I said, "I suppose you're going to watch television again this evening."

Darlene started to raise her voice. "I knew you were going to nag at me and find fault. . . ." Our conversation was moving toward a blowup. Then, all of a sudden, she shouted, "You've ruined my whole schedule. I want to sit in front of this television set and not be bothered, and now you're home. I'm trying to go off drugs!"

"How did you feel, when you heard that?"

Later, Darlene told me that she had thought that I would be destroyed once I found out that she was taking drugs. Instead I became very calm. Yes, she was behaving obnoxiously and horribly, but,"What else is new?" Vera laughs. Darlene had always been a moody teenager. For me, knowing that she was on drugs explained her recent, bizarre behavior. I was actually relieved. Now everything fitted together.

"What did you say to her next?"

There was a long silence. Then Darlene declared, "I'm never going to speak to you or my dad again." I replied, "I can understand how you might feel this way." By this time, I had had enough. I wanted to get out of the house. So I told her, "I'm going shopping. I'll see you later."

I went to Westlake Mall, bought a pair of navy blue shorts and came home. Darlene was on the phone with her dad. I heard her telling him, "I've destroyed Mom. She's probably sitting in a parking lot somewhere crying her eyes out."

"Hi, Darlene; I'm back!" I called out cheerfully. She was very surprised. "What's going on?" she shouted. "I bought these shorts for myself and some frozen yogurt for you. Strawberry, your favorite!" I answered. At that moment, our relationship completely turned around. She realized that I wasn't going to reject her and that I could handle her addiction.

Since then, our relationship has steadily improved. This past Sunday, I was on the phone with her for almost 2 hours. She said to me, "I don't need drugs to deaden my pain anymore. Now I can just 'be with' whatever is happening to me.

I cannot believe how understanding and accepting you have been, Mom. Before, I wanted to take everything that I could—money, food and love—from you. Whatever you gave me, it was never enough. At the dinner table, I would eat two helpings and then ask for a third. I would listen to you sigh and then eat that third helping. I'd eat a fourth, when you left the table. Not anymore."

She continued, "You are my role model now, Mom. Do you remember, when we moved to Denver, how you fixed up our house with second-hand furniture and 'made do?' Well, I'm doing the same in my efficiency apartment. I'm even making my own curtains! I'm also learning to manage on my own income."

Until then, I had been so worried about Darlene—about her weight, about her overspending and about her living alone. Now that we are really listening to each other, I have confidence in my daughter.

"You really broke your communication barrier. What you did and said must have meant a great deal to her."

I was determined to stick with her—to reach out to her somehow.

Vera had reached out to Darlene first by taking dramatic action to show that she cared and then by really listening to her. As Darlene became aware that her mother wanted to share her problem, rather than dominate her, lecture her or judge her, their communication became mutually empowering.

When Communication Is Not Empowering

There is more than one way to run away from a relationship. Of course, you can physically leave. But you can also remain in the relationship without totally participating—which is far less obvious and much more painful. People in power-over relationships shut each other out.

Although two people in a power-over relationship may be physically and even legally connected, at least one of them is not really "there." Even though both of them may sleep next to each other at night, they might as well be 1,000 miles apart. They prevent empowering communication either by not expressing their true feelings or by refusing to receive whatever their partner shares.

You, as well as your partner, are responsible for the quality of your communication. If you want to change a power-over relationship to one where you are empowered together with your partner, start by changing the tone of your conversations. If your partner will not take the lead, it is up to you to show him or her a different way of talking and listening.

Breaking Down Barriers

Empowering communication doesn't just happen. You have to initiate it. The hardest part is to get past your own fear of breaking down the barriers between you and someone else.

Let me give you an example from my own experience. My son and I had been exchanging angry letters for about 6 weeks. For the first time in 3 years, he was coming home for Christmas—for just 2 days. I did not know what to expect. An hour after he walked in, he said to me, "Mom, let's make sure we talk." But, deep within, I was reluctant to have a confrontation with him. If my son left without our talking, at least he would have pleasant memories of his stay. But if my son and I were to sit down and try to resolve our differences, we might not succeed. We might even get into an argument that would take us further apart.

So we ate meals, read books, watched videotapes, opened gifts and chattered about superficialities. I did everything I could to avoid accepting my son's invitation to talk. At 10:00 on the final night of his stay, my son put on his pajamas and lay down on the couch in the living room, instead of on his bed in the bedroom. Perhaps this was a sign that he was making himself available for a discussion. In any case, I knew that it was up to me to take the initiative.

When I said, "Good night," to my husband, I told him about all the reasons I had been angry at my son. "But I cannot get up the nerve to have a discussion with him," I concluded. My husband said nothing.

I started getting ready for bed. But a small voice within stopped me from continuing. It said to me, "You and your son have always talked honestly with each other. Over the years, you have shared your deepest fears, frustrations, hopes and dreams. Why can't you do this now? Even if your son never speaks to you again after tonight, at least you will have reached out to him. You will have showed him that you cared enough to tell him what is on your mind."

One of the most difficult things I have ever done was to go over to the couch where my son was resting, open my mouth, and say, "Let's talk." "Yes, Mom, let's talk. We have a lot to discuss," he answered simply and gently. Three hours later, we were both satisfied. We hugged each other and said, "Good night." I had initiated a conversation that my son told me later was the best thing that had happened to him while he was home. If I had not acted, this opportunity to strengthen our relationship would have been lost forever.

How to Start a Fruitful Conversation

Would you like to talk with someone else like Shana did with Max, Vera did with Darlene, and I did with my husband and my son? You can. This is how to start a fruitful conversation. Empowering communication is made up of many conversations like this:

Step #1: Pick a quiet, private time to talk. After dinner, when children are asleep, or early in the morning, before you start your day, are both possibilities. It is usually best to set a time limit, like Shana and Max did, say 15 or 30 minutes.

Step #2: Have in mind one subject that you would like to discuss. For example, "How can we be better parents to our children?" Or, "What can we do to cut our monthly expenses?" Or, "Why I would like to spend more time with you." Ask yourself, "Why is it important to me to talk about this subject? What mutual purpose will we share, once my concern is resolved?"

Step #3: Take the time to consider the approach you will use. How will you start the conversation? What kind of resistance will the other person most likely show? If you reach an impasse, how will you handle it?

Step #4: Get in touch with your feelings beforehand, so that you can express them honestly. You will also avoid triggering deep, unexpressed anger within you.

Step #5: When the other person talks, just listen. Do not argue, interrupt, put him down or make sarcastic remarks. Simply receive what he says. Look directly into his eyes and pay attention to his words. You might indicate that you are "with him" by saying "yes," or "mm hmm" or "I understand" at appropriate times. Your purpose is not to dominate the conversation, but to give the other person room to express himself. If there is a long silence, you might ask him if he has anything more to say.

Step # 6: After the other person is finished talking, briefly share your own feelings. They do not necessarily have to be the same as his. If the other person has not yet learned how to really listen, express yourself clearly and simply. Speak in a calm voice. Avoid shouting or crying, which he may interpret as manipulative or threatening.

Step #7: Then give the other person a chance to speak again. Listen to him the same way as you did before. Let him talk as long as he wants. Nurturing conversation, which is mutual, autonomous and authentic, is something that everyone seeks.

Step #8: If, at any point, you start feeling very angry, tell the other person immediately that you would like to continue your conversation at another time. Make it clear to the other person that he may end the conversation as well, if he experiences an upset. If you hurt or embarrass each other, both of you will be unwilling to have another dialogue like this.

When you have a two-way conversation where each of you shares your own feelings honestly and accepts what the other person is saying, you have taken a big first step toward creating a mutually empowering relationship.

While some of your conversations will be mutually satisfying, others will make you feel as if you never want to try again. Don't quit. Empowering communication is an ongoing process. Eventually, your obstacles will become stepping stones.

Empowerment Exercises

1. Focus on Your Feelings: Sit down in a quiet place, close your eyes, and relax. Ask yourself, "How do I feel right now?" Check out what you are experiencing in your body. See if a particular word like "sad" or "angry" or "scared" comes to your mind. If it does, say to yourself, "I feel (sad or angry or scared) because _____." If nothing comes up for you, then say to yourself, "I feel (sad or angry or scared), but I don't know why . . . ." Repeat this sentence at least 10 times. Do this exercise at least once a day for a week. As you become more aware of your feelings, and the reasons for them, you may want to write down what you have learned in your Empowerment Journal. You may also want to share them with someone else by having a fruitful conversation.

2. What Kind of Listener Are You? The next time you have a conversation with someone important to you, be a "fly on the wall." Notice how you listen, and respond to, what you hear. Are you a "sponge," passively sitting back and soaking up the words you hear? Or are you a "center stage celebrity," waiting to speak as soon as the other person takes a breath? Are you a "helper," eager to provide a quick solution to a problem? Or are you "judge, jury and executioner," ready to tell the other person why he or she is wrong? Could it be that you are you an empowered listener, first receiving carefully what the other person says and then doing your best to let him that know you understand?

3. *Is Your Communication Empowering?* Think about all the conversations you had with your partner, during the past week. Did you tell him or her what was really on your mind or did you chat about impersonal subjects, like politics and sports? If you discussed a subject that mattered to you, did you tell him or her how you really felt? When your partner talked to you, did you give him or her your full attention or did you allow your mind to wander? Can you name the three problems that your partner is most concerned about right now? If so, you might ask your partner if you are correct, the next time you talk together.

Empowering communication is only the beginning. To fully empower yourself in your personal and professional lives, you must discard the old myths that blind you to new realities. What are they? Let's find out!

SAY "GOODBYE" TO THE MYTHS: FINDING A "PERFECT MATE," "HAVING IT ALL" AND "LIVING HAPPILY EVER AFTER"

5

> TORVALD. *"Before all else, you're a wife and a mother."*
>
> NORA. *"I don't believe in that anymore. I believe that, before all else, I'm a human being, no less than you—or anyway, I ought to try to become one. I know the majority thinks you're right, Torvald, and plenty of books agree with you, too. But I can't go on believing what the majority says, or what's written in books. I have to think over these things myself and try to understand them."*

> Henrik Ibsen
> *A Doll's House*

Once upon a time there was a "perfect woman" who married the "perfect mate," "had it all" and lived "happily ever after." Oh, if it were only that easy! Yet women have always believed that life is a fairy tale just like this. If you think back to your old book of *Grimm's*, you will remember that your favorite fairy tales usually ended in a burst of glory, as the heroine was rescued in the nick of time by a "handsome prince."

These fairy tales actually ruin women's lives. They are destructive myths, which have been handed down from generation to generation in our male-oriented society. Women who accept them cannot become empowered.

Farewell, Old Myths; Hello, New Reality!

As long as you believe what male-oriented society tells you, you cannot act in your own best interest. Like dragons, men's old myths spit forth smoke and fire, which blind you to your own feminine reality. How do you overcome them? How do you find real solutions to your real problems? It is not easy. Let's consider them, one at a time.

There is No "Handsome Prince."
(Even If There Were, You Wouldn't Want Him!)

Old Myth: You are made "happy" by a magical "handsome prince," who is always romantic and gives you wonderful material things.

New Reality: You are empowered by forming a partnership with a real man, who allows you to be yourself.

The characteristics women usually seek in a partner are those that lead to power-over relationships. A tall, handsome, aloof, successful man usually is not interested in sharing power together with someone else. He doesn't want to let a woman be her own person or to listen to her tell him the truth about herself. As one of the women I interviewed, who was in a power-over relationship told me:

I didn't select the relationship because I could grow in it; I selected it for other qualities. Ray had broad shoulders. I would just lay my head on his shoulder, and something would happen to me inside. Perhaps it was a flashback to my childhood, or something. He was a great dancer; he complimented me every day; he brought me perfume and scarves and jewelry. Nobody had ever treated me this way before.

The very qualities that make a man an excellent "handsome prince" make him a poor mutual partner. Typically, a "handsome prince" is neither available nor compassionate nor willing to share. These three qualities are the cornerstones of mutuality.

I ask Denise and Dan, a couple with a mutually empowering relationship, to tell me about their courtship. Dan begins:

Denise and I were very good friends, before we had a sexual relationship. Ours was a very small university—a community of no more than 600 people. Everyone knew everyone else. We had both been active in a Christian group and had attended its events, before we started dating. We also played squash with each other.

"The opposite happens in Saturday night 'prince and princess" dating, doesn't it? Both people get swept away by sex and romance. He's playing a 'macho' role, and she's being a 'darling little lady.' It's not real. When you saw Denise on a squash court with perspiration dripping all over her face, then you were able to go beyond the glitter and establish a friendship. Your marriage was based on this friendship, wasn't it?"

"Yes," Dan replies. Denise adds,"We always had a good time together. I figured I could be my own person with him. I had been engaged to a medical student, but I didn't want to be a doctor's wife. A doctor, maybe, but not a doctor's wife."

How can you increase your chances for creating a lasting mutual partnership? Dr. Jacqueline Light offers these insights:

How long your marriage lasts may be pure luck. But a lot depends on making a good choice in the first place and not paying attention to what the public says is "the right choice."

Whom you choose when you are 22 is not necessarily whom you would choose when you are 42. You might choose a good dancer when you are 22, perhaps someone who looks good in his clothes. You might walk all over the man who is always "there" for you and who really loves you, because he's not Lochinvar from the West on his horse—who treats you badly. Some women seem to thrive on being treated badly. And they "respect" a man who does not let them call the shots. Remember the Groucho Marx saying, "Any club which wants me for a member can't be much of a club?" Many women have been conditioned to like a man better if he doesn't like them very well.

Women go into a relationship with a set of adolescent qualifications that the male must meet, which are detrimental later on. But marriage is not a temporary relationship, like courtship or even living together. It's a basic companionship with someone who likes to do the things you like to do. It's being with somebody you want to see every single day.

"And the very qualities of Lochinvar on a horse—good looks, aloofness and even callousness—won't make him a very good husband?"

This is exactly my point. Lochinvar is the kind of man with whom it's great to go out on dates or to have an adventure, maybe an affair. But he may not be the person who will sit with you while you are nursing the baby and talk to you.

"But Lochinvar's 'exciting.'"

That's what we seem to say! Then we sit there alone with the baby, while he's out there having adventures! But marriage is an everyday experience. The excitement comes out of the things you do together, like having children, celebrating holidays, taking walks, watching a movie or cooking dinner. No one can live a life of peak excitement all of the time. Both of you need to be enthusiastic about your everyday life together and be happy to see each other at the end of each day.

You have got to find someone who is able to care about you; otherwise nothing that you do makes any difference. Compassion is most important—what lasts.

"So by choosing the right person, you are off to a running start. While there are no guarantees, creating a partnership is a lot easier. If you want a partnership and the other person does not, you won't succeed. Period."

Right. He may just lack compassion—for everybody. And he is not willing to make you an exception.

"I agree with you that wealth, age, education, good looks and social status are far less important than a loving heart. But the courtship system puts a premium on excitement and adventure."

It used to. The young people now see each other in an "un-made-up" state in co-ed dorms. We didn't. We were the "Friday, Saturday, Sunday princesses"—hair all done up, always clean and sweet smelling. What we have lost is a certain amount of excitement, which came from well-defined male and female roles. The men don't feel called upon anymore to get on a horse to fetch a woman from anywhere. Let her open her own door! So some of the feeling of being treated in a special way, because you are a female, is now gone.

Men have dropped their "super-masculine" behavior, in many cases, because we have wanted them to. What do we put in its place? A kind of companionship, where we can both have exciting adventures together. Young women feel just as entitled to do dangerous things as young men. We are no longer accepting the passive role assigned to us in the past.

"Do we women now play an important role in the selection process?"

Yes, we do. When selecting a partner, the big question to ask yourself is, "How does he make me feel, when I am with him?" You have to examine your feelings honestly. Is his eye roving while the two of you are talking? Do you feel scared, anxious, worried or intimidated by him? Is he interested in listening to you? Does he makes you feel as if he likes talking to you—and being with you? Do you enjoy being with him? When you are not with him, do you miss him? Do you feel as if you can't wait to tell him what you have been doing?

Above all, you need to find someone who will allow you to be yourself—and will not be overly critical of you.

"Someone who will be accepting of your real self, as opposed to someone who likes you only when you act the way he wants you to act."

That's it. He needs to understand that this is you—that you have flaws and he has flaws, but he still loves the essential you. It sounds so trivial when I say it, but this is the secret of making it happen.

"It's not trivial at all. There are a lot of marriages, many of them with small children, which are falling apart because this basic ingredient is not there. If I had known this when I was 21, I would have selected a different person."

When people are in their 20s, they are mostly interested in someone with the right image. When people are in their 30s, they start getting interested in someone who can help them. "You have a career; I have a career. How can we assist each other?" When people are in their 40s and 50s, they start getting interested in companionship as a primary reason for being with somebody.

"When companionship should actually have been there as a value all the way through. . . ."

Right. But many 20-year-old women mainly care about how a prospective partner looks—and maybe how large his bank account is. These are the first things they notice. Twenty-year-old marriages are often based on these values.

"Finding a suitable partner is not easy. You meet dozens of men, most of whom are not right for you. After a while, the selection process gets tiring. So, when you meet someone who is at least "possible," you start asking yourself, "How much longer can I wait to get married?"

"And how much longer can I wait to have children—and to have a home?" Women feel pressure. "Is there someone out there for me? Where is he?"

A woman tends to project onto a man what she is looking for. She sees the tall, dark stranger and learns that he is a social worker. So she projects compassion onto him. He has ignored what she was saying three evenings in a row, but this experience does not touch her romantic fantasy. It somehow gets swept under the rug and ignored.

This woman gets married and finds out that her husband is really not compassionate. Then she panics, because she is not sure that she can live with him. So she starts trying to change him, which is a fruitless effort. No one changes, just because someone else wants him to. Everyone wants to be loved for himself.

Infatuation is the beginning of any relationship. After that, you have to adjust yourself to who your partner is. You think, "This is the real person I am married to. Can I stay married to him?" Lots of women have this decision to make, depending on how awake or asleep they were during courtship. If you were completely asleep, you wake up married to someone you don't know. And then what? If you believe in the institution of marriage, you have to say,

"I did this. I married a stranger. Is there enough to keep the relationship going? Or is this situation just plain impossible?" Sometimes women just walk away."

"And sometimes women believe so deeply in the institution of marriage that they build a relationship."

The success of a partnership depends on not just what the two people bring to the table but on how much each of them is willing to do to make it work. Once you are in a solid relationship more than 5 or 6 years, each of you is rewriting the contract. Inevitably, your careers, your families, your communities and the world are all different. You need to accommodate and change, too. Your motivation must come from within. Dr. Light stands up and gestures dramatically to make her point.

Men and women who discuss these issues before they get married find out the answers. Young people in their 20s are now asking each other, "What do you want to do with your life? How do you want to raise children, if we have them? How would you feel if . . ." If you are approaching a commitment, you should talk about these things. Don't go into a marriage blindly and assume it's going to work out. These are the nuts and bolts issues you should both be discussing, not how big is the diamond.

I smile and then sigh. Like most women, I am reluctant to say "goodbye" to my "handsome prince" fantasy, even if the tradeoff is a satisfying partnership!

There Is No "Perfect Woman"

Old Myth: Yes, Virginia, there is a perfect woman. If you only try hard enough, you can become one.

New Reality: No woman is perfect. As you become empowered, you get to know your strengths—and accept your limitations.

Contemporary women have not only taken *Cosmopolitan* Magazine editor Helen Gurley Brown's phrase, "having it all," as a motto; they have exaggerated it—well beyond her wildest dreams. According to a group of 30 women at a Harvard Medical School Department of Continuing Education workshop that I attended, a typical woman who "has it all" has all of this:

1. Personal well-being, including
   - a strong sense of identity
   - self-respect
   - self-confidence
   - good health
   - personal fulfillment

2. Achievement, including
- a challenging career
- money
- power
- success
- status

3. Satisfying relationships, including
- children and family
- a desirable romantic partner
- sexual fulfillment
- good friends
- a support system
- time alone

. . . all on the bedrock of beauty, health, and calmness! Sound like a lot? Well, it is!

Encouraged by male-oriented society, we women have invented a new fairy tale: the perfect woman leading the perfect life. Then we have expected ourselves to live up to our exorbitant expectations. As a colleague of mine laughingly remarked, after listening to Colette Dowling discuss her book, *Perfect Women*, on the Phil Donahue Show, "Only women would buy into this. Who ever heard of the cult of a 'perfect man?'"

Sometimes this womanly obsession with perfection can be downright dangerous. I interviewed Marie, a woman who was being beaten up regularly by her husband, but continued to stay in the relationship for over 5 years. When I asked her, "Why?" she answered:

Everything looked so "picture perfect" on the outside that I felt that I couldn't explain my decision to leave to anyone, even my friends and family.

Marie had a stake in maintaining her illusion of the "perfect woman with the perfect marriage." She found it hard to let go of her dream of "living happily ever after." Other women starve themselves or have major plastic surgery to create a "perfect body." The truth is that no woman is perfect—physically, mentally or emotionally. Women who pretend they are perfect usually feel inadequate and embarrassed about themselves. Empowerment means accepting and appreciating your entire self, both your virtues *and* your flaws.

Accept Your Limitations

An empowered woman accepts her limitations. Society's myths notwithstanding, no woman can do everything. Our bodies, our minds and our emotions have weaknesses as well as strengths. The secret is to know them—and then to have the courage to accept them.

Sophie, one of the women I interviewed, was a spunky, petite 55-year-old woman who had recently fallen and broken her hip and her right arm. Confined to a walker, she still would not accept her injury. She was so embarrassed about her condition that she did not have the courage to talk about it with other people. She would spend 2 hours getting herself dressed in the morning rather than ask someone else to assist her. During our interview, I pointed out that there were still many functions her body could perform. By allowing others to assist her, she would create opportunities for mutually empowering relationships.

For each of us, there are things we just can't do. For example, I have a back disability. Twenty years ago, my doctor told me not to lift any object over 15 pounds. For 19 years, I refused to accept what he had told me, even though I knew deep within that it was true. It was painful to ask other people for help, and even more agonizing to confront my own realization that I wasn't omnipotent. So I ended up moving furniture or cartons of books and spending about a month each year flat on my back.

Just last year, I was finally able to accept what I have always known—that I can swim half a mile, do aerobics for 45 minutes and run around a track half a dozen times, but I cannot lift heavy objects. To appreciate what I can do, I have had to come to grips with what I cannot do.

You Cannot "Have It All"

Old Myth: You can "have it all." Life is like a huge banquet. You can stuff as much food into your mouth as you want without getting sick.

New Reality: You can have "what you want most." If you eat too much rich food, you will get a stomach ache—or gain 5 extra pounds. There are tradeoffs.

The most recent—and most destructive—myth is the virtue of "having it all." In her book by the same name, Helen Gurley Brown suggested that women can have a full-time career, a husband, children and personal fulfillment all at the same time. Not realizing that this is a myth perpetuated by our male-oriented society, a generation of women have taken this suggestion to heart. As one of my interviewees remarked, "After all, men don't have to choose between marriage, family or a career, so why should we?" Do you agree?

Would You Like to Be Elise?

Elise is a 39-year-old married attorney. Her co-workers say that she "has it all." She is both a partner at a prominent New York law firm and a mother of a recently adopted son.

How does she do it? Elise took just a few days off when her son arrived. Within 6 weeks, she was back working full-time. Elise employs both a live-in housekeeper and a live-in nanny. She does not spend a moment on activities that are not related to her family or her work. She compensates for her 60-hour week and frequent overseas trips by sleeping very little and organizing her time efficiently. Although Elise admits that she spends a limited amount of time with her son, she devotes a lot of effort to planning activities for him. Enjoying these activities with the baby is delegated to the nanny.

As you read about Elise, did you identify with her? Rushing from here to there trying to "do it all?" Does this lifestyle make sense to you?

Empowered Women Decide Their Priorities

The problem with "having it all" is that women's reality is different from men's. We have the potential to bear and nurture children. Many of us are finally starting to realize this. Here are some of the comments that were made by some of my interviewees:

- "Having it all" is garbage. You can't "have it all" unless you are a "walking zombie'—or you have a totally supportive husband and full-time household help. Even then you'll miss watching the kids grow up.

- I believe that some of these "supermoms" are so busy trying to do so many different things at the same time that they are actually very unhappy. They are not satisfied emotionally. If you don't do the things you enjoy, or do things for yourself, your life is not fulfilling. An unhappy woman is not empowered.

- In life, there is nothing for free. Each thing you choose has a cost. I have paid for each choice that I have made, but I would have paid, one way or another, if I had made another choice. I could have crumbled when my husband left, but that was not an acceptable alternative for me; the consequences would have been too terrible. Sometimes I feel trapped, when I have put myself in a certain position by making a choice. For example, I have to get up and go to work every day. But this is because I have chosen to have a job in the first place.

- I don't think that any woman can "have it all." We always pay a price for whatever we do. Any choice we make closes doors to other options.

- "Having it all" is as foolish as "one size fits all." Nothing can be right for everyone. Maybe a few women may be comfortable "having it all," but

certainly not most of them. And certainly not me. I do not want to "have
it all." My goal is to be an individual who leads the life she chooses,
pursues her own desires and is happy.

"Having it all" really means that, unlike men, women are not okay
the way they are. Although the expression was coined by a woman, it
was popularized by men—and by women who have been taught to
think like men. Did you ever notice that, in our society, men are
praised for "winning," but not for nurturing? Only women receive ac-
colades for doing both at the same time. To "have it all," a woman has
to live not only by her own values but also by men's. A logical and
practical impossibility to be sure.

A woman who is determined to "have it all" does not have her own
agenda. She is living her life according to the values of male-oriented
society. To become an empowered woman, she has to start living according to her own feminine standards. She needs to make choices
among options, rather than allowing only one option, "the choice of
not making a choice" to be forced on her.

How About Choosing What You Want, Instead of "Having It All?"

"Having it all" is just another fairy tale. To get what she wants from
life, an empowered woman creates her own "reality tale" by making
wise and careful decisions.

Dr. Jacqueline Light told me about an important decision that she
made, which might have been difficult for many women:

I had my first child when I was a junior in medical school, and my second,
when I was an intern. I made all my career decisions on the basis of what
would be better for my family. I did not choose an internship or residencies
that would have kept me in the hospital every other night for years.

In fact, I attained the first black pediatric residency at a major hospital
and turned it down, because I didn't want to be away from my infant daughter. She had been born in February, and I would have had to leave her in
July to be on duty every other night for the next 2 years. I didn't want to
do that. And let me tell you, the walk over to the hospital to say "No" was
a long one!

What was interesting was that I really didn't care. I was sure that I was
doing the right thing. I knew that I could not be away from her that much,
when she was that tiny. And I didn't want to be. I felt that, if I didn't want to
be away from her, then I shouldn't go.

"You valued your mothering role. You were willing to stand up and
say to the world, 'Being a mother is worthwhile. I choose it with
pride.'"

My desire to be a mother rose from deep within me. It overwhelmed the honor of being chosen for the position and my enthusiasm for the opportunity to study under a great physician. I respected both my career role and my mothering role, but I knew what I was feeling. Thank goodness I did! I have never had a second of regret. Women have to be able to respect and follow their feelings.

It turned out that it was absolutely the right thing to do. I got a better residency in psychiatry—at a less well-known hospital. Since I had won a psychiatry prize when I graduated from medical school, my husband said to me, "Why don't you become a psychiatrist?" Eventually I decided I did not want to be a pediatrician after all.

Knowing yourself, knowing your instincts and knowing what's best for you makes you able to make a decision like this. If you know yourself, if you feel confident that you can survive no matter what, you will not be afraid of offending these "big, powerful people," who have deigned to give you a plum in the first place. You will be able to stand up for what you want.

Dr. Light eventually became a psychoanalyst and continued to practice after her second daughter was born. To women who want both to work and to raise children, she offers this advice:

If you have a commitment to very young children, they don't understand that you have another job to do. You are either there—or not there—for them. When your children are sick, they prefer to have you with them. You have obligations to them, too.

But, if you are with your children, your work is going to suffer in some way. So do your best to avoid being "boxed in" at work, when they are very little. You might want to advance your career a little more slowly, during this period of time. You don't necessarily have to stay at home full-time, as women in the '50s did. But choose the kind of full-time job which will allow you to take leave. Or work part-time. Or work for less money. "Do with less and do less," while your children are small. They won't notice whether or not the family car is brand-new. But they will notice whether or not you are there. A lot of "things" do not compensate for the lack of your attention.

My motto is, "You don't have to bake cookies every day, but you should bake them some days." You need to be there when they wake up from their naps—not every day, but sometimes. You have to drive your own carpool occasionally, because that's where the information is. You don't learn much from your children 4 hours after they have arrived home from school; they've already forgotten what happened that day! When they jump in the car, or off the bus, they tell you what their first grade teacher did. If you are going to have children, be there for them.

It takes a lot of time to take care of your children—and yourself. You also have to keep your eyes on your husband and not allow him to feel that he is second. It's so easy not to see him clearly, when you are consumed with raising children. Being a mother is such an empowering experience.

"Ideally you should have built a team with your husband, before these lovable, loving, demanding children come along."

Right. Whatever the rules are, they are made by your team. Other people may not understand—or even respect—the team's rules, but it doesn't matter. As long as the rules work for your team, that's all that counts.

"What do you think about a man assuming half of the nurturing role?"

Sharing parenthood is a fine idea. But it is never 50-50; it is more like 51-49. There will always be a primary parent—either the mother or a father or else a big sister, grandmother or aunt.

"What about total role reversal?"

A househusband would never work for me. I couldn't tolerate a total invasion of my role. Who's going to play the father's role? I'm not!

For role reversal to work, both people have to be willing to play a role that is not theirs biologically. The woman has to reverse her role, too. If he wants to reverse, and she doesn't, then the children will be raised by two people playing female roles.

Right now, many children are being raised by two people playing male roles, and no one is doing the nurturing. This is a serious problem.

Choosing everything diminishes, instead of enhances, the quality of your life. By trying to be all things to all people, you usually end up sacrificing your essential self. Most women who "have it all" will admit under pressure that they, in fact, feel overwhelmed by their responsibilities, torn by conflicting desires and frustrated by endless "juggling" and "balancing." They have only a limited amount of time to sit back and enjoy life and do what they want to do most. By trying to "have it all," you avoid making choices, which is an integral part of empowerment.

Guilt is what paralyzes women more than anything else. We feel guilty no matter what we do. If we decide to stay home with our children, we feel guilty because we're not achieving. We think we are "selling out" to our children, giving up our individuality and letting our husbands take advantage of us. If we go to work, we feel guilty because we're neglecting these very same children and this very same husband.

But there is a difference between true guilt and false guilt. True guilt is what we experience when we do not live up to our own standards of right and wrong. False guilt is feeling that we have failed to live up to someone else's values.

Male-oriented society heaps false guilt upon women. For centuries, our culture has told us that women should be "limitless fountains of giving." Not giving is very difficult for us; women who don't give experience torrents of false guilt. To have healthy relationships with other people, especially men and children, we need to set limits. Yet it is very hard for us to do this. Our culture supports men who make these kinds of declarations: "I refuse to put up with this" or "I need this for myself." Women are not supposed to say these things. Yet we must—for our own sanity and self-respect.

You have an inner voice. Male-oriented society is a cacophony of conflicting outer voices. Whose voice do you listen to and trust? If you listen to society's voice, you will experience endless false guilt, because there will always be people, your feminist friends, your traditional husband or your mother, whom you will never totally please. If you listen to your own voice, you will experience integrity and true personal autonomy.

Take the time to ask yourself, "Who am I and what makes me happy? What do I really want? What is important to me in life? Being home with my children? Devoting myself to my career? Getting or staying married? What can I do to feel satisfied with myself in the long run? Which choice, or combination of choices, will give me the most inner peace?" Listen carefully to your answers and then honor them. Being true to yourself is the ointment that will heal your wounds.

An empowered woman makes choices without false guilt. Yes, choosing a full-time career without marriage and children may seem "unfeminine" to some men and women. Deciding to devote yourself to your husband and young children, while working only a few hours a week, may be labeled "unliberated" by others. But the critical question is not, "What do other people think?" but, "Which path feels right for me?" When you absolutely refuse to "have it all" and commit yourself instead to weighing your own priorities, you have reached a milestone in empowerment.

You Will Never Live "Happily Ever After"

Old Myth: Happiness is an end point—a glorious, permanent state which you finally achieve.

New Reality: Empowerment evolves—gradually and sometimes painfully. It never ends.

When we are blinded by a fairy tale outlook, good things somehow "happen" to us; in the nick of time, we are rescued by magic, or else by a brave hero. So, naively and passively, we wait for him to arrive. He will marry us, make us rich and make us like ourselves.

An empowered woman does not delude herself with fantasies. She faces the real issues and asks the hard questions. If she loses her job, if her husband leaves her or if she faces illness, she does not harbor any illusions that she will be rescued either by someone else or by some supernatural force. She knows that is up to *her* to find a solution to her problems. She is bold enough to say to herself, "Everything may *not* turn out the way it's supposed to be!"

The path to empowerment can be long and difficult. There are at least two stepping stones. The first, and most important one is becoming aware of your own potential as a woman. Many of us are still not aware of the incredible strength we possess within.

The second stepping stone is realizing that becoming empowered is difficult. It may take years for you to recognize your own inner potential and even longer for you to express it. Sometimes you may feel as if you are not making any progress at all. Relationships that you thought would be empowering may turn out to be controlling. You may experience mutuality often, but not always. You may express the truth about yourself to some people, but not others. Before you begin to see results, you will probably experience dozens of failures and make hundreds of mistakes.

You may have developed a plan for empowerment that is ideal for you now. But circumstances may change. What seems right when you are 20 and childless may be a disaster when you are 30 and have two children. What works for you alone may not fit your needs a decade later, when you are in a mutual partnership. This is what one of my interviewees told me:

When I was growing up, I thought that I would go to college, get married, have children and raise a family for about 20 years. Then I would go to law school when I was about 45. After my children were grown, I would become a lawyer. After I graduated from college, I went to work. My job didn't "fit" my ambition at all. After my first child was born, I realized that my plan was backward, and I should go to law school first. Even if I got a menial law job after that, at least it would help me toward what I was going to do when I was 45. So I reversed the plan.

Two steps forward, and one step back. You reach a temporary resting place and then the journey resumes. This is how you become empowered.

When You Feel Discouraged

Sometimes, you may feel like Heidi, a woman I interviewed recently:

I've made such a mess of my life that there's no point in doing anything. Today's just going to be another awful day; why should I even bother to get out of bed?"

I replied, "You can do something, Heidi. You are stronger than you think you are. Even if you don't want to get out of bed, do it anyway. If you simply cannot, make a phone call to someone who will support you or offer your support to that person. Or perhaps you prefer to write down your negative feelings in a journal or talk about them into a tape recorder and then share what you have written with a friend. After you take the first step, the next ones will be easier. And, once you have created a mutual relationship, you will begin to experience empowerment."

Even when you yourself reach a high level of empowermmnt you may occisionally experience the feeling, "I can't do this." Do not resist this feeling; it will pass. Seek a mutually empowering relationship with another person, perhaps in an empowerment community, so that this obstacle becomes a stepping stone. The only thing you must not do is completely give up.

Empowerment Exercises

1. *Focus on Your Feelings about "Having It All"*: Sit down in a quiet place with your eyes closed. Repeat the sentence, "I have it all," to yourself at least 10 times. Then stop and see what comes up for you. Which people, if any, are you thinking about? What thoughts are you having about each one? How does your body feel? Are you tense or relaxed? Do you feel any physical discomfort? Where? What kind of emotions are you experiencing? Can you find a word that describes what you are feeling, for example, happy, sad or angry? You may want to repeat this exercise several times, to get fully in touch with all your feelings.

2. *Journal Writing: What Are My Life Choices?* In your Empowerment Journal, write down your thoughts about what is most important to you in life. Is it achieving? Making money? Having a mutually satisfying marriage? Bearing and raising a child? Doing something to preserve the environment? Keep coming back to this theme for at least 2 weeks, so that you record your thoughts at different moments in time. You may speak into a tape recorder instead, if it is more comfortable for you.

3. *Make Up Your Own "Reality Tale"*: Sit down with a pencil and your Empowerment Journal, or a tape recorder. Write down these words in your Empowerment Journal, or say them into the tape re-

corder: "Once upon a time there was a girl named. . ." Then say your name. Now make up a story about your future life. In your story, a "handsome prince" does not come to find you; you are not "perfect"; and you do not "have it all." Now start thinking of the real problems you will face in your new reality scenario. Once you perceive the actual difficulties, you are ready to start finding solutions to them. Remember, only fairy tales end with "and she lived happily ever after."

The best way to come to grips with your new reality is to find out who you really are. How do you begin the quest for your unique personal identity?

BECOME THE KEY
TO YOUR
OWN IGNITION

6

Who are you?
You are a rare and special woman.
A patterned snowflake,
a single fingerprint,
a molecule of DNA.
No one else offers
what you offer
to the world.

r. r. j.

You are unique. You have a special set of qualities that makes you the woman you are. Do you know yourself? Before you can give of yourself to other people, you have to have a self to give. When you do, you will experience a certain sense of wholeness. You will be at one with yourself.

The best way to discover who you are is to form empowering relationships with other women. After you get in touch with your true self, you will be ready to enter into an authentic, mutual and autonomous partnership.

Because women have the capacity to have children, we face a confusing array of options. The pressure used to be on us to be devoted wives and mothers. It seemed natural to make our husband and children the center of our lives. Then the pendulum swung in the opposite direction. We were told we must have a career to fulfill ourselves—as long as it was not the career of being a housewife. Now many of us are becoming disillusioned with full-time careers and are opting to have children and stay home with them.

Times will change, and the pressures will again be different. But the important questions will always remain the same: "What do I want to do? Who am I and what makes me happy? What can I do to feel satisfied with myself in the long run? Which choice, or combination of choices, will give me the most inner peace?"

Your personal identity is one of your most precious resources. Until you discover it, empowerment will elude you. When my friend, Vicki, realized that she had no clear-cut sense of self, she risked everything to find it.

Vicki: "I Left My Husband to Find Myself."

I am sitting in Vicki's living room. Although the furniture is elegant and colorful, most of it has been purchased in thrift stores. I have not seen Vicki recently. Her thin arms and legs give her a deceptively fragile appearance, as does her soft voice.

"These are my children now." Vicki smiles. She picks up a small antique picture frame with three panels, each with a picture of a smiling, robust teenager. "Craig's at Ohio State University now. He'll go on to law school, when he graduates next June. Richard's in his junior year; he's also at Ohio State. He plans to get a Master's degree in business administration and then go into business for himself. And Katharine is a freshman at Vassar. She wants to major in Spanish and become a translator."

Vicki smiles again. "I don't miss the children as much as I used to, because Larry and I have grown much closer recently. We are getting married in June. No, I'm not planning to go back to college. I've gone two years; perhaps I'll finish someday. Right now I want to work for a while. I love my job as administrative assistant to the President of the Apex Corporation. In my spare time, I act in a local theater group. I have even begun to write a play." Vicki pauses, looks up at the ceiling and back at me. "I guess everyone did turn out all right, after all!" she bursts out. "Including me! You know it's been 15 years since I left my husband to find myself."

But, when Vicki made her fateful decision to discover her own identity, she had no guarantees. At age 17, she had decided to marry her boyfriend, Ivan, who was about to be sent to California on a military assignment. She continues:

Basically I didn't know what to do with my life. He was tall, dark and charismatic, and I was a young, impressionable, bored kid in love. I didn't want him to go away and never see me again, so marriage sounded like a good idea. I told my parents, "I'm getting married the day after tomorrow. You can come, if you want." They were very upset, but off I went to a small town in California and became pregnant immediately. I had one kid after the next.

Three pregnancies in 3 years. By the time I was 20, I was a mother of three children.

Life was hard. We were poor, and he was ambitious. Ivan decided to become a stockbroker and go with one of those big East Coast brokerage firms. His goal was to be a millionaire by age 40, which he managed to do. But it was hell getting there. We had a real poverty-level kind of existence. I knew he was making a lot of money, but he was investing every single penny trying to become a millionaire. It was very difficult for me and the kids, because we were sacrificing everything for his ambition. Nothing was being brought back to us. And we're talking basics.

I remember standing in line for the bus with the kids in the dead of winter. I was taking them to a free reading program at the library, which I did every week, and they were complaining bitterly about how cold it was. Suddenly I saw a chauffeur-driven Rolls Royce drive by, with two men in the back seat. Immediately, I felt a flash of recognition: there was Ivan with a wealthy client.. Here we were ankle-deep in the snow waiting 45 minutes for the bus to take us from our inner-city home—and he's going by in this luxury car headed for a luncheon date! It just kind of swept me away, because it didn't seem real. And it was the downfall of our marriage. I decided I wouldn't have this kind of lifestyle; it wasn't fair to the kids—or to me.

For the last 7 years, I had done nothing except work my fingers to the bone and take care of my children 18 hours a day. Now, here I was, 25 years old. When was I ever going to find an identity of my own? All I knew about myself was that material things weren't very important to me and that my calling might be someplace in the arts.

A few months later, I went into a deep depression. I told a minister at our church, whom I had become close to, that I was feeling suicidal. Then I actually attempted to kill myself. Thank goodness I lived! I can't even think about how close I came to dying.

In the hospital emergency room, I remember a nurse yelling at me,"How could you do this to yourself? You have a loving husband; you've got kids." She was some big help! I was crying and saying to her, "No, I don't know how I could do this." The doctor on duty sent me to a clinic, where I was given a lot of tests. No one could find any reason why I would attempt to kill myself. So they kept me in the hospital.

One night, I woke up about 3:00 in the morning and heard strange noises. The woman who was my hospital roommate had so completely retreated from the world that she had created her own language. When her husband had died, she had mentally fallen apart. Listening to her absolutely terrified me. I thought, "What am I doing here? This place is for crazy people. It's not for me. I must get out." As she says these words, Vicki sits up straight in her chair.

I remember wearing my white hospital gown, sitting cross-legged on my bed the next morning, and saying to myself, "Well Vicki, you've really done it. This is the end of the line. After this place, there is no place to go but up! You are going to get better and get out of here forever." It was a very profound moment. What I realized—in the starkest terms—was that I really wanted to live very much. My will to survive has been with me ever since. Vicki's soft voice has become loud.

My hospital stay was very short—only 6 days. The hospital psychiatrist told me, "I don't know what's wrong with you, but I'll put you on these pills and then you can go home." I asked him, "Will these pills help me? How long will it be before I get better?" He gave me no answer. Since I distrusted the pills—and him—I quit taking them.

When I came back to see the hospital psychiatrist 2 weeks later, I told him that I was no longer on the medication. He said, "You don't need me; it's clear to me that you are going to do exactly what you want to do." I replied, "You're right. I guess I don't need you." And I walked out of his office. When I came home, I threw the pills away. I never saw the psychiatrist again. As far as he was concerned, I was a "difficult patient." As far as I was concerned, I was someone who had discovered something very important about myself.

Vicki strokes her long, blonde hair with her right hand. I needed to understand what reality was, and the pills weren't going to teach me reality. If I was feeling better, I wanted to know that it was because something was actually happening to me, not because the pills were giving me an illusion that I had improved.

"What do you need to do, Vicki?" I asked myself, as a therapist might. From deep within, I heard the answer. "You need to get your emotional and mental stamina back, so you can separate from your husband. This is what your survival is about."

Ivan was a very controlling person. I don't necessarily mean this in a bad sense. He was just a very extroverted person who was totally driven toward his goal: making lots of money. Ivan had created a very repressive reality. He dominated everyone around him, including me and the kids. In order to find out what was within me, I had to get away from him physically. As long as I stayed close to Ivan, I woudd never know who I was. My psychic survival was at stake.

Had I had money of my own, I might have been able to forge my own reality within the marriage. My mother had managed to create her own identity and stay with my father. Because she had an inheritance, she could do what she wanted. But I did not have a "nest egg" like my mother did.

A few weeks later, Ivan and I were sitting alone in the kitchen about 11:00 at night. All the children were asleep. Out of the blue, I said to him, "I've got to get out of this craziness, Ivan. Go make your million dollars. You're going to have to do it by yourself. This is the children's childhood, and all they're going to remember is that they're poor. It doesn't matter how many stock certificates they'll have in their portfolios 20 years from now. You can't recreate their childhood. You just can't. And you can't ever make these years of my life up to me, Ivan. I need to see what my life is all about. You're going to have to leave."

I was petrified when I said these words, because I didn't know what I was going to do next. I would be on my own for the first time in my life. I had three little babies ages 7, 6 and 5. I did not have a college education. I had never worked, except as a lifeguard during summer vacations. I didn't have any money. I didn't have hot water in the apartment. I didn't even have a telephone. My parents were still angry at me for running off, so I had no family support. I was completely alone.

The next day, Ivan packed his suitcase and left. Two weeks later, I got myself a job as a secretary. . . . Eventually he started paying child support . . . . Somehow I made it.

Yes, I really went through some tough times. Especially when I would give myself a huge guilt trip. "Am I doing all this for me? Breaking up my family and taking Daddy away from my kids, just so I can find my identity?" But I couldn't help it; my feelings were so intense. I had to risk telling Ivan the truth.

The sun is coming in through Vicki's living room window. It shines directly on her blond hair, creating a halo-like effect. Her dark brown chair is a silhouetted background. What a lovely scene! We pause for a moment. "I like your living room furniture, Vicki. It's elegant," I remark. Vicki replies:

A few pieces are family heirlooms, but most of it was bought at thrift stores. It reminds me, no matter how far I go, to always remember where I came from—and what I have gone through to find out who I really am.

A woman cannot be who she is, when she is controlled by someone else. To discover her identity, Vicki had to break away from her husband. How could she fill the void? Only in a mutually empowering relationship would her deepest self emerge. Vicki needed at least one person with whom she could be real, someone who would allow her the space to develop in her own directions. Unfortunately, her therapist discouraged self-disclosure and exercised power over her.

Eventually Vicki found her own self through her relationships with her children. As she told me:

Because I was a single parent for many years, all the children became very involved with my struggles. I have had an extremely close relationship with my kids, much more so than if I had been married.

After Vicki left her husband, she created mutually empowering relationships with her two sons and her daughter.

Sophie, another woman I interviewed, also left her husband to find herself. Unlike Vicki, Sophie became empowered through her relationship with a therapist.

Sophie: "I Had a Problem That No Pill Could Cure."

Sophie is a petite senior citizen who has the sparkle of a teenager. When I meet her, I cannot help but notice that her right arm is in a sling and she is using a walker. Sophie does not wait for me to ask her why.

Two weeks ago, I fell down, for the first time in my life. But I'm not about to let this stop me. Would you like to go somewhere and talk?

We proceed side by side to her room on the third floor. Sophie will not even let me help her in and out of the elevator. Once in her room, she steps out of her walker and gets herself seated in a straight brown chair. "Well", she asks. "What now?" Her strawberry-blond wavy hair frames her bright blue eyes and her square determined jaw. Clearly Sophie is a force to be reckoned with.

For once, I do not know what to say to her first. I take a stab in the dark and begin, "Sophie, you strike me as a person who has had a lot of difficult experiences and has overcome a lot."

Don't be fooled. It has taken me a long time to become an integrated person. Most people aren't really willing to be themselves; they're afraid, and I understand that. We go through a whole lifetime, tiptoeing around and focusing on peripheral, superficial issues, but I'm not interested in talking this way. Sophie's words are sharp and biting.

Suddenly her tone of voice becomes gentle, almost melodramatic. "I have so many stories to tell. I think that sometimes I could be Scheherazade. This is what comes up for me right now":

When my husband and I separated 20 years ago, I was left with $7,000, two children and no family. I didn't know what I was going to do. I've come a long, long way since then. I don't think I accomplished it all myself either. I really think a Power higher than myself was beside me all the time. I really do.

During the early years of my marriage, I felt unprepared to take care of my family. Although I had gone to night school, I didn't have a college education. I was always trying to cheer my husband up and to encourage him. I would say to my husband, "I'll go to work so you can go to school. I'll do this and I'll do that for you." No matter what I did . . . She pounds her fist on the desk nearby. Her voice is angry. No matter what I did; no matter what I said, it was not acceptable to him. *I* was not acceptable to him.

The last 3 years that my husband and I were together, I was getting disturbing reports that my daughter was having difficulties in nursery school. I wanted to put her in another school and have her see a child psychiatrist. My husband didn't want to talk about my daughter's problems at school; when I brought them up, he would scream, "What do you want me to do?" and he would rant and rave. Then he would drive up to the mountains and disappear for a few nights. We never resolved anything.

Finally I took matters into my own hands. I went to visit another nursery school, where the board was made up of psychoanalysts and other psychoanalytically oriented people. I was very impressed. I came home and told my husband, "I have found an excellent school for our daughter. I am willing to go out to work, if we don't have the money to pay her tuition." My husband said to me, "I don't want you to work; a mother belongs at home with her children."

A few days later, I took my son and daughter for a picnic on the beach. I was driving along the highway, when a 20-ton truck, loaded with gravel, overturned. My car was hurled into the air. For a little while, I lost consciousness—I don't know for how long. After I awoke, I got out of the car, walked into a pharmacy across the street, bought first-aid equipment and took care of everyone else's cuts and scratches. All that went through my mind was, "First things, first."

Later on, a policeman, who was at the scene of the accident said to me, "Lady, I've seen cool customers, but never one like you!" This was the first moment I had felt good about myself in a long time.

The next day, when my children and I went to the doctor, he told me that they were okay, but I had suffered a brain concussion. I had to rest for 6 weeks. While I was in bed, I put together a jigsaw puzzle that I had never been able to complete before. Finally its pieces fitted together, just like the pieces of my life. . . .

My relationship with my husband was deteriorating, and I was feeling worse. I called the doctor; he prescribed some tablets for me. I took some, and I couldn't get off the sofa for 2 days. On the third day I walked into his office and asked him, "Why are you just giving me pills? Is this all I have to expect out of my life—to live at half-mast? This is not what I want. I want to live fully." I didn't go back to this doctor again.

Deep inside, I knew I had a problem that no pill could cure. I called some of the board members at my daughter's new nursery school and they gave the names of five psychiatrists. I went to all of them; each one had a different opinion. One said, "I don't think you need psychiatric help at all. You're just taking your money out of your pocket and putting it in someone else's pocket." Although none of the psychiatrists ever told me there was something wrong with me, I was sure there was. Sophie sighs. There are tears in her eyes.

The last psychiatrist I saw said to me, "It sounds as if you are very frustrated. You can't do anything more for your children, and you can't do anything at all about your husband. So why don't you do something for yourself? Why don't you begin psychoanalysis?" I said, "I can't afford it." Do you know what she replied? "I'll bet, if you could afford it, you wouldn't do it anyway." She made me so angry!

A week later, I came back to this doctor's office and said, "Well, I am going to start psychoanalysis. I don't have any money, and I don't have a job. Whom do you recommend?" She gave me the name of an analyst. I'll never forget our first session. He asked me, "How are you going to pay for your analysis?" I answered, "I don't know; God is going to help me!" He asked me, "How long a time will it be until you get a job?" I replied, "I don't know, but I promise you that I will get one.'

So I started psychoanalysis. My husband thought I was crazy. After all, he had told me many times that only crazy people go to psychiatrists. He said to me, "You'll go once; it'll be enough." But I kept on going. Just as I had promised my analyst, I got a job. It was in a furniture store. Although I had wanted to begin a career in design, I put it off, so that my husband would feel less "threatened." My earnings paid for my daughter's nursery school tuition—and my psychoanalysis.

Now my husband and I started having terrible fights. He told me, "I am not going to give you another dime. You'd better get yourself an attorney." Within 6 months, we were separated. So now I had to work from 9:00 in the morning until 9:00 in the evening at two jobs. I had my appointments with my analyst before I went to work, and I spent the evenings with my children. Two nights a week I attended classes at night school. You can see that I was very busy! Sophie has spoken these words very quickly; she is almost out of breath. Now she pauses for a moment to collect her thoughts.

After I had been in analysis for 9 years, I had major surgery. I was very disappointed that my analyst never called me or came to see me. I could not understand how he could ignore me during such a difficult time in my life. I thought it was very inhuman of him. But, although I was deeply disappointed in my analyst personally, I did complete the last few months of my analysis.

People ask me, "How do you feel about your psychoanalysis? Nine years is a lot of time—and a lot of money." I reply, "It was the beginning of my journey." While I was not entirely satisfied with my analysis, I do agree with what my analyst used to say to me: "I've kept you out of the hospital, haven't I?" After spending almost 2,000 hours on the couch getting in touch with myself, I've learned to take care of my own needs, instead of expecting other people to take care of me. Every week that I earned enough money to pay for my analysis—and all my other expenses—I realized that I could take care of my financial needs, as well as my emotional ones.

During my psychoanalysis, I opened up to another person for the first time. Until I started seeing an analyst, I had never let anyone know what was going on in my life. No one. When I wasn't getting along with my husband or my children, I used to hold counsel with myself. I never told anyone my problems; I never shared my responsibilities. When the going got rough, I'd stay up all night and then make a decision. That was it. My husband and I never really talked to each other. My psychiatrist and I never had many dialogues either, but at least I shared myself with him.

Now I have paid off my mortgage, and I have money in the bank. I have my B.A. and my Ph.D. in design. I have had a fascinating career, which has included teaching at the college level, before I retired last year. I am living my life fully. My flag is fully unfurled—no longer at half-mast.

Yes, I have learned a lot and overcome a lot, and I still have more ahead. I don't think I'll ever be finished until I die. I refuse to grow old gracefully. I believe in dying with your boots on. Sophie says this last sentence with passion. Her eyes actually seem to emit sparks. Yes, Sophie's spirit is unquenchable.

Now she stops talking and thinks for a while. Then she remarks, "By the way, you may be interested to know that my son has become a psychoanalyst. Through the years, I think he has fully understood how important my psychoanalysis has been to me."

Like Vicki, Sophie was playing a power-under role in a rigid power-over marriage. Both women had to leave their husbands, in order to get to know themselves and realize their full potentials. Unlike Vicki, Sophie empowered herself in her relationship with a therapist. Her psychoanalyst gave her a place to open up, share and discover herself. Although their relationship was not mutual—and imperfect—it was a bridge to Sophie's eventually forming other mutually empowering relationships, particularly with her children. Although each took a different path, both Vicki and Sophie ended up knowing who they really were.

Self-knowledge is the stepping stone to authenticity, autonomy and a satisfying partnership. To be authentic, you have to know who you are. A woman's true feelings are expressions of her innermost self. To be autonomous in a relationship, you must first discover your identity. Every woman who acts in her own behalf is in touch with her own self. To have a satisfying mutual partnership, you—as well as your partner—must be able to know and to share what is really important to you.

Priority Number One: Explore Your Deepest Self

"How do I feel?" and "What do I want? are subjects worthy of your deepest consideration. Devote at least as much time and effort to pondering their answers, as you would to questions such as," What groceries do we need for dinner tonight?" or "What shall I say at the next staff meeting?" Every day spend at least 5 minutes finding out the truth about yourself.

According to psychologist Dr. Nathaniel Branden, your self-esteem, which is crucial to your empowerment, is made up of self-respect and self-confidence. In order to respect yourself and believe in yourself, you must know yourself. Self-knowledge is a foundation of self-esteem.

Discovering yourself is the most exciting adventure you will ever have. You have a special set of qualities that makes you who you are. When you know exactly what they are and how you want to use them, you will experience a special sense of wholeness.

What I am talking about is discovering yourself, not "fixing" yourself or "changing" yourself. There is no one else like you. You are a unique person. Finding out how much good there is in you can be a thrilling experience.

Although you will grow and become different as time passes, you will always respect the uniqueness within you. As one woman I interviewed said to me:

Self-knowledge is a continuous labor; at the end of it is a beginning. We turn in darkness in our dreams. Establish what matters to you at the time—and then live by these values.

Empowerment does not come from pleasing someone else, being like someone else or being different from someone else. Empowerment comes from knowing yourself and being yourself.

To have a unique self is the birthright of every woman. What stands in the way of your self-discovery?

Dare to Be Different

Some women fear their own uniqueness. From early childhood, they have been taught to "fit in," to be just like everyone else. What might happen if they "stand out" instead?

Nora, the television marketing executive whom I talked with, had been aware of her "differentness" since she was a child.

I always felt as if I was "a silly millimeter off." In other words, as if didn't quite belong anywhere. I have never fit into a group; I have never had anyone else whom I could talk to about what I was doing, someone who could say to me, "I understand." Nothing I ever do is done in a conventional way.

And I have always done things at a different time from everyone else. For example, in the '60s, I was wearing business suits when everyone else was wearing scruffy jeans. Later on, when I had my children and continued to work, my woman friends had made a choice between one or the other. It may surprise you, but it never bothered me.

Nora saw herself as special, not as "peculiar." She was proud, not ashamed, that she was not exactly like her relatives, friends and co-workers. Nora appreciated the personal qualities that made her different—and special. Every woman can learn from her example.

Unlike Nora, Dale, a lesbian therapist and playwright with whom I spoke at length, learned to accept her uniqueness very gradually. As she told me:

It has taken me a long time to accept my own special kind of brightness, which is different from that of scholars. During my childhood, I knew I had something special within, but I did not know what it was. When I was in high school, I felt that my brightness was trapped inside. When I took a test, I would get nervous and forget how to spell. This happened once when I was taking a history test, and I finally made my point in by creating a picture-story. I was so ashamed of what I had done.

When I got my paper back, my teacher had drawn an eye and then the letter "C" on it. She gave me full credit for my work. This teacher saw that I had all the answers within me even though I did not express them in a conventional way. Now I know that I am an auditory learner; I hear something once and remember it. Although I did not fill a single notebook during college and graduate school, I understood how to take information to a deep place and work with it.

Like many women, Dale was ashamed that she was not the same as other people. As Dale continued to discover who she really was, she realized that her differentness actually enhanced her inner beauty.

Playing a Role Rather Than Being a Person

Who are you? Are you, (your name), a woman? Or are you your husband's wife, your ex-husband's ex-wife or your friend's lover? If you gave one of the last three answers, stop and think.

Who you are is not defined by someone else. To always follow another person is not to be true to yourself. Ask yourself, "Why don't I listen to my own voice within? Why don't I take a stand and say, "This is all I can do." Why don't I confront other people more often and say 'No?'" "Because," you may reply, "I am afraid to damage the relationship."

If you are in a relationship where another person has power over you, you are harming yourself by always going along with him or her. Every time you fail to state your own needs and limits, you are missing an opportunity to define who you are. Every moment you pretend to be someone you are not, you are violating your own integrity.

When you are not your own true self, you also keep the other person in the relationship from being who he or she really is. Two persons are playing the roles of "husband" and "wife" or "girlfriend" and "lover," rather than being authentic together. This harms the relationship far more in the long run than saying, "I choose not to do this. It is uncomfortable for me."

Any persistent feelings on your part need to be expressed, because the other person will inevitably sense them. The sooner you can take care of these feelings and get them out of the way, the closer both of you will feel to each other. Share your emotions with conviction, rather than hesitation. "This is how I feel; it has nothing to do with you." You don't have to be defensive; explain that your anger or fear or boredom is about you, not the other person. Being genuine with someone else is a marvelously freeing experience.

You will inevitably feel frustrated and resentful, if you do something you don't want to do. No matter how much you try to hide your feelings, they will simmer beneath the surface, like a volcano waiting to explode. At a moment when you least expect it, a chance remark from the other person will cause your "volcano" to explode. Had you said "No," in the first place, neither of you would have been hurt.

So long as women play roles, instead of being people, everyone loses. Never mind what a wife, or an ex-wife or a lover is "supposed to" do. You don't have to change like a chameleon to meet someone else's expectations. Just because someone else is happy or sad or angry, you don't have to act the same way. Just because someone else asks you to do something doesn't mean you have to do it. If you show your real feelings, you will like yourself better—and so will everyone else.

Since we have been trained to meet other people's expectations from the time we were little girls, we need support from other women to behave differently. We must look for friends and acquaintances who are not afraid to say "No," or else join or form a community of men and women who feel the same way. Together we can become aware of, get comfortable with and learn to express our true feelings.

Be Who You Really Are

Do you feel frustrated that you cannot measure up to the ideal you have of yourself? Would you buy a dress that was much too big for you, even though it looked beautiful? If your ideal self does not fit your true self, you will never discover who you really are. Dr. Jacqueline Light puts it this way:

If you don't have a lot of energy, don't become a trial attorney or have six children! If you take on these "super-responsibilities," you will always be behind schedule and always be unhappy. Pay attention to what kind of person you really are, and then make your life decisions accordingly.

I myself would like to have had more children. But I quickly realized that my emotional resources were insufficient. When I had my third child, I said to myself, "This is it. I've had enough." That's something else you, as a woman, have to know—when you've had enough!

You cannot be authentic, if you are not being the person who you really are. One woman I interviewed spent almost 15 years in religious communities trying to become "totally spiritual," until she realized that she was not a very spiritual person at all.

Take a good, honest look at yourself. What you want to be is you, not a poor imitation of someone else. The woman you saw on television last night can fly a jet plane, but maybe you cannot. The model on the cover of your favorite fashion magazine may look thin as a twig, but not like you. Vera's 23-year-old daughter Darlene described to me how she gradually accepted her unique physical self:

I got the idea that "thin is beautiful" from fashion magazines. It didn't help me either to see all the slender girls in high school getting all the dates. In college, I observed that the men liked to go out with 5-foot-tall, 102-pound, blond, suntanned "beach bunnies." In order to deal with their "weightism," I had to develop a sense of myself. Then I had to experience my own anger. I had to get outraged before I could walk into a room and say to myself, "Who cares. She's thin, but I'm me."

You alone decide what you will aspire to—and whether or not you have measured up to your own standards. Just make sure not to set your sights too high. If you have chosen to be a full-time mother to one child—and are proud of your accomplishment—it does not matter if:

- Someone else has been a good mother to *two* children.
- Your best friend thinks that your child is "spoiled" or "neglected."
- The magazine you pick up at a doctor's office tells you that full-time motherhood is "out" and having a career is "in."

Un"self"ishness

Traditionally, women have been taught not to have a separate "self," literally to be un"self"ish. Did you learn that unselfishness is the highest good? This is what happened to Jayne, a woman I interviewed:

The main thing I learned at home was not to think about myself. That would be "selfish." When I was in high school, altruism was my "religion." I believed that unselfishness was the ultimate good. My mother had always taught me this. It was her early training. None of it was conscious—or malicious. As a teenager, Mom took care of her mother. Afterwards Mom went to nursing school, and she supported her entire family. She couldn't take advantage of her options without thinking that she would be selfish—a failure as a human being. I was expected to follow in her footsteps. I became Mom's parent; I took care of her emotionally. You know, I still grieve for my lost childhood.

It was difficult for Jayne to discover her own self, when she had learned to give it away to others instead. But somehow she prevailed.

In spite of my mother's influence, I didn't give my "self" up. Even as a child, I was always making choices; I just didn't realize it. Later on, I realized that, if I had the tools to identify what I wanted, I could do just about anything. I started asking myself, "Jayne, do you know what you want?" What kept coming up was that I wanted a career in science, but one that did not require taking care of patients. I had already spent enough time taking care of Mom!

Because my mother has continued to insist that life is to be lived unselfishly, she has become more and more unhappy. After I left for college, she told me that she did not feel that her life was worthwhile. When I told her that I wanted to be a scientist in a laboratory, not a medical doctor, she didn't speak to me for 3 months. Now she can't understand why I don't want to have children right away. The truth is that, after I get married, I'll hardly be home. What kind of life would that be for a child?

The more I saw Mom falling apart, the more terrified I was to get involved in a relationship. But one afternoon, while I was waiting for the subway, a sweet-looking guy started talking to me. He told me that his name was Ed. Much to my surprise, I found myself enjoying our conversation. Ed and I started seeing each other 3 or 4 times a week. He said that he would love me, no matter what kind of career I pursued. Little by little I began to feel safe with him. Now I have a relationship with someone I love, who allows me to care about "me," as well as him.

What I'm trying to do now is to create a separate self. It's a learning process, a growing up. Emotionally, I'm still very much an infant. I am still unsure of my identity—that funny sense of self, when you're sitting by yourself. In my relationship with Ed, I'm slowly starting to find Jayne.

When Jayne stopped being un"self"ish, she started discovering her "self." She was able to recognize that she was playing a power-under role in her relationship with her mother. Slowly she created a mutually empowering relationship with her fiance, Ed.

Put Yourself in Center Stage

Many women do not know who they are, because they are busy obsessing themselves with men. Some value themselves because of their wealthy, accomplished or handsome husband. Other women distort their identities by pleasing men or by imitating men.

Codependent women usually focus their energy on the man in their lives. Sometimes they obsess themselves with a female friend, their children, their father, or their mother. As Wendy put it, "When women want to do something, we always make excuses: 'I can't do it because of my parents, my husband, my kids, my dog. . . .'" At the opposite extreme, radical feminists sacrifice themselves for the "movement." Self-fulfillment means not giving up your individuality for anyone or anything at all.

For women who have their minds on someone else, self-discovery is not easy. I remember sitting in a San Francisco coffee shop and taking a personality test together with a friend. My score indicated that I was excessively concerned with pleasing other people, particularly men. After that, I did some serious soul-searching. I realized that, if my husband wanted to go to a science fiction movie, then I wanted to go; if he didn't, then I didn't. If he liked tennis, then I took up the sport. And so on. It took me 3 more years to find out who I was and what I wanted—and then gather the courage to do it.

If you can care that much about someone else, you can truly care about yourself. Codependent women, who focus their energy on other people, have this hidden strength. Self-discovery is much more difficult for depressed women, who do not care about anyone or anything at all.

Depression: An Obstacle to Self-Discovery

The most common emotional problem of women today is depression. Unlike a sad woman, a depressed woman cannot get in touch with her own self, or move forward in her life, because she has lost touch with her emotions. A sad woman feels intense grief, usually because she has recently experienced a loss or a disappointment. She may have a lump in her throat and want to cry, or else may be on the verge of tears or weeping outright. A depressed woman feels nothing; she is numb, even dead, inside. Having lost touch with her original sad feelings, she hides her grief even from herself. She experiences the world as a dark, empty place.

Dr. Irene P. Stiver and Dr. Jean Baker Miller of the Stone Center for Developmental Services and Studies at Wellesley College have developed a theory of how women's depression originates—and is healed—in relationships. Sad women who are in isolating power-over relationships cannot express their sadness. Without an outlet for their sadness, they lose touch with it and become depressed. When these women enter an empowering relationship, their depression can disappear as they reconnect with their original sad feelings.

Depression is usually experienced by women who are "stuck" in static, rigid relationships, where there is no room for them to express their emotions. A depressed woman is someone whose sad feelings are not responded to. There is no one who recognizes her sadness, who takes it seriously, who understands that it is valid and legitimate under the circumstances, and who responds to it in some meaningful way. The way out of depression is to be truly listened to by someone else.

I have often experienced depression myself. My breakthrough came while I was researching this book. While deciding which seminars to attend in order to enrich my knowledge of women's empowerment, I selected one sponsored by the Center for Studies of the Person, which had been founded by the late psychologist, Dr. Carl Rogers. The La Jolla Program, as it was called, was unique: 35 men and women meeting in groups 10 hours a day for 2 weeks with no agenda except to see what comes up and trust in the process. This was the ultimate group experience! Although I attended the seminar as a professional, I was amazed to find a place where I could begin to come to terms with my own emotions.

A few weeks later, I went to Cape Cod and heard Dr. Irene P. Stiver of the Stone Center speak about depression. Now I was empowered to look hard at my own feelings for the first time. Before I could go out and work with other people, I had to honestly examine myself. Why was it that I sometimes couldn't get out of bed in the morning?

Climbing out of the dark pit of my depression was no easy task. Because depression had helped me to survive, it had become a way of life. The first step was to get in touch with all the sadness and frustration that had been buried inside me for half my lifetime. I realized that, as a child, I had been grieving for the caring mother I never had. After I gave birth to my own children, I had been mourning the loss of my professional self. As I learned from listening to Dr. Stiver, many women prefer to be depressed, rather than to get in touch with their sad feelings, which can be very painful at first. As I begin to experience my emotions, my eyes would often be full of tears.

The second step was to express them to someone who would understand. When a depressed woman says, "Leave me alone," she often means that she lacks a safe place to express her emotions, and so feels less vulnerable if she hides them. As I interviewed women for this book, I was able to share the truth of my life experience with them. Often I was surprised to find that their private reality, as well as mine, was vastly different from what we were "supposed to" feel. Other women besides myself had suffered terrible losses in their relationships; what we all needed was a forum to express our grief and frustration. Then we could rebuild our lives.

Once I got in touch with my feelings, and shared them with other women, I felt genuinely connected for the first time in my life. I didn't *need* to talk on the telephone for an hour a day to try to escape my self-imposed isolation. I no longer felt lonely. Although I was physically alone as I wrote at home every day, I felt that I was part of the greater unity of all women.

For the first time, I was able to move full speed ahead with my career. I began to feel good about myself. As I heard women describe how they were struggling to become empowered, I became proud to have been born a woman. As my interviewees told me stories of their courage in their relationships, I became convinced that a woman's ability to connect with other people is her greatest strength. If she can form even one relationship where she can be true to herself, she will realize that it is possible for her to do it again. Inevitably she will create other empowering relationships in her life.

Get Past Your Emotions

I have sometimes been told, "You're too emotional." Has anyone ever told you this? Actually, being emotional can be an asset, is well as a liability. If you are passionate, you are open to experiencing the full range of your emotions. This is a sign that you are already empowered in your capacity to feel. What you need to do is to get beyond the sad or angry place where you are, so that you can see yourself in a clear perspective.

If you are depressed, the first step is to create a mutually empowering relationship with someone else, preferably a therapist. Once you get past your depression, you will come face to face with your sadness. You will have reached the first stage of empowerment: feeling—with your deepest emotions and with your intuition. The second stage will be knowing and choosing your heart's desire—with your mind. The third stage will be acting to get what you want—with your strength and energy.

When you are an empowered woman, you know what you want; you choose it and you act to make it happen. As you become empowered together with someone else, you experience autonomy.

Listen to Other People; Then Decide for Yourself

Once you have discovered your own identity, you make your own decisions; you do not let other people make them for you. This is the essence of autonomy. You pay attention to what other people have to say, but, in the last analysis, you listen to your own voice.

Ask yourself these questions:

- "If every book I read and every person I know tells me, 'No man wants to marry a woman over 45'—and my inner voice tells me, 'That's a lie!'—whom am I going to believe?"
- "If my mother, my father, my sister, my brother and my best friend all think that I should get married to someone—and my inner voice tells me that he is not a suitable lifelong partner—whom am I going to listen to?"
- "If my husband says that I am an inadequate mother, a poor cook or a 'dud' in bed—and my inner voice denies his accusation—whom am I going to trust?"

Your answer to all these questions should be, "Me!"

One empowered woman I interviewed describes how she makes decisions:

Empowerment is listening to your own inner voice, even if it is different from what everyone else is saying. As women we have been conditioned to believe that, if we don't agree with the other people around us, we must be wrong. But that's nonsense. When you hear or see something that doesn't "feel right," it doesn't mean that you are "exaggerating" or that you are "crazy." You need to have enough confidence in yourself to believe that what doesn't "feel right" isn't right, even if you think that you're the only one in the world who feels this way. Somewhere else, other women are also grappling with the same concern. You are not alone.

You Discover Your Identity in Empowering Relationships

You discover yourself in authentic, mutual and autonomous relationships. Are your relationships two for two, rather than "two for one?" Are you your own person in them? Do they allow you to be yourself ? Then your relationships are fertile soil in which your own self will grow.

Or do you find yourself playing a power-under role in a power-over relationship again and again? Do you follow another person and allow him or her to control you? Or else are you codependent? Do you focus all your energy on someone else, rather than yourself? In either case, you are not taking a stand for your own self. Instead, you are preserving an unsatisfying relationship in which you yourself cannot develop.

You cannot discover your identity in relationships which do not empower you. You develop your own self in mutual relationships with other selves. You constantly learn about yourself, as well as the other person. As you recognize your weaknesses, you also discover your strengths. Your personal strength to take the initiative, speak your truth, make decisions and take action develops, as you relate to others. Paradoxically, the more you share power together with someone else, the more each of you becomes a distinct individual. Empowerment begins, when you start to realize both how very special you are—and how very connected you are with others.

Empowerment is most dramatic when you relate to other women. Women who are role models, mirrors and message bearers enable you to see dimensions of yourself that you would never discover alone. Let each woman you meet be your teacher. As you discover new role models, mirrors and message bearers, be authentic with them. Share what you really feel, what you really think and what you really want. Let other people see who you really are. Let them hear the beautiful music inside of you.

As you increase your self-knowledge, you will be proud of who you are as a woman. You will appreciate that women's contributions, nurturing others and creating mutually empowering relationships, are as valuable as men's values of financial gain and professional success.

The Value of Time Alone

Time alone is for building a relationship with yourself and the universe. If you are in an empowering relationship, you are learning who you are in relation to another person. Nevertheless, you will want a room of your own" (or even "a car of your own") where you can pursue your self-exploration further in privacy.

Self-discovery is like making a journey into the desert alone with your eyes closed. Although you cannot see where you are going, you can always feel where the sun is.

Terri, a military executive whom I interviewed, described her discovery of her own self like this:

When I was a teenager, I consciously said to myself, "I have to be true to myself. I must do what I think is best. I'm not going to spend a lot of my energy shopping for ruffled clothes and pastel shades of makeup. I'm not going to spend most of my waking moments thinking about boys. I don't want to wind up just being someone's wife or someone's mother. I want to get away from my family. I want to achieve something that I can be proud of. I want to be me."

For the last 20 years, I have dedicated myself to working hard at a job I like. Now, as a high-ranking executive in the military, I have enough money to support myself. Finally, I am free to chart the course of my life.

What I have learned is this: Every woman has discretion about how she uses her time and energy; many of us just don't exercise it. If you want to achieve something extraordinary, you have to be dedicated and focused.

While self-discovery takes place in relationships, it continues when you are by yourself.

Empowerment Exercises

l. *Design a Self-Portrait in Words:* Imagine that you have almost reached the end of your life. You are describing to someone you love what your life was about and what meant the most to you, as you look back. Use these questions as a guideline for your answers. You may either write them down in your Empowerment Journal or speak into a tape recorder. If you have a flair for verse, you may want to express some of your answers in a poem. Those of you who like to draw may prefer to sketch pictures of yourself living your life.

   a. *Introduction:*
      1) How would I describe myself—in two adjectives?
      2) What were the three most significant choices I made in my life?
      3) In a sentence, how would I like to be remembered?

   b. *My Relationship to Myself:*
      1) What were my best personality traits?
      2) How did I feel about my body?
      3) What was the quality of my sexual experience?
      4) What kind of recreation did I enjoy most?
      5) What spiritual beliefs did I adhere to?
      6) What was my preferred lifestyle?
      7) Why was I unique?

   c. *My Relationships with Other People:*

1) In what ways was I similar to my parents?
2) In what ways was I different from my parents?
3) Which people did I care about the most?
4) What kind of a relationship did I have with each of these people?
5) How important was marriage—or an exclusive relationship—to me?
6) Was being a mother necessary for my self-fulfillment? Why or why not?

d. *My Relationship to My Work:*
1) What were my greatest talents?
2) What was my life's work, as I envisioned it?
3) Did it matter to me whether or not I made a lot of money?
4) Which accomplishments gave me the most satisfaction?
5) Of all my accomplishments, which one was I most proud of?
6) What contribution did I make to the world during my lifetime?

e. *Conclusion:*
1) What, if anything, would have been worth risking my life for?
2) What do I regret doing—or not having done?

2. *Explore New Directions:* You have a chance, right now, to start living your life without regrets. Ask yourself these five questions. You may either write down your answers in your Empowerment Journal or speak into a tape recorder.

   • If I could be anything I wanted, what would I be?
   • If I could do anything I wanted, what would I do?
   • If I could say anything I wanted, what would I say?
   • If I could go anywhere I wanted, where would I go?
   • If I could have anything I wanted, what would I have?

   If nothing comes up for you, refer to your self-portrait in words, which you have just completed, to give yourself ideas.

3. *Focus on How You See Yourself, Not How Others See You:* Sit down in a quiet place, relax and close your eyes. Turn your attention to yourself. Visualize your face and body, hear your voice and touch your clothes. Do you experience any sensations or tension anywhere in your body? If so, where? How does this part of your body feel? What words or phrases come to your mind? Does anything else come up for you?

   Now open your eyes, get up and go to a full-length mirror. Look in it. Move around. Say something. Take off your clothes, look in the mirror and move around again. Put on another outfit, if you like. How do you experience yourself now? The same way? Differently? Think of at least three adjectives that you think describe you accurately. You may want to write a few paragraphs, "How I See Myself" in your Empowerment Journal, or else record your words on tape. If you have ever described yourself in the past, you might learn something about your growth and development by comparing your self-portrait with the earlier one.

4. *Keep a Daily Log of Your Authentic Self:* Each time that you say or do something that expresses your genuine self, note it in your Empowerment Journal. Do thas every day for at least a week. At the end of the week, read back what you have written. With who were you able to be authentic? Did you initiate dialogues or did you respond to other people who opened up first to you? What was the outcome of each encounter? How did you feel afterwards? How do you think the other person felt? How did each of you benefit? Did either of you grow?

5. *Pay Attention to Your Inner Voice:* Whenever you feel confused, *stop, look and listen.* If possible, *stop* what you are doing, close your eyes and relax. *Look* inward at yourself, not outward at other people. Believe that you have an inner voice—and that you can hear it. Know how to tune into it, by means of focusing, journal writing or any other technique you find helpful. Then *listen* to what your inner voice says. Pay attention to it, when it speaks. It tells you what is most precious to you—your values, your lifestyle and your philosophy of life.

Now you are ready to tune into other people's messages and decide which of them are valid for you. After you weigh the advice of others, make your own decision. Then trust it. Act promptly, so that you create the reality you want. In the last analysis, always be true to yourself. "Follow your gut," as one therapist I interviewed put it.

6. *Realize the Choice is Yours:* Whenever you feel pressured, sit down, relax and say to yourself, "This is my day to make choices." Each time you feel that you "have to" do something, ask yourself, "What will happen to me if I don't?" What you will soon realize is that you always have the prerogative to choose. When you do something you "have to" do, it is simply because you prefer not to endure the consequences of making the other choice. (I do this exercise regularly, and it really works!)

Once you have discovered who you are, the next step is to find your calling and empower yourself in the workplace. Would you like to know how? In the next chapter, you will discover how the obstacle of frustration in the workplace can be turned into a stepping stone.

EMPOWER YOURSELF IN THE WORKPLACE

"What lies behind us and what lies before us are tiny matters compared to what lies within us."

Ralph Waldo Emerson

What does work mean to you? Every woman has a different view. When I interviewed Kim, a successful financial consultant, she told me that her answer was vastly different from her mother's. "Work is a way to get money," her mother had once told her. "I don't know why you feel you have to be challenged in your job." Kim had retorted, "I want to be interested in what I am doing, Mom. I'm not going to work every morning just to get money or simply because I don't have a husband and children to take care of."

What Is Your Calling?

Your identity is your sense of who you are—and who you can be. Your calling is your special life's work that develops from your unique self. Each of us has a different calling, something of value we want to do during our lives. This is how Stacey, a 23-year-old newspaper reporter, found hers:

Realizing I would spend almost half my life at work, I always intended to find something to do that I adored. I knew I was curious, because I enjoyed exploring and finding out new things. I was also aware that I was creative and that I liked to talk to people.

I didn't become interested in writing until I was a junior in college. Then I knew that I had found my niche. By trying a lot of different writing jobs, I found out what I liked and learned to avoid what I didn't like. I really enjoy my job now as a reporter for a local newspaper. It fits well with my personality. I have the freedom to decide what's new and interesting and worth writing about. Then I go and talk to people, which I love to do. Since I am a highly curious person, I can also be as nosy as I like, or as they let me be. Then I write. For me, it's fun to play with words.

At this particular moment, you may not yet be fully conscious of your talents and strengths—and the purpose for which they are uniquely suited. You may discover your calling gradually, the way Stacey did and the way I did.

Before you find your calling, you may have to explore several different careers. Chances are that you will have more than one career during your lifetime. As time passes, you enter different stages of life, and your relationships change. I myself have had two careers so far. Besides being a writer-editor, I have been a teacher in both colleges and elementary schools. Because teaching had shorter work hours, it suited my needs while my children were growing up.

To pursue your calling may mean breaking with tradition—and doing something very different from what you are doing now. You may need the support of an empowerment community to gain the courage to take the leap.

After you have decided upon a career, finding the right job is often the result of trial and error. Try on jobs as you would try on shoes. Ask yourself each time, "Am I comfortable in this job? How do I feel about what I do, the workplace and my co-workers?" One day, perhaps by accident, you may find a job that fits you well. Although you may have several jobs during your lifetime, each new one should feel right to you, when you embark upon it.

If you like what you are doing, you have a head start on empowering yourself in the workplace: You see your job as part of your own self-fulfillment. As Kim put it, "When the pressure gets too heavy, I say to myself, 'Am I doing this work for me or for my boss?' Then, if I need a break, I take it."

Even if you *have* to take a job just for money, keep a clear vision in your mind of what you really want to do as soon as you get the chance. See what opportunities you can find at your present job to further your long-term career goals.

What Is Your Personal Rhythm?

Take the time to discover your personal rhythm. Kim told me:

I am happy being a consultant, because it suits my style. I like to work in peaks and valleys. I'm willing to work 14 hours a day, 7 days a week to get the job done, and then slack off for a while. When I was putting in 8-hour days as an accountant, I went berserk.

Sometimes it takes a drastic change of pace to empower yourself in the workplace. During the three years I spent working in offices, I never felt empowered. The nadir was when I was the only woman executive in a consulting firm—and the only one not invited to strategy meetings. I used to think that there was something wrong with my "bosses," my co-workers, and of course, me, as I bounced from job to job.

Finally I had two realizations. First, I was not feeling empowered in any of these jobs, because I was not doing the work I really wanted to do. Second, working in an office didn't fit my personal rhythm.

I like to write from 5:00 in the evening until 1:00 in the morning, a time when most offices are closed. Iam most comfortable wearing a sweatsuit, attire that most offices consider grossly inappropriate. Because I do not drink caffeinated beverages, soda or liquor, I feel awkward during coffee breaks and office parties.

The truth is that I took these office jobs just to make money. Following my own advice, I waited until I was financially secure enough to do what I loved full-time—free-lance writing. Now, at last, I am empowered in the workplace. My late hour, no-break work style fits my rhythm excellently. Best of all, my sweatsuits offend no one; if they do, neither my dog nor my computer can complain!

Margaret is another woman who has been struggling to find her calling and a job that fits her personal rhythm. In the empowerment community where we met, she experienced a dramatic breakthrough. Let her tell you about it, in her own words.

Margaret: "No More Pain for This Lady!"

At age 37, Margaret has ulcers, colitis and chronic migraine headaches. A tall, strikingly attrictive woman, Margaret does not appear to be ill at all. But, after we introduce ourselves, I can see the pain in her eyes. "Make yourself comfortable," she says. As we sit on her bed directly across from each other, I ask her, "Why are you hurting, Margaret?" She begins:

I graduated from high school one year early, so about 2 weeks after I was 17 years old, I had my first full-time job. It was a secretarial position at an insurance company. At age 18, I marriel my high school sweetheart, Brian. About 3 years later, our first daughter, Claire, was born. Our second daughter, Jessica, arrived 2 1/2 years later.

I stayed home until Jessica was 5. Then I felt a real pressure to go to work. I had read stories, baked cookies, made playdough and driven the girls to lessons—all the things a "good mother" was supposed to do. Going back to work was really scary, after 7 years of dealing only with toddlers. But there was something inside me that wanted more. And we needed the extra money. Although my husband had taken over his father's business, agriculture had taken a downturn. Fortunately, I found a job as a secretary for Al Blank, a state senator.

When Al lost the primary for lieutenant governor, my employment with him came to a grinding halt. Then he got appointed the director of a state administrative agency. One hour after he had accepted the position, he called me up and asked me, "Would you like to be my assistant?" "Yes," I replied, without out a moment's hesitation. A few months later, I was promoted to senior personnel officer. I've held this job during the past 4 years.

Once Al was in charge of a government agency, our relationship became very strained. One problem was that my duties weren't clear-cut. Since I did not want to be a secretary anymore, I began to do other jobs around the office, mostly ones that other people didn't want to do. My specialties were patting everybody on the head and wiping everyone's tears. I wrote my own job description which read something like, "This employee does everything that needs to be done that nobody else can handle!"

Al was now having problems at home. His own personal tension spilled over to the office. The pressure on me at work—to get everything done right—became unreal. Most of the time, I did not understand what Al wanted. He would ask me to do something right away, but I often did not know what it was. If I asked him a direct question like, "Is this what you mean?" he would get very angry. It became a "no-win" situation. I could either do what I thought he wanted—and possibly have to do the job over again—or I could risk asking him what he wanted and have him scream at me.

One day I was thrown out of Al's office. I had gone in there to ask him whether or not he had any questions about a new employee I was supervising. All of a sudden Al became very angry and started blaming me. I could tell immediately that I was not being understood. For the first time in 8 years on the job, I began to cry. Immediately Al said that our conversation was over. I sat down in a chair for a few moments to compose myself, but he got up and opened the door of his office for me to leave. As I look at Margaret, I notice how pale her face is—almost like a piece of marble sculpture. It strikes me as odd that she is talking about this emotionally charged incident in such a monotone voice.

I was extremely hurt. But no matter how badly I wanted to walk out at that time, it would have caused our family severe financial hardship. My husband was in the process of selling his father's business, and we needed my income. Since it would have been impossible for me to find another job at the same salary level, I swallowed my pride for 6 more months. Margaret's voice remains flat, but her words betray her despair.

Now the business has been sold. We have enough money to live on. I don't need this job any longer. Why am I staying in a situation that is making me ill? Margaret pulls out a soda cracker and starts munching on it.

I am almost always in constant physical pain. My ulcers have made it impossible for me to eat. My colitis has been so bad that I often have to find a place to lie down at work. My migraine headaches have become so intense that sometimes I have to go home early. My job is literally making me sick. Why should I continue to suffer like this? Life is too short. . . . Margaret clasps her hands on her head, leans back and pauses for a moment. I wonder, "What is she thinking?""

I don't really like pushing papers around a desk, and I don't like following office procedures. I do these tasks well, but I don't enjoy them; they drain me. What really gives me pleasure are sewing clothes and decorating my house. I can go into a fabric store, and I can find a pattern and a fabric that fits any picture in my head. To find out exactly what kind of work I want to do, I'm going to take some college courses.

Margaret's face suddenly becomes very serious. My friends are going to think that I am insane, because I am making a very high salary for someone without a college degree. They do not understand how intense the pressure is in my office, and there is no way I can explain it to them. Several of them have already told me, "Before you quit, go and see what is out there." Well, I don't know what is out there, but I know what is here for me now—a very unhappy lady with major health problems.

And my husband, Brian, is going to want me to stay as long as I can. Maybe our marriage will fall apart if I quit my job, but I know that we haven't got much of a future together the way things are right now. How agreeable can I be if I am in constant pain and depression? How much time can we share, if I come home from work at 5:00 in the afternoon, go to bed immediately, and sleep until 7:00 the next morning? Recently I haven't even cooked any meals. I haven't had the energy.

This morning, I awoke at 4:30 in the morning, and I felt rested for the first time in 4 years. I said to myself, "You started out as a secretary and now you're a senior personnel officer. If you've done it once, you can do it again somewhere else, maybe in a line of work that's more to your liking." For the first time, Margaret smiles a radiant smile and her whole face bursts into light! As she gazes at me intelligently, I notice that her eyes are a lovely hazel.

A few days later, I stop by to check on Margaret. "How are you oing?" I begin. I am surprised to hear her answer. "Not so great. Everyone else expects me to feel terrific, and I don't. I've lost my desire to help myself. Maybe I should go back to my old job, after all!"

I am suddenly moved to ask her, "Margaret, at the end of your life, do you think that your boss, your husband, your children or your friends will thank you for 'sacrificing' yourself for this job?" "Heck, no," she replies. I continue to question her: "What do you think the people you love will say about you, if you continue in the same direction? That Margaret should have taken the time to enjoy herself. . .to smell a rose, swim in the ocean, play ball with her kids, go to the movies with her husband. . . ." She nods her head, "Yes," in silent agreement.

The next time I see Margaret, she is stretched out on a living room couch with her eyes completely closed. All the lines in her foreheadhave disappeared; her lips are soft and relaxed; and her cheeks are slightly pink. When I say her name, she opens her eyes quickly and sits up. For the first time, I hear a note of animation in Margaret's voice.

I called him long distance today. My boss, Al. At the end of the conversation, he said, "See you, Monday." I answered, "Al, I may not be coming back. I'm a different person now." I didn't even bother to listen to his reaction. I just hung up the phone. Margaret giggles like a schoolgirl who has just played a prank.

Eight days later, Margaret telephones me. Guess what? I'm calling you from the office, and I've just stopped the clock! When I first came back, everyone was saying, "You look great—not pale like you used to." I felt well for 2 1/2 days, but then I became as sick as ever. So I went to Al and told him, "I am leaving." Just like that.

Six weeks from now, I'll be out of here. I'm still at my desk, but I feel amazingly calm. No more pain for this lady!

As Margaret becomes more aware of her potential, she will be able to find a career, and a job, where she can fully express herself. Finally she will become her own person.

Your work is one of your best friends. Each job you choose is an investment of your time and energy in your future. The most important commitment you will ever make to yourself is to make your life's work an expression of your unique talents, skills and interests. Career counseling, psychological testing and quiet introspection can help you make the right choice.

Autonomy in the Workplace

For many women, autonomy is the key to empowerment in the

workplace. They need to follow their own star, rather than to fit in with someone else's requirements. How can women do this, in a hierarchical corporation with rigid rules?

I asked Dr. Jacqueline Light, "What do you suggest to women who want to empower themselves in a male-oriented workplace?" This is what she replied:

The main difference between women and men in their attitudes toward work is that men are generally freer to put their work first. And they do! This is a characteristic of the male in the workplace—and in life. One of the biggest difficulties in marriage is that men give their work a higher priority than their family and their emotions. Women tend to put their relationships with their spouses and children first.

What happens when you put a woman in the workplace, particularly in a big corporation that expects that employees will identify with the organization and put it first? What is best for the organization is supposed to be best for everyone. In fact, what's best for the organization is *not* always best for everyone—especially if you are a woman. What if you have a big corporate meeting this morning and your child just came down with the measles last night? What is best for you is to be home with your sick child. So you end up in a terrible squeeze. You are caught between your work life and your private life.

Of course, there are different kinds of women. The woman who chooses to make money and gain power over others may decide not to have children. The woman who defines herself mainly by her relationships, but who also likes to work, is more likely to opt for the "Mommy Track." I certainly have chosen it, and I think I am in good company. Making money and gaining power over other people in the workplace is not as important to most women as it is to most men. What really matters to most women is doing a good job.

"Isn't the 'Mommy Track' followed by women who have feminine values?"

Yes. This is why a lot of people say that the "Mommy Track" is second rate.

"Both men and feminists put the 'Mommy Track' down. Especially the feminists. The women who cannot give themselves permission to both work and have children are sucked into the male value system—"

—and end up trying to compete with the men. And it is just this kind of set-up that keeps women from being successful. Women shouldn't fall for men's propaganda: "Compete with us on our own terms or don't compete at all."

"But you don't have to."

Exactly. If you buy into this male value system, you will not like yourself. You will forever think you're second rate and second class and second best—all of the "seconds."

"You will be standing there with your newborn baby in your arms—wanting to be with that baby and being torn to pieces."

Instead of realizing, "I can be with the baby and leave work for a while."

"In fact, if feminine values ruled our society, men would think in these terms, too."

Women have to define themselves. We cannot allow men to define us. For this reason, any job that a woman can put together which allows her to have autonomy in the workplace is a good deal for her.

"What do you mean by autonomy in the workplace?"

Being your own boss. Running your own show. Then you have more flexibility. You don't have someone standing over you and judging you—telling you that you have succeeded or failed. You do this for yourself.

In the corporate workplace, you cannot advance without good ratings. There are some real, unescapable problems for women who work in a corporate team.

"A male-oriented corporate team."

Yes. Some of our sisters enforce male values more vigorously than the men. One of the worst things a woman can run into is a female boss who plays by men's rules. This is a nightmare that I've encountered myself. When I was a medical intern, there were female nurses who didn't want me to go home to nurse my baby at dinner time.

"Are you serious?"

Yes, oh yes, oh yes! They would downgrade me to the male chief of service, even though I might have worked all day long to take good care of my patients, so that I could go home for 2 hours—home being across the street! These success-oriented women were antagonistic toward me and the other women in the hospital with feminine values. I guess there will always be women who will buy into the male-oriented value system—and enforce it.

"Yes. In the workplace, the woman who chooses feminine values is going to have to confront the men and women who choose masculine ones."

That's why reaching for autonomy in the workplace is an important goal for women. Learn to prioritize for yourself, not on the basis of what someone else thinks. Check out your feelings. Ask yourself, "Do I feel best when I'm in balance or when I'm totally stressed out?" Some people love stress! She laughs. "Do I feel best when I'm not working at all? Am I one of these women who would rather be at home?"

These are all questions for upper-class and middle-class women. Lower-class women don't have a choice. They have to work to support themselves and their families. If this is the case, you should check out workplaces that allow you to feel good. If you do not feel good where you are working, then get out. You can move! Always understand that if you are doing an excellent job in the organization where you are working, you can always go somewhere else.

Dr. Light suggests that in a male-oriented workplace, you must become autonomous. What strategies can you use? Most important, select a job with a schedule that fits your needs. Perhaps you can:

- Work flexible hours.
- Work part-time.
- Share a job.
- Work for an understanding boss.
- Be a consultant.
- Be self-employed.

Self-employment has been the answer for Julia, an attractive, red-haired woman in her mid-30s. When I first interviewed Julia 5 years ago, she had told me how unhappy she was with her work. Now she tells me:

The kind of job I have now empowers me. I can say, "I don't want to work on this project," or "I'm not coming in until 10:00," or "I can't work late tonight" or "I'm taking next week off."

"In your new position, you are not required to follow other people's rules?"

Yes. I manage my time so that I meet my goal—whether it is to work 30 hours a week so that I can enjoy extra free time, or to get a certain project finished.

"How did you become autonomous? Your job wasn't always like this."

Remember when I was employed in the marketing department of a large corporation? After a while, I became very unhappy. I wasn't enjoying my work anymore. After 3 years, I was offered an opportunity to go on as a consultant for a firm that was one of my customers. They guaranteed me 6 months' work.

Up to that time, I had always been afraid to go out on my own, because most people I had known who started their own businesses had ended up working 80 hours a week. In graduate school, I had decided that I would never allow myself to work more than 40 hours. I wouldn't "break my neck" working nights and weekends while I was young. But this consulting firm had a rule that you had to get special permission to work overtime. So I decided to take the leap.

"You were not afraid to leave a 40-hour-a-week full-time job with a complete benefit package for a 6-month temporary job?"

I was not afraid at all. Actually there was nothing binding; the 6-month "guarantee" was only verbal! I figured that there was always "Plan A" and "Plan B" and "Plan C." What was the worst that could happen to me? Not that I don't enjoy my possessions, but if I had to change my lifestyle—sell my townhouse and live in an apartment—I wouldn't be devastated.

Remember, I don't have children who depend upon me for income. It would be much easier to say to myself, "I'm not going to have dessert tonight," than to say to a child, "You can't have an ice cream cone; we can't afford it."

"What I hear is that you are happier now, even though you don't have job security—a contract or a slot."

I am my own best resource. I have to count on myself. Not that I can't count on other people; I can't just depend on someone else to read my mind—or intuit my feelings. I'm the one who has to determine what it is that I want and what I need from other people. Then I can ask them.

My most reliable investment is what I create. I believe in myself and what I am doing. Since I have started being self-employed, I have actually had to turn work down!

Trina, an Hispanic obstetrician-gynecologist with an 8-year-old son, achieved autonomy in the workplace by finding a job with a flexible schedule. This is what she told me:

The kind of career I have chosen has its limits. I am not out there making great advances in medicine. Instead I am letting other people do this and then applying their knowledge.

I am a single parent. A lot of the reason why I am here in a Health Maintenance Organization is that I can have more time to spend with my son. Although my parents have moved nearby to be with me, and I have "instant child care," I still feel that I want to be with my son much of the time.

"Working at a Health Maintenance Organization gives you an opportunity to be of service to women and, at the same time, to have regular contact with your son. Do you have a fair amount of autonomy in your job?"

Yes. The hours are very regular. I know, weeks in advance, when I am going to be on call and when I am going to do surgery.

"You picked a job where you could schedule your own free time, rather than getting stuck in the demanding structure of a hospital, which would require you to work long hours, including nights and weekends?"

Right. But, by the same token, I have limited what I am accomplishing professionally. It is a fair exchange. I'm not going to make great strides in advancing knowledge in obstetrics or gynecology—

"—but you have a son."

"He means the world to me!" Trina's voice trembles. Behind her words, I sense a great deal of emotion.

For Lynda, a mother of three and a former legislative assistant and practicing attorney, part-time employment has been the way to achieve autonomy in the workplace:

All of my children were born while I worked on Capitol Hill. I took 3 weeks off for each child. I always thought that we deserved this time together.

While the children were growing up, I always worked part-time. Senator Stan Bradford was very nice to me. I saw him right before an election campaign, right before my first baby was born. I told him, "I would really like to come back after the baby is born, but only if I can work 3 days a week." "Are you sure you want to do that?" he asked me. "Yes, this is really what I want to do," I said. It was that easy. But this happened only because I had worked for him a long time. You need to build your professional reputation first before you ask for this kind of set-up. You should work full-time for a few years before you ask for part-time employment.

I am very glad that I have stayed home. If I hadn't, I would have missed the most important moments of my life. But I also really liked my job; it kept my brain alive. If I had to choose between working full-time, after my children were born, and staying home full-time, I would have quit my job. Fortunately, I was able to work part-time, which I think is the ideal arrangement. I worked 3 days a week at the Senate and stayed at home the other 2.

This story tells you how happy I was with my choice: One day, after I had worked in the Senate, I came home, my husband asked me, "What did you do today?" I said, "I marked up a gun control bill and showed it to two senators. Tomorrow it will be on the news." The following day, I stayed home and took care of my son, Todd. When my husband came home, he asked me, "What happened today?" "Todd peed standing up," I replied. I realized what a contrast there was between my two kinds of days. But I was just as excited and happy about one day as the other. Only one kind of day would not have worked well for me.

Lynda, who is now an editorial writer for one of the country's leading newspapers, frequently advises women about how to achieve autonomy in the workplace, after they give birth to a child. This is what she says to them:

You have to have a certain confidence in yourself and say, "I am going to follow this track, and not follow these other tracks, whether other people like it or not." If you reason like this, you wind up happier, no matter what your choice.

I think that the women who go back to work full-time, full speed ahead after their children are born are going to be very sorry later on. I'm not sure whether or not the children suffer, but you miss the best part of your life. I don't understand married couples fighting about who has to do the "terrible" job of raising the children and who does the "glamorous" job of working in an office. The thing to do is to share both.

I meet so many women who are very unhappy with their lives; they feel terrified and trapped. They start on the Total Career Track. Once they are on it, they feel they have to stay on it. They are pushing for a promotion, and they don't want to show a sign of weakness. These women are making tremendous money, but the tradeoff is that they have sold all their time. They complain, "I'm not married, and I don't see any prospect of it. I never meet anyone; I never go out; all I do is work." I've also seen young married women who work 80 to 90 hours a week and say to me, "I don't have enough time to have a child." I say to all of them, "Honey, you have a choice. You can quit. You don't have to stay. I left. And I wound up happier."

Expect to "make waves," if you stand up for feminine values in a male-oriented workplace. Whether you decide to leave an uncomfortable job, or opt for a more flexible schedule, you will run into opposition from men—and from women who support the male value system.

Men will typically say, "You took the job, and now you're leaving us in the lurch. We knew you wouldn't stay. Just like a woman! Don't ever try to convince us again that you're qualified for a job." Women who support the male value system are programmed to react like this, "You've sold out to our enemies! Now you've ruined it for all of us. We'll never get another job." Or "We've worked our tails off. Why shouldn't you? You don't deserve any special privileges!" Just shrug your shoulders and go on. This is the price you pay for the privilege of achieving feminine autonomy in a male-oriented workplace.

Find a Role Model—and a Mentor

In the workplace, role models and mentors are your staunchest allies. One woman I interviewed put it this way:

The difference between women who end up with achievements they feel good about and those who don't is that the achievers have a vision of what they want and a mentor or a model who helps them get there. It is especially helpful if the mentor or model is a woman.

In today's male-oriented workplace, finding an appropriate role model is not easy. As Lynda told me:

The problem is that women today lack suitable role models. Women are buying into men as role models, but not vice versa. Most men are interested in making a lot of money and totally immersing themselves in their work. I am interested in neither. During my 15 years on Capitol Hill working for the Senate, I did very exciting and interesting work. Then I went downtown and practiced law for 4 years, but I didn't like it. I was not interested either in making a fortune or in working day and night. And I never thought I was doing anything really "important" representing the interests of clients I did not necessarily care about.

For a lawyer, it can be a challenge to find a role model who embodies feminine values. In Lynda's words:

The only role models we lawyers have is that of the male attorney who goes to Wall Street, works day and night for 7 years, becomes a partner in a law firm and ends up making hundreds of thousands of dollars a year. I tried this for one summer, and I hated every minute of it. It was very boring—not satisfying at all.

As more and more women become lawyers, appropriate role models should become easier to find.

Do you have a mentor—a woman who is committed to helping you get ahead in your field? If not, follow these three steps:

1. Think of a woman in your field of work whom you admire.

2. Ask yourself, "What personal qualities and professional skills does she possess? Which ones do I already have? Which ones would I like to have? How has she achieved autonomy in the workplace? What might I learn from her?"

3. Devise a strategy to get introduced to her, or to get to know her better.

During your first 2 years in your chosen field, a mentor can be particularly valuable. Sheila, who had a successful political career, told me that her mentor had given her a big boost at the beginning:

Right before my marriage, I had worked for a politician for about 6 months. I had met a woman who was clever and taught me most of what I know about politics. I reconnected with her; the two of us got involved in a political campaign, and our candidate won. Although I saw all the people around me cashing in, I didn't get a political position. But I learned a lot.

Ignore Sex Discrimination, If You Can

Sex discrimination, or sexism, as it is sometimes called, is power-over in its most virulent form. In a sexist relationship, you hear: "I'm a man. I'm superior to you, because you are a woman. So I can control you. I can keep you from fulfilling your potential." In a relationship where you are empowered together with someone else, you get a different message, "Since we're both valuable people, let's empower each other."

Sexist relationships are created by men obsessed with the ideology of dominating or submitting, "winning" or "losing," and being "better than" or "worse than" someone else. A sexist relationship will destroy you, instead of empowering you. Never allow someone else to tell you what you are worth; appreciate the value of your own contributions, instead. If you refuse to pay attention to sexist talk, eventually it will cease. For there to be a conversation, there has to be both a talker and a listener.

If you encounter sex discrimination, you have a choice. You can either fight it, ignore it or distance yourself from it. Most of the women I interviewed decided not to pay attention to it, or else to find another job. They preferred not to get involved in a pitched battle that would distract them from their own career development.

If you walk into a workplace with the attitude, "I'm a woman, they're going to discriminate against me," it's more likely to happen. You can avoid a lot of sex discrimination by simply disregarding it. A well-known female district attorney in the New England area, whom I interviewed, told me this:

I think that if women are out there looking to find sex discrimination, then they will find it. I think that this is true in any sphere. If you are looking to find insults, you'll find them, because a lot of what you find is what you perceive. I've heard many men say privately that most women do things better than men anyway. If women would just take the chip off their shoulder, go out there and do what they do best, there wouldn't be as much discrimination.

To some extent, there will always be sex discrimination, but if women would just ignore it, much of it would go away. I happen to think that if you're not looking for it, you don't see it and you don't feel it. When I first started this job as assistant attorney general, the police were difficult to deal with—perhaps because I was a woman or maybe because I was new. But I would just ignore their behavior and go about my business. I haven't had any serious problems.

Trina's approach to sex discrimination was similar. When I asked her if she had ever encountered sexism, she replied:

I never heard anyone say anything sexually discriminatory to me either in medical school, internship or residency. People simply never said things like that. Either I was very lucky, or I happened to meet the right kind of men and women.

Choose a workplace where the worth of every person, both male and female, is recognized and appreciated. It doesn't matter what the gender of your co-workers is; what matters is their attitude. This is how Quincy, the widowed mother of three, empowered herself in the workplace:

When I made my decision to become an office manager for an all-male law firm, a friend of mine tried to convince me not to do this. But I refused to listen to him. I knew that this was the right job for me. I have a very nice situation now. All three lawyers treat me like a professional. They are about my age; we are all part of the team.

If All Else Fails, Change Jobs

Every woman who chooses not to work for an employer who blatantly discriminates against women is making a difference. When sex discrimination cannot be ignored, the best alternative is to leave gracefully and find another job. Nora, the television marketing executive, did exactly this, with the help of her mentor. As she told me:

I continued climbing professionally until I reached a level where I could not get promoted to general manager, because I was a woman. Up to then, I had never encountered sexism. The same woman who had helped me get started in the radio business reached out to help me again. She told me, "Get out of radio; you don't need this." Then she got me started managing a travel agency that she had acquired. So I walked away from broadcasting.

Three months later, I got a call from a television station whg needed someone to head up their marketing department. They made me a financial offer that I could not refuse. My mentor said, "Nora, here is a great opportunity for you. I think you can manage to do this job and continue to oversee the travel agency as well."

Julia, now a self-employed businesswoman, dealt with sex discrimination in her workplace just like Nora did—by finding another job.

I was in a work situation once where I was one of six section managers. The next level up was department manager. The department manager was leaving, and she recommended that I fill her spot, as I was the most qualified person for the job. I was not given this position, because a man at the next level up did not want to deal with an "aggressive woman." He actually went outside the company to hire somebody. Some excuse or another was made up.

The department manager who had recommended me was a woman whom I looked up to and respected. Her husband had left her with four small children. She had started as a secretary in the company and kept moving up. By always saying what she thought, she helped me to be freer in expressing myself at work.

"Did you try to fight the decision?"

There was no way that I could. I went for an interview and expressed my interest in the position. Then the decision was made to bring in someone else from the outside. This did not happen to me just because I was female. I believe that I lost this job—and a hefty raise in salary—because I was regarded as both aggressive and female. I was very surprised. As a mathematics major, I was accustomed to being valued for my capabilities. I had become used to being dealt with as a person, not just as a woman.

"How long did you stay with the company after that?"

I left the following year. I said to myself, "I've done my best, but I don't see how I am going to move up anymore here."

"What did it feel like—being without a job?

I always knew that I could quit and begin again, because I had done it before. Ten years earlier, I had left another position to go off on a 2-year sailing trip. I learned that the world did not fall apart, if I didn't have a job. Knowing that I could start over really empowered me. When I went back to work, I did my best to be effective. But if I didn't like something that was going on, I had the inner strength to speak up and fight for what I believed in. I knew that I could handle leaving a job.

Nancy, a retired senior citizen, echoed the same theme when she talked with me about the sex discrimination she had encountered many years ago. Our conversation went like this:

"When you began working as a professional during the '30s, you must have encountered a great deal of sex discrimination. How did you handle it? You really were a pioneer."

I wasn't able to do much about it. Women got paid much less than men for the same jobs. We were expected to prepare food and do secretarial tasks, in addition to the rest of our work. It was awfully hard to be a professional.

Forty years ago, I was at a university running their Bachelor's of Social Work Program and teaching a couple of classes as well. The Assistant Dean who was in charge of the undergraduate program said to me, "We have to have a man as coordinator because all the other departments have men in this position." Apparently, he had gone behind my back to replace me, without even saying "boo" to me!

"Did you feel angry?"

Yes, I felt angry and also disgusted. But I just went my own way. Although

I had received a great performance review, I chose not to take my case up to the National Foundation Board. I also could have fought the Dean's decision at a State Board meeting that I attended, but I did not. I was just sick at heart that this kind of incident had happened in such an outstanding group.

"What I hear is that you distanced yourself."

"I had other resources—I became a social worker."

Create Mutual Relationships with Your Co-Workers

You influence your co-workers, including your "boss," by accepting or rejecting their power-over behavior. If you expect to work together with them, rather than simply to give and follow orders, you will set a tone for their relationships with you. Kim told me about how she handled Mr. Preston, the demanding president of her consulting firm.

When he gives me orders, I have no problems telling him that I won't do something and my reasons for it. We'll talk about it and reach a decision together. Sometimes, I'll admit I'm wrong. Other people might find him intimidating, but not me.

The benefits of creating mutually empowering relationships in the workplace can be enormous. You give support; you gain support. Nora gave me an example from her experience:

I am very clear that I have never done anything of significance by myself. I have always had people who reached out to me when I needed help in my career. When I went to visit my college radio station, I decided to become the station's sales manager. I got the job and then hired someone to work under me, whose father owned three television stations. It was he who taught me how to sell advertising.

I stumbled into media marketing at an early age. I didn't have a "connection" like most people did; I walked blindly into the offices of complete strangers. Fortunately, most of them were very kind to me. Now I do my best to help other people in my field, whenever I can.

Mutual relationships were very important to Nora in her career climb.

The Workplace Is a "Mixed Bag"

In the last analysis, the workplace is a "mixed bag." No one can ever be completely autonomous or authentic. No matter what your work situation, you will never be able to do exactly what you want—and say exactly what you want—much of the time. If you work for a small business, you have to defer to the wishes of your "boss." Even if you work for yourself, there are clients, investors or government agencies to whom you are accountable. If you are a government employee, or work for a large corporation, you operate under bureaucratic constraints.

Although it is more difficult to create mutually empowering relationships in the workplace than it is at home, nevertheless it can be done. How successful you are depends upon these three factors:

1. How you perceive yourself,
2. How you perceive other people, and
3. How you handle yourself and other people, in the light of your perceptions.

Consider these experiences of women who have attended my **Empowered Woman**™ Seminar. Which sound more like you?

Dealing with a client :
Recently, I was being "jerked around" by a client, who was stopping my work in the middle of the project. I took the bull by the horns, went to confer with the principal party and negotiated for what I wanted.

or

A client of mine has constantly been belittling my ideas. Since he's not willing to even entertain the possibility that I may be right, our project is at a standstill.

Asking for a raise in salary :
For over 2 years, I had been asking to have my job upgraded, in order to increase my financial base. Finally, they gave in.

or

I was told I was not aggressive enough to deserve a raise in salary. That was it.

Talking to the "boss":
Last week, I politely told my new boss either he could shape up and treat me as a professional, or I was leaving. He is shaping up.

or

Yes, I let my boss treat me like I'm a naughty teenager; I allow him to do this because nothing I do can turn a U. S. Navy Captain who's a "* % ! ?" into a rational human being.

Dealing with co-workers:

Some of my male co-workers see my persistence as being aggressive, but I refuse to give up. I just keep on telling them what I want.

or

Keith, one of my co-workers, irritates me no end, but I just swallow my increasing anger.

All the empowered women realized that they risked upsetting the apple cart by speaking their minds. But, by not communicating, they risked being unhappy at work and ultimately having their job performance suffer. Every working woman experiences frustration, and many of us also experience intimidation, sex discrimination and sexual harassment as well. But, if you are aware of your strengths and work to create mutually empowering relationships, you can get what you want, more often than not.

Terri, a woman who worked her way up in the military, finally became empowered when she gave up power over her associates. This is her story, in her own words:

My family didn't have any money, so I couldn't apply to college right away. The moment I finished high school, I went to work for the government as a clerk typist. I started working on my bachelor's degree at night. When I started going to college, I really didn't know how it would help me professionally. Then I realized, if I studied English, I could become an editor. It took me 6 1/2 years, but I finally got my degree in English and history. I became a technical editor, got three promotions in 8 years and read every publication put out by my department in the process. Then I decided I wanted a higher-paying job: I would become a writer. I told my supervisor that she should give me a chance. Since I had been rewriting all the copy anyway, she said, "All right."

I got two more promotions, but was denied a third. So I went to the director of the agency and asked him, "Why?" He said that if I could get accepted to a war college, I would be eligible. So I had identified exactly what I had to have to get to the next threshold—more education. It took me 4 years to get the paperwork through the system. I don't know if I wore them down or what, but I got accepted by a prestigious war college.

The moment I started classes, the job I wanted opened up. I didn't know what to do. I said to myself, "If you don't ask for something, you don't get it." So I went back to the agency director and told him, "I think I should have this job, because I am the best person for it. This is a chance of a lifetime for me." I talked to everyone on the director's staff. I ended up getting the job and taking the courses at the war college at the same time. It was a very hectic, but wonderful, year. I found myself sitting in classrooms next to generals and colonels. They knew that they had to take me seriously then.

After I got this promotion, I still had to prove myself. You see, I've always been self-confident. But I've also been aware that anyone who picks up my easy self-assurance starts dressing me down. The top military men I was working with appreciated that I did my job well but they still felt that they constantly had to put me in my place. It was a real challenge! First I had to become technically competent and then I had to learn to deal with the people around me. It made them angry to see me go into a meeting thoroughly prepared, when everyone else wasn't prepared at all.

I studied the behavior of my new associates and asked myself, "What sets these high level people apart from the people at the worker-bee level?" Then I answered my own question. The executives always appear to be calm—to act as if they had not worked very hard to get where they were. So I started not to get so prepared for meetings. My boss liked it better. Instead of circulating a two- or three-page memo, I said two or three sentences. Less was more. Overpreparation had helped me get my promotion; now that I had reached a higher level, overpreparation was self-defeating. To move up, you have to be willing to change—to let go of old habits in new situations. At each higher level you reach, you have to look around and see what you have to do differently to work well with the people around you.

Even if you've done your job thoroughly, you have to leave something for other people to do. At the very least, leave the people at the next level up the option to say "Yes" or "No." Consider how what you do affects other people, before you do it. Sometimes it's more effective to pose the question than to give the answer.

Rene, another woman I interviewed, empowered herself in the workplace by creating a network of mutually empowering relationships, which attacted capable people. As she put it:

A number of people who now work at my agency have told me that they originally came here because they thought very highly of my work and wanted to work with me. Over the years, this message has been passed around within certain circles.

Although Rene had outstanding training in her field, she attributes her success to creating empowering relationships and avoiding power-over ones. She told me, "I have made it my business to notice what is going on, to tactfully stay out of difficult situations and not to be openly hostile toward someone I did not agree with." Rene did not just rely on her intellectual credentials; she developed her relationship skills as well.

Let Other People Empower You

Sheila, a woman with a successful political career, told me how she reached out to other people who empowered her:

I was aware that I wanted to do something in the arts, but I didn't know what. So I went to a women's job counseling center, and they said to me, "Well, you've done fundraising; why don't you work for a nonprofit association?" I said, "What a good idea!" So I started cold-calling the nonprofits. Wasn't I afraid of being rejected? No. I figure that the person I'm calling has feelings and smiles and laughs—just like me. So why should I be afraid of him or her? Most people are just as shy as I am. A few people were nice to me on the phone; one said he'd see me. He gave me the confidence I needed to press on.

Sheila was pro-active. She did not wait for something to happen and then react to it. She acted first.

I never imagined that I would end up being a presidential appointee. But friends on the Hill encouraged me to lobby for a newly created job and I got it. I talked to a Senator who pulled me through. The lesson that has stayed with me is that, in politics, as in all organizations, there is always one key person that you have to reach, to get what you want. You might need the help of five other people to get to him or her, but the secret is to reach that special one.

Another lesson I have learned is to play by your own rules. It took some clever maneuvering to get my current job in the arts; I didn't do everything other people told me to do. I did things the way I thought they should be done.

Although many other people supported Sheila in her job search, she did not always take their advice. In the end, she listened to her own voice.

She's a Partner, Not a Competitor

Many women do not really want a conventional career, because the world of work is still based on the male value of competition. Competition is another way of saying power-over. If you compete, someone "wins" and someone "loses."

In mutually empowering relationships, there is collaboration instead of competition. Every person in your workplace, male and female, is a potential source of strength, assistance and advice. If you encounter a woman who is better trained, more capable or more accomplished than you, you see her as a resource. You think, *"If you are better than I am or if you have something that I don't, it does not diminish me. On the contrary, it enhances us both!"*

An empowered woman sees the workplace as a place of abundance, not scarcity. There are enough tasks, enough projects and even enough promotions for everyone. Women empower each other by working together, not by competing with each other.

Although you cannot change other people's attitudes, you can determine yours. Workers with male-oriented values will continue to seek power over other people. As an empowered woman, you will prefer to cooperate and share resources, especially with other women.

Are You Empowered in the Workplace?

How do you know when you have finally become an empowered worker? To find out, ask yourself these questions:

I have empowered myself in the workplace if . . .

1. I have, or have had, a mentor in my chosen field.
2. I have created my own job description.
3. My hours are flexible; I don't "punch a clock."
4. I feel free to take time off for necessary personal business.
5. At the end of the week, I usually feel good about what I have accomplished.
6. When there is a difference of opinion between me and my supervisor, I feel free to discuss it openly.
7. When I make a mistake, I am gently corrected, not scolded like a child.
8. My immediate supervisor confers with me, instead of telling me what to do.
9. When I am given a task to do, I do what I believe needs to be done, rather than simply following someone else's instructions.
10. If I see something wrong going on, there is someone who will listen to me sympathetically—and take action, if necessary.
11. I communicate well with most of my co-workers.
12. My views are taken into account in company policy making.
13. My company hires lesbian, handicapped, black and Hispanic employees.
14. Management is aware of salary discrepancies between men and women and is working to correct them.
15. I would recommend my company to a woman friend looking for a job.

The more "yes" answers you give, the greater the chances that work is an empowering experience for you.

Empowerment Exercises

1. Journal Writing: My Work History: Past, Present and Future: List each job you have had since you began to work. Next to each one, write down how you felt about it. For example, one of your items might be: "Computer Programmer, Software Corporation—generally bored, but liked one of my co-workers." If you have not held many jobs, write down how you felt about each of your school or volunteer experiences.

By writing this "feelings resume," you will know which jobs you liked and why. As you list the workplaces where you felt most comfortable and fulfilled, you will help yourself find your calling.

2. Focus on Your Calling: Now sit down in a quiet place, relax and close your eyes. Go over in your mind everything that you have liked in your past jobs. Allow yourself to re-experience the satisfaction, accomplishment or challenge you have had. As you focus on each one, what do you feel in your body? Do you experience pleasure or tension in any particular part of it? Can you find a name for what you are experiencing? What thoughts come to your mind? Now re-experience all your pleasurable feelings and review the words you used to describe them. Can you think of a single job, or career, where you could experience all of them? For example, if you felt "contented" in your work as a lab technician and "stimulated" by a brief summer job as an artist, might you consider a career as a scientific artist?

3. Visualize Yourself in a Leaderless Situation: Would you like not to be told what to do? Imagine yourself in a work community where no one was the "boss." No one told anyone else what to say or what to do. Would you be comfortable? If not, what would bother you? Continue to ask yourself this question until you come up with an answer. It will help you understand what difficulties you may have becoming empowered together with other people in the workplace.

4. Keep Track of Your On-the-Job Empowerment: In your Empowerment Journal, write down at the end of each day a brief note about any empowering experiences you had. Did you share, cooperate or collaborate with a co-worker? Did you politely tell him or her about something that was on your mind? Did you take a step toward creating flexibility for yourself in your workplace? Did you take action on your own, instead of reacting to what someone else had already done?

Empowerment does not end in the workplace. An empowered woman seeks mutuality, autonomy and authenticity "after hours." Are you satisfied in your sexual relationship? If not, perhaps you need to turn this obstacle into a stepping stone by uncovering your sexual blueprint and becoming sexually empowered.

UNCOVER YOUR SEXUAL BLUEPRINT

8

"Exploring our sexuality is a journey that begins at birth and continues throughout life. . . . The longer we explore and the deeper we delve, the more intimately we know the sexual terrain and the richer the experience becomes."

Lonnie Barbach, Ph.D.
For Each Other

Your sexual blueprint is an essential part of your unique personal identity. Every woman's is different.

Uncovering your unique sexual blueprint is the first step in becoming a sexually empowered woman. By going back to your childhood, you can find out the special mix of beliefs about sex that you have acquired. Then you can decide which ones you want to keep, and which ones you now want to discard. The issue is not what other people consider to be "good," "moral" or "ladylike," but what is sexually comfortable for you.

Complex social forces have shaped your sexual attitudes and behavior. While you were growing up, your parents, teachers, brothers, sisters, friends, and neighbors gave you messages about sex. In all likelihood, your mother was your model. On some level you picked up how she felt about her body, and about sex. Once you became an adult, the people you had sexual experiences with, particularly those with whom you had long-term relationships, had their own special impact on your sexuality. The books, newspapers and magazines you read, the radio programs you listened to, and the movies and television programs you watched also influenced your attitudes toward sex.

The kind of information you received about sex depends on when you were born. Until about 25 years ago, women were consistently told to "save ourselves" for our husband. Since then, we have received mixed messages about sex. On the one hand, we have been warned about its dangers. On the other hand, we have been encouraged to express our sexuality freely—one authority going so far as to say that a woman should feel free to have sex with more than one man at a time.

Which Messages about Sex Did You Receive?

How do you uncover your sexual blueprint? Look at the messages below:

"Sex is to be saved for marriage."
"Virginity is the greatest gift a woman can give her husband."

"'Nice' women aren't sexy."
"Sex is dirty."
"You shouldn't touch your 'private parts.'"
"You shouldn't talk about sex."

"Men ask for sex; women say, 'No.'"
"Men enjoy sex; women don't."
"For a woman, sex is a duty of marriage."

"People who think about sex a lot are 'crazy.'"
"A woman isn't supposed to have sexual needs."

"Men use women for sex."
"A woman who has sex with many men cheapens herself."
"It is terrible for a woman to be unfaithful to her husband."

"Sex should always be romantic."
"Your partner should 'know' how to please you sexually."
"You must be the 'perfect lover.'"

"A pretty woman is a 'sex object.'"
"Sex is a way to get a man."

"Homosexuality is evil."
"Lesbian women usually have short haircuts, wear clothes that resemble men's and teach physical education."

"Gay men are 'sissies'; you should avoid them."

"If your body doesn't look like a 'cover girl's,' then it's ugly."
"No woman's body is flawless."

"A successful woman is a sexual threat to men."
"Be all you can be; some man will like you for it."
"A sexually experienced woman is a better lover."

"Sex is not a commodity; it is mutual sharing."
"No one should ever use sex to manipulate someone else."

"Sex is the ultimate expression of love between two people."
"Sexual pleasure is the birthright of every woman."

"There is always more to learn about sex; no one 'knows it all.'"

Which of these messages did you hear most frequently, while you were growing up? Which ones do you strongly believe now? Which of these did you formerly believe, but are ready to discard?

You need to understand your past, because it will be difficult for you to depart radically from it. What you absorbed during your early years has filtered what you learned afterwards. For example, if you learned that sex is painful when you were a little girl, since then you have probably blocked out messages that sex is pleasurable. You must be prepared to accept your existing sexual self. It is the starting point from which you can begin to grow.

Although it is difficult to re-examine feelings you may have hidden from yourself for a lifetime, it is possible. New lines can be added to your sexual blueprint. You can start doing what you feel is right, not what others told you to do long ago.

Creating an Empowering Sexual Relationship

Uncovering your sexual blueprint is an enlightening experience. Yet it is only the beginning of sexual empowerment. Whether your sexual identity is heterosexual, bisexual or lesbian, you want a sexual relationship that is satisfying for you as well as your partner.

Is your sexual relationship autonomous, authentic and mutual? Ask yourself these questions:

1. Can I initiate sex and say "No" to sex comfortably?
2. Do I let my sexual partner know my deepest desires?

3. Do my sexual partner and I both give pleasure to each other?

If you can honestly answer "Yes" to all three of these questions, then you have an empowering sexual relationship. If you cannot, this is how to create one.

Sexual Autonomy: Acting, As Well As Reacting

Sexual autonomy is acting on your own to get what you want, or don't want, sexually. If a stranger makes sexual advances, you are comfortable refusing him or her. Conversely, if you want sex more frequently, you do not just sit back and always expect your partner to make overtures to you.

Machi, a Japanese college student, became sexually autonomous in her relationships with men. Rather than always waiting for a man to act first and then responding to him, she decided to become the seducer. When she realized that she could play an active role in her relationships with men, she experienced sexual empowerment.

Machi: "I Want to Seduce a Man"

I am sitting in a circle of 12 women. Although many have talked, only one stands out. Machi's features are as delicate as a Japanese painting: clear black eyes, a chiseled nose and a pink, sculptured mouth. Although she looks petite and fragile, she could knock a man down with one karate blow.

Afterwards, I ask Machi if I can come to her room and talk. Although she is occupying a dormitory room, she has beautified it with Japanese paintings, calendars and small sculptured objects. Very politely, she asks me to sit down.

How will I communicate with a woman whose native tongue is Japanese? It turns out that language is not a problem. Machi speaks English fluently, only occasionally stopping to look up a word in her Japanese-English dictionary. Her voice is soft—almost childlike—but her words are clear. She begins:

I like men more than women. I am more comfortable with my male friends than I am with my women friends. Usually I feel relaxed when I am with a man, especially when he is my lover. But there is a problem. Men, of course, exist as human beings. On the other hand, men also exist as sexual beings. The problem is that men sometimes change very suddenly from human beings to sexual beings. I understand that this is natural. But when this happens, I feel a terrible fear. I am afraid when, in a single moment, a man becomes a "wolf man." She takes a deep breath and then laughs a deep, bubbling laugh.

Yes, I like "wolf!" I have sexual feelings, too. Still, at the moment a man suddenly changes from a human being to a sexual being, I get very scared.

The word "suddenly" is important. It may be difficult for a man to understand, but I fear his "suddenliness." At the moment when he becomes sexual, I experience my own passivity. Sometimes I think that, if I seduce a man, I will not be afraid anymore . By seduce I mean that I, not he, would be the first one to be sexual. I need men, in order to have a sexual life. But my passivity is my problem.

"You would feel better if you seduced, if you initiated sex?"

Right. With me, the man usually becomes sexual first. When this happens, I am afraid because I do not feel ready for sex.

"You enjoy sex more—and are not afraid of it—if you have had time to get yourself ready for it?

Yes. But it as difficult for me to say "No" when a man seduces me, if he is my lover and I love him. At such a time, I cannot say "No," because his sexual desire is part of his affection for me. When someone acts toward me with good feelings, kindness, gentleness and love, it is difficult for me to say "No." I worry that, if I do, I may hurt him. I know that, if I were to seduce a man, I would feel hurt if he refused.

I am not afraid to have sex with a man. What I am afraid of is the moment sex begins—his activity and my passivity. It is almost a physical fear. She reaches for her Japanese-English dictionary. "Physical, yes physical."

"It is in your body?"

Yes. You know, I cannot control this feeling. At the beginning of making love, sometimes I experience this feeling of fear all over my body. I think it is difficult for a man to understand how I feel. If I could make him understand, we would have a better relationship, mentally and physically. I think so. She speaks these words slowly. Her voice has become very low and gentle, almost sensuous.

I have not paid attention to my fear for a long time. When I used to have this feeling, I would think, "I don't like this man. I don't love him. I feel sorry for him." But this was not true. What I did not like was his aggressiveness and my own passivity. I was hurting. Once I understood my feeling, I was less afraid. I was able to respond better to the man with whom I was making love.

My sexual fear may be connected to my relationship with my father. Why? When I am with a man, I want always to feel comfortable with him. While I was growing up, my father sometimes acted like a mother. Often what I want a man to do is just hold me—put his arm around my shoulders—just like my father did. We would care about each other, just as my father and I used to. He would not suddenly become sexual.

Let me tell you why, as a Japanese woman, I have always liked my father better than my mother. My father was strong and active, and my mother was weak and passive. My mother always accepted my father's decisions. But she used her weakness as a tool. I don't want to be like my mother. Machi shakes her head from side to side, to emphasize "No."

"I have always wanted to be a strong woman. I don't ever want to use my weakness to control my husband." She points to her hand, searches quickly through her dictionary and then states even more emphatically,"The Japanese wife has her husband in the palm of her hand."

"She manipulates him?"

Right. I don't want to manipulate a man; I would hate to play such a role. I want not only to be feminine but also to be strong and honest. Femininity is a very important word in my language. The Japanese word "femininity" actually means, "looks like a woman." Yes, I would like to look more elegant and sophisticated—and act more gently and kindly. But, at the same time, I would like to become more honest and stronger inside. I think other Japanese women would like to be this way, too. Machi's giggle is infectious. We laugh together, closely and deeply. Despite our language difference, we understand each other completely.

"You would like to become more active, more honest and more open in your sexual relationships with men?"

Yes. I want to seduce a man. I want to begin sex—to choose the time when we change from human beings to sexual ones. Sometimes I will be sexually passive. That's okay. But let me decide for myself whether to be active or passive. I don't want a man always to make this decision for me.

As a teenager, I used to be very boyish. I couldn't dress up; I couldn't "decorate myself" with earrings, rings, bracelets or cosmetics. It was only when I started to notice my fear of my own passivity and to become more active during sex, that I was able to dress up. Now I can enjoy my femininity. Being feminine doesn't mean always being sexually passive.

I have not talked about my sexual problems with other Japanese women; I do not know why. But I did share my feelings about sex in the women's group yesterday. Some of the American women told me later that they felt the same way as I did. I used to think that I was a strange woman and what I thought about men and sex was peculiar. Now I do not think so. I am glad to know that my feelings are international!

"Do you have any more questions? No? That's okay. My brain is empty now." Machi points to a green-and-white picture of a rabbit, executed with the delicate strokes of a Japanese brush. "Would you like to have it? Yes? Good. Take it so you will remember me—and what I have said to you. I think Japanese women will be very interested in what you are writing about."

Machi's message is that women can initiate sex. They can seduce, not just wait until their partner makes the first move. Machi wants to communicate her desire for sex in an appropriate way, so that she can create a sexual experience that she enjoys, as well as her partner.

Conversely, a woman who is sexually autonomous can say "No," to sexual advances she does *not* welcome. She knows what she does not want, as well as what she wants. She can both initiate sex and decline sex comfortably.

If you suggest a sexual rendezvous, do not expect that your partner will always want to make love to you immediately. Sometimes he or she will feel like saying "No." In an empowered sexual relationship, there is a give-and-take as both partners reach out, and respond, to each other.

Being Sexually Authentic

Do you know what would make you happy in bed? Can you tell your partner what you really desire, even if it is not something you have never done together before? Then you are sexually authentic.

Being sexually authentic does not mean that you exercise power over your partner in bed. You do not demand that your partner do this or that. You let him or her know, with words, gestures or actions, what you would like. Then you wait for his or her response. In an empowering relationship, both you and your partner are free to express your individual sexual desires. But, since human beings are imperfect, there is no ironclad guarantee that you or your partner will always be satisfied. "Most of the time" is about as much as you can hope for.

You cannot expect your partner to be a mind reader. To enjoy sex, you have to know what you want and then be able to ask for it, directly or subtly. Julia, the self-employed businesswoman, had not achieved sexual autonomy, when I first interviewed her. I asked her to tell me what was holding her back.

I didn't enjoy sex, because I didn't know how to ask for what I needed. So my friend, Ted, didn't know how to give it to me. For a while I went through a stage where I had sex with him because I thought I owed it to him. I was suppressing my own desire.

Ted and I talked about why I was holding my real sexual self back. The reason was, because I never believed that my parents loved me, I felt that I couldn't trust Ted. Since it seemed to me that our relationship was not going to last, I held tightly onto my feelings. I was not willing to tell Ted what I wanted sexually and then open up and receive it.

Like many women, Julia needed to get in touch with and express her deepest sexual desires. Only then would she and her partner have an empowering sexual relationship.

As an empowered woman, you can reject the messages about sex that no longer fit your authentic sexual self. You can experience your true sexuality. Dale is one woman who made this daring decision.

Dale: "I Am a Lesbian"

I meet Dale at a therapists' professional conference. Surrounded by 50 women, I am sitting quietly and wondering, "How can I *discreetly* find a lesbian woman to talk to." I lean over and ask the woman sitting next to me, "Is there a lesbian discussion group? Who's the leader?" She points across the room to a tall, poised woman with dark brown hair softly curling around her face. "That's Dale."

I get up from my chair and go over where Dale is standing. I ask myself, "How do I start a conversation with her? I don't want her to be offended." Suddenly the words start tumbling out of my mouth. I hear her say, "Yes, let's talk tomorrow. I'll ask my friend if we can use her room." I do not sleep very well that night. Our connection is still so fragile.

The news is good; the following afternoon, she shows me her friend's key. A few moments later I find myself sitting across from Dale in an armchair, with a square wooden table between us. I am looking at a well-dressed, attractive woman. In an instant, the lesbian stereotypes I have been carrying around with me are all demolished. As I listen to her story, I begin to understand the discomfort of wearing a sexual facade—and the relief of discarding it. Dale begins:

I would never have found my lesbianism as a teenager. Although women were always my primary emotional attachment, I did not buck the system. I was 30 before I started rebelling against my parents. That's when I came out—when I was 30!

For a teenage girl to be socially acceptable in my hometown, she had to have a boyfriend. So when I was 17, I started going with a boy, who later became my husband. I married George right out of college. Six months later, while I was in graduate school, I got pregnant . A year later, George, infant Sara and I moved to New Jersey, and I got pregnant again. Right after our second daughter Allison was born, I got a job as a school social worker. I also began teaching two courses at the local community college. Dale takes her hands off her lap, folds them and puts them on the table.

Although I was a mother of two small children, I was still a child. I had never gone away to summer camp. I had never lived on my own, except when I was away at college. Even then I had taken on a responsible position as a resident advisor for over 30 girls, to help pay my tuition. I had never rebelled; I had never goofed off. I didn't have the slightest sense of who I was.

Now here I was in New Jersey, 1,000 miles away from my family. Although I had no connections with other women, I soon started hearing about the feminist movement. One day I read in the paper about a women's coffee house where some women were doing theater. Acting had always been a secret ambition of mine. So I went for an evening. You know, I absolutely loved it. Everyone was so nurturing, gay and straight women alike. The more I tried, the more they encouraged me.

At the end of the evening, one of the women asked, "Would any of you like to get together and start a theater workshop?" I know now that I was really excited by this possibility, but at the same time I felt afraid. I was aware that several of the women were lesbians and I was thinking, "If I join, they're going to jump on me." Since I had heard stories of lesbians going after straight women, I made sure that I let everyone know that I was married. Later on I saw, during my "coming out" process, that no one in the group would have ever made a move unless I had expressed interest first.

For the next couple of years, I worked very closely with these women. The theater workshop was a wonderful place to be. I could get as close to the lesbian culture as I wanted without having to show my cards. Of course, I still was not consciously aware of my lesbianism. Sometimes I would say to my husband, "I can understand women loving each other—the intense feeling that they must have." But our conversation never went any further than this. A breeze moves through the window and blows Dale's brown hair gently.

One day I was asked to co-direct a women's camping week where there would be a series of workshops. I was a "straight" woman; the co-director was a lesbian. There would be something for everyone. I accepted. For the first time I would be completely on my own, away from my parents, my husband and my children. Dale's voice has become loud and strong.

All of a sudden I found myself alone with 75 women. Fifty percent of them were lesbians! And none of them knew me. Immediately, a woman approached me and wanted to have a "relationship"—to get to know me in a different way. This absolutely freaked me out, because up to now I had never had this kind of experience. I gave her all the reasons why she shouldn't be approaching me. "Don't you understand who I am? I'm the resident straight woman, who can be very close to you, but . . ." I went on and on.

This woman kept saying to me, "All you have to say is 'No.'" Actually, what she was asking me to do was to take responsibility for my decision, something that no one in my life had ever asked me to do before. My ambivalence was showing. There was a part of me that just didn't want to walk away from her. I could not say "No."

It was an extremely painful week for me. Lesbian women have since told me that their "coming out" has normally taken about 5 years—from first awareness to total self-integration. For me, it felt like these 5 years were consolidated in 1 week. It was incredibly intense. I was the caretaker for all these women, plus I was dealing with my "stuff" inside. I stopped eating, and I stopped sleeping.

By the end of the week, the woman who had approached me had already decided that I wasn't interested in a lesbian relationship, even though I hadn't actually said "No." She was amazed when, the night before we were due to leave, I just collapsed into her arms. Had I not done so, I probably would have continued to submerge my true sexuality, because I was so involved with my husband and two small children. In the back of my mind, I would always know that I would have to deal with it someday. Dale swallows hard, after she says these words.

Up to then, I had never been sexual with anyone but my husband. Both my parents had told me that sex is always associated with love. So I went home thinking that I was in love with this woman. Within 24 hours, I told my husband, George, about her. I thought he would understand. Instead his response was, "You've betrayed me!" Soon afterwards he told me, "I don't love you anymore, Dale." He exited from our bedroom and asked for a divorce.

Six months later, I was on my own. Although I felt terribly hurt at the time, I now realize that my husband was actually helping me out. How could I have ever left him, and my two small children? The stark, cold outline of the motel armchair contrasts sharply with Dale's warm, intense discourse. I think to myself, "How odd to be sharing such an intimate story in such a sterile place."

On my 30th birthday, I moved out of my beautiful three-story house to a one-room apartment. My new kitchen was so small you could touch all four walls if you stood in the middle. I felt very poor and very isolated—but very free. My husband and I had joint custody, so half the time I didn't have to take care of the children. If I had them Friday, Saturday and Sunday, I could take Monday off and just cruise. I was so excited about being single again.

Finally, I gave myself permission to act like an adolescent. I went out without telling anyone where I was going. I had fun!

A few months later, I got a job producing plays about community social issues and family problems. It was a nice blend of theater and social work. I have continued in it for the past 8 years. I have also taken a half-time job as a social worker and spent time developing my skills as a therapist.

I guess you can say that my story is one of empowerment. I found out who I really was and then used this knowledge to change my life. Now I am working to share my gift with others. In my private therapy practice, over 80 percent of my clients are lesbian or gay. I am still working in the theater. Recently I have written three plays, which I hope to have produced in the near future. Right now I am exactly where I want to be.

Dale became empowered in a women's community. By observing other women who were models and mirrors of lesbianism, she was able to discover her own sexual identity—which was completely different from the heterosexual one she had previously assumed. Because she was honest with herself, she was finally able to experience mutually satisfying sex.

She continues:

For the past 7 years, I have lived with a woman who has helped co-parent my children. She's a few years older than I am and has allowed me plenty of room for growth. After we moved in together, I finally told my parents about her. Although I was afraid that I would lose their love forever, I had come to a point where I could not continue to live in "unreality" any longer. For the first time in my life, I went home all by myself. Dale and I look straight into each other's eyes.

My mom's reaction was funny. She was in the kitchen cooking a very traditional Polish dish, and we started talking. Somehow the conversation turned to Karen, the woman I had been living with. There was a long silence. I took a deep breath. Then I said to my mom, "By now you must know that Karen is a very important person in my life." "What are you trying to tell me?" she whispered, her eyes fixed on the stove. "That she's not only my friend; she's also my lover," I replied. My mom turned around very quickly and said to me, "I always knew that there was something different about you, Dale." There were tears in her eyes. I felt very moved.

I said to my mom,"I don't know how to tell Dad." She replied, "Well, maybe we don't need to tell him right away. Let's just think about it." So I went out to the store to get some flour. As I was walking back, I was thinking, "I don't want Mom to have this secret from Dad." I was just about to tell her this, but when she opened the back door, she said to me,"I just told your father." So I walked in, with the flour in my hand, and there was my dad sitting at the kitchen table. I just freaked out. I had always felt a lot of anger toward my father; it had seemed to me that he did not like women at all. So I did not know what to expect from him. All my dad said was, "You know, Dale, I've had this feeling about you for a long time."

All I could think was, "Here they are, two social workers, and neither one of them had ever discussed their daughter's sexuality with the other!" Both of them in hindsight said, "Yes, I sensed that Dale was different," but they had never shared their feelings. Now finally we were all able to talk. It was one of the most touching moments I have ever had in my life. Dale and I look across the table at each other in silent understanding. After about 30 seconds, she resumes speaking.

"What we want is for you to be happy," my dad said. "Yes, I am happy, Dad, happier than I have ever been," I replied. "I've always felt that I was looking for something. For the first time in my life, I feel like I've found it." "You've always seemed so unsatisfied," said my mom. "Yes, I was, Mom. I wasn't in the right place," I answered. Then I started weeping.

"What are you crying about?" my dad demanded. There was a long pause. Finally I replied, "I had so much to lose by coming home and telling you the truth, Dad. Now I feel that I am closer to you than I have ever felt before." And he cried with me. But his were not tears of disappointment. He was very deeply moved.

The next morning, my parents asked me if I wanted to go to church. Although I hadn't been to church in years, I said,"Yes." We went to the church where I used to go to as a child, the one where I had been baptized and confirmed. My father was sitting next to me. He was holding my hand and letting himself cry. I was crying, too. Dale's eyes are moist. "Would you like a tissue?" I ask Dale. "No," she replies.

I've always been so frightened of my father. My mother has always warned me, "Watch out when your dad gets angry. Stay away from him." But the flip side of my dad's anger is his ability to be emotional, to have feelings and to be touched. My mother isn't able to do this; she's always placid. When I was a child, I never heard her raise her voice. When she would cry, she would go into the other room. She would always tell me, "Dale, you're so emotional; you're so dramatic." That morning, in church, I felt a real kinship with my dad. You know, I still do. He and I share the same kind of emotional drama. Although we continue to have great struggles in our relationship, my connection with my father has become much stronger.

You see, for most of my life, I had not been a "real" person. I had been doing my best to minimize my rage, which is like my father's. So I didn't present as "real." What I found out during that weekend at home was that when I took the risk to be real, I got "realness" back. My father's "realness" with me touched me so deeply. Dale gestures dramatically. A joyous smile is on her face.

Acknowledging her lesbianism was a major breakthrough for Dale. She became authentic not only with her husband but also with her mother and father. Interestingly enough, she had not really concealed her secret from her parents very well. Both of them had known, or at least had strongly suspected, that she was a lesbian.

How many of you have once thought that you were hiding something from a person close to you? More often than not, your secret is perceived on some level. The other person in the relationship distorts his or her behavior to deal with the false self you are projecting. Both of you end up feeling isolated. For many years, Dale, her mother and her father were all actors in a charade that drove them further and further apart. By sharing her revelation, Dale allowed them all to be themselves. Not just Dale but actually three people ended up "coming out."

Amy is another woman who found out that she was a lesbian. She came to terms with her true sexual self during her teenage years. In a conversation I had with her, she told me about her experience:

In my junior year in high school, I went to a camp. There was a girl there that I was very attracted to—almost like "best friends." I can remember wanting to kiss her. When I shared that with her, she was scared to death. She said to me,"You know what you are?" I had heard the word "fag" before, but I hadn't ever heard of the term "dyke." I was very sheltered. Remember, I lived in the middle of Nebraska, where these terms were not brought up. If they were, it was in a derogatory sense. I could never imagine myself being this way. So I thought, "I don't know what these words mean, but I really am attracted to this girl."

"She wanted to give what you were feeling a name—a category."

Right. I should tell you that, up until then, I had been sleeping with boys. I dated in high school. I even had a high school sweetheart.

Then I went to an all-woman's college, where I had my first lesbian experience. I fell in love, really puppy love. But I still continued to go out with men and deny my true sexuality.

One day I told my "special friend "at college about what had happened to me at summer camp. She took me straight to the university library, and we went through all the sexuality books. After reading the material about lesbianism, I realized, "This is who I am. This is what's happening to me." It made me feel better to know that there were other people out there with the same feelings as mine.

Then I went through a whole stage of denial. Thoughts would race through my mind like, "I don't really want to be this way. I wasn't raised to be this way." After my freshman year, I transferred to a large coed university. I joined a sorority. I joined the gay and lesbian association on campus. Slowly, I stopped denying my sexuality.

"Was it easier for you to "come out," because there were other women at college who let you know, 'I am this way, too'?"

"Yes."

"What would you have done if you had not found other lesbians?"

I would have sought them out. That's what happened when I went to the university and I joined that sorority, even though there were no overt lesbians. I couldn't deny my true self, even though it sometimes screwed me up. Even though my lesbianism kept me from really concentrating on my studies, I knew that I had to come to terms with it.

"Coming out" is really a long process. You go through anger, and you go through denial You're sort of re-evaluating everything. "How do I feel about myself? How do I feel toward my family? What kind of future will I have, if I'm not going to get married, live in suburbia and have children?"

"You were questioning a lot of society's values. Did you tell your parents about your revelation?"

Yes. When I did, the weight of the world went off my chest. I said to myself, "Okay, this is it. There's no turning back now." Telling my mother and father was the best thing I ever did. It was also the hardest.

"How did you tell them?"

I dropped the initial bomb over the phone. Afterwards they told me that they had suspected for a long time—that they had had a gut feeling. They asked me, "Why didn't you tell us earlier?" I said, "Because I knew exactly how you would react. I wasn't ready to deal with you."

It turns out that I was right. My mother still keeps on bringing up the issue of my sexual preference. The other day she asked me, "Have you thought about giving men another chance?" I said, "Mom, it's not simply a question of 'giving men another chance.' I wouldn't wish lesbianism upon anybody. But I can't do anything about it at this point. All I can do is accept who I am."

"Was there any particular person who was very supportive—someone who made it easier for you to travel this road?"

I would have to say that it was my mother, even though she wasn't with me at college. She taught me to be myself. She told me that women can do whatever they want to. My mother was a feminist back in the '70s, when the movement started. There she was all by herself in suburban Nebraska, and she decided to go back to school. She was there for me as a role model.

Later on, I had some very close friendships with gay men. They listened to me; they held my hand; and they supported me.

It was only with the support of other people that Dale and Amy had the courage to embrace their true sexual identities.

One obstacle to discovering your true sexual identity is the rigid ideas developed by our male-oriented society about what lesbian and heterosexual women look like. A stereotypical lesbian woman has short hair, masculine mannerisms and a deep voice. A stereotypical highly-sexed heterosexual woman has large breasts, long legs and a sultry voice. The truth is that few women fit these general descriptions. To discover your own special sexual self, you have to disregard all of them.

Amy shared with me how she managed to shed her stereotypes about lesbians, so that she could accept her own unique sexuality.

After I told my mother that I was a lesbian, she and I went to the movies. As we walked out, the people who were waiting for the second show were staring at those who were leaving. After we got in the car, Mom said, "A lot of people were staring at us." "Yes," I replied, "I noticed that." "Do you think people were looking at us, because they thought we were a lesbian couple?" she asked. Amy laughs. Wasn't that an off-the wall comment?

Mom went on, "I'm a naive Nebraska girl in the big city. Will you help me?" She stared straight at me and asked me, "Do you look gay, Amy?" "What do you mean?" I said. "When people look at you, do they see a lesbian woman?" Mom asked. "I don't think so," I answered. "People have been surprised, once they have found out. I don't try to hide it, but I'm not consciously doing anything to show it off either."

I'm not a radical lesbian feminist. I'm not trying to shock my parents or make myself unappealing to men. Sometimes I think I overcompensate by trying to look extremely feminine in a traditional way. I put on a plain T-shirt and say to myself, "You look like a dyke." So I take it off.

As a matter of fact, I am not athletic whatsoever! When I used to meet a stereotypical "dyke," I could not stand her. I would say to myself, "That's not you. If that's what being a lesbian is, then I am not a lesbian."

"There are as many kinds of lesbian women as there are 'straight' women."

Yes. But I was "hung up" on the stereotypes, because of the way I had been taught by society to view homosexuality. Up to that point, I had not met an outwardly lesbian person whom I could really connect with. All I kept seeing were these radical, short-haired, army-jacket-wearing women. I wanted to be who I was: Amy, a lesbian.

"Now there is a range of choices; there are fewer stereotypical lesbians."

You are absolutely right. There are still lesbians out there, but we come in all shapes and sizes. We are proud of who we are; if you have a problem with it, that's your problem. Over 10 percent of the American population is gay. You can't ignore that.

"It's probably higher than that, if you count bisexual men and women."

I often think about the women who have decided that being a lesbian is okay. Then I think about all the ones who don't feel this way at all. I know lesbian women who are married and have children. Their spouses don't know. I think this is very sad.

"You told me that it was easier for you, after you told your parents—"

—And my co-workers and my family and my friends. I said, "You don't have to understand completely, but accept me as I am."

Heterosexual women also benefit from being sexually authentic. In order to do this, we need to ignore the messages of the mass media. Our male-oriented culture continues to perpetuate the myth that a woman should be a "Barbie doll," when she has sex. Every month the mass circulation women's magazines repeat the message, "Please your man in bed." Supposedly, men are the only ones who have sexual needs and preferences.

Nothing could be further from the truth. To become sexually authentic, you must acknowledge your own sexual desire. There is nothing wrong with being sexy. Most men like a woman who expresses an interest in, and an enjoyment of, sex. Not only is their sexual pleasure enhanced but also they are complimented when a woman responds to their advances. Many men will not excite you, but a few will. When this happens, be honest—and let go!

Being sexually authentic also means paying attention to your own sexual preferences. You have to know what you want before you can ask for it. You also have to know what you *don't* want before you can say "No." Pam, one of my interviewees, put it this way, "When my husband Tyrone asks me to put on see-through underwear, I just say, 'I don't want to. It's not me. I accept that.'" Although Tyrone was initially frustrated when she did not do what he asked her to do, he eventually preferred to make love in the nude—because *both* of them enjoyed it.

Above all, sexual authenticity means not faking—anything. Pretending to be sexually excited or to have an orgasm will not help you make a lasting connection with your partner. Pam told me that, in her previous marriage, she used to let her husband think that she had had an orgasm when she really hadn't. As she explained, "I didn't want to hurt his feelings by making him think he wasn't a 'superstud.'" Perhaps she never did hurt his feelings, but they ended up getting divorced. She now has a satisfying—and sexually authentic—relationship with Tyrone. As Pam says, "I only faked once—and he caught me. Never again."

If you are not your true self in bed, you will eventually get disenchanted. Your partner will inevitably sense your dissatisfaction and distance himself. You owe it to yourself—and to him or her—to make the effort to find out what really pleases you in bed and then to let him or her know what it is. Actors and actresses in a sexual charade get tired of playing their parts. Mutual sex lasts.

Mutual Sex: It Should Be Good for You, Too!

Like everything else in an empowering relationship, sex is experienced in partnership. Sex is not something done by a man to a woman, or by one woman to another.

In our culture, with its emphasis on power-over and control, the values we learn are men's. To most teenage girls, intercourse, rather than menstruation, is the most important rite of puberty. Dominance, mastery and performance describe the male sexual experience; submission and passivity, the female one. We hear "I got her to go to bed with me" or "I finally gave in," rather than "We decided to make love, to express our deep mutual caring and respect."

Since sex is defined mainly as male sexuality, how do women get in touch with and describe their own sexual desires? How does one solitary woman speak out and say, "My orgasm is not just a physical release; it is an expression of my deep connection with another human being." To speak up as a lone voice in a crowd is a formidable undertaking. Most women remain silent about themselves as sexual beings; some feel ashamed of their sexuality, when they compare it to men's.

To become empowered, women need to find a way to talk about what is going on for them in a sexual relationship. Empowerment groups are a good place to begin conversations. Women who meet in groups share common experiences, including sexual ones. It makes all the difference in the world to know that you are not alone. Finding out that what you have been feeling is not "sick" or "weird" can be exhilarating. "I'm always on the bottom and I hate it!" "You know, I feel the same way." "I want to tell him that I'd rather be on top sometimes." "Me, too." Through dialogues like these, women find their individual, and collective, voices.

If you are empowered together with your partner, he or she will be as concerned about your sexual pleasure as you will be about his or hers. Whether your lover is male or female, sex can be enjoyable for both of you, if neither of you has power over the other.

Are you a sexually empowered woman? Answer these questions silently:

1. Do I let my partner know what I like sexually, and what I don't like?
2. Do I allow myself to fully experience my sexual feelings?
3. After I have sex, am I, as well as my partner, generally satisfied?
4. Am I able to let my partner know when I want—and don't want—to have sex?
5. Do I refuse to play a sexual role that does not fit me?
6. Have I uncovered my sexual blueprint and sketched a new one?

The more questions you answer "Yes," the greater the likelihood that you are now a sexually empowered woman. If your "no" answers outnumber your "yes" ones, you may have sexual resistances that you need to deal with.

Your Sexual Resistances

Do you believe any of these statements? "Nice 'ladies' shouldn't be sexy." "Women over 50 shouldn't be sexy." "Mothers and grandmothers shouldn't be sexy." All of them are myths. The truth is that we are all sexual beings from the time we are born until the time we die. Every woman, with the possible exception of the very young, senile or infirm, has some sexual desire.

Are you a woman who doesn't dare to be sexual at all? What is stopping you? To fully experience your sexuality, you need to get rid of whatever kind of resistance you have.

After you do Exercise 2 below, say to yourself, "I do not allow myself to fully experience my sexual feelings because . . ." Once you find out what is blocking you, you can then decide whether or not you want to hold onto your resistance, or start working to overcome it.

Empowerment Exercises

1. *Where Did Your Sexual Blueprint Come From?* Your sexual beliefs were formed from information you received, and experiences

you had, early in your life. As a child, what did you learn about sex? Can you remember even bits and pieces of the answers to these questions?

a. Childhood Experiences:

1) How did your mother feel about her own body and her own sexuality? What did you learn from observing her?

2) What were your impressions, when you saw your mother and father together? Did they express affection openly in front of you?

3) While you were growing up, did you feel respected as a female? Was it suggested to you that girls were less valuable than boys?

4) Did either of your parents explain the facts of life to you? If so, how did you feel afterwards?

5) During your childhood, what kind of information about sex did you get from books, articles, movies, and radio and television programs?

6) By the age of 12, which of the following did you conclude? That sex was good and enjoyable? That sex was harmful? Or that sex was something to be afraid of?

b. Adolescent Experiences:

1) How did your parents react, when you became a woman? Did your father let you know that you were attractive? Did your mother envy you?

2) If you had a sister, did you talk about sex and boys with her? If so, did she teach you anything?

3) If you had a brother, how did he treat you, after you reached puberty?

4) What were your first teenage sexual encounters like? Were they satisfying or frustrating?

5) At age 18, was sex delightful, unpleasant or frightening for you?

c. Adult Experiences:

1) Were your adult sexual experiences different from your teenage ones? If so, how?

2) What was your most satisfying sexual experience of all? What was your most frustrating one?

3) Did you feel that you could "be yourself" sexually with any of your partners? If so, with whom?

4) How do you feel about sex right now?

2. *Overcoming Your Sexual Resistances:* If you are hesitant to fully experience your sexuality, it may be because you are experiencing

some kind of resistance. Which kind of sexual resistance may be blocking you? Answer these questions silently:

a. *Your Own Fears:*

1) Are you afraid that you may "fail" at sex? Or do you fear that you may "succeed"—and wind up in an intimate relationship?

2) Are you worried that you will become "unfeminine?" Or are you concerned that you may lose the respect of your feminist friends?

3) Are you in a painful relationship which you are reluctant to end? Or have your recently lost a partner and are feeling sad or depressed?

4) Are you simply reluctant to change and grow?

b. *Other People's Reactions:*

1) Are you inhibited because you have recently had a hysterectomy or a mastectomy?

2) Are you embarrassed, because you have a sexually transmitted disease?

3) Are you concerned about displeasing members of your family or your religious group?

4) Do you believe that, if you empower yourself sexually, you will be pursued by suitors you don't want?

If you want to overcome your resistance, identifying it is the first step. The second step is being honest about your resistance with other people. While not everyone will accept you exactly as you are, somebody eventually will. Open your heart and share what is in it. Being authentic can make you more sexually attractive than wearing the latest fragrance or a designer dress.

Does a sexually empowered woman necessarily look "sexy?" No. Sexual empowerment has nothing to do with the stereotype of "sexiness" developed by our male-oriented society This is another obstacle that must be turned into a stepping stone. The truth is that a sexually empowered woman is sexually satisfied, most of the time. So is her partner. A "sexy" appearance has nothing to do with sexual satisfaction.

Do you have to look "sexy" to be truly feminine? Let's find out.

APPRECIATE
WHAT FEMININITY
REALLY IS

9

If there has been one more kiss or one less tear,
one more garden, one less death,
If someone else has found
joy or beauty or love
because of me,
That's femininity!

r. r. j.

"You're unfeminine" is one of the most hurtful insults a woman can receive. Almost all of us embrace femininity. But what exactly does it mean to be feminine? In essence, it is having the chromosomes and reproductive organs of a woman. In a related sense, it consists of being a caregiver, that is, nurturing and loving other people. A woman who truly cares for others will form mutually empowering relationships with them.

After this, femininity definitions go haywire. Femininity has come to connote:

- Looking "sexy."
- Being soft and gentle.
- Being small, delicate and fragile.
- Having full breasts, a small waist and rounded hips.
- Wearing ruffles, lace or high heels.
- Having a husband or a boyfriend.
- Being emotional and sentimental.
- Being weak and submissive.

171

- Being "unselfish"; putting other people's needs ahead of your own.

This kind of "femininity" describes what makes us acceptable and attractive to others, according to men. As long as we believe that we must have these so-called "feminine" qualities, to love ourselves and to make others love us, we will poison, rather than empower, our relationships. A fragile, weak, submissive and "unselfish" woman can never be an equal partner.

When we force ourselves into a stereotyped "feminine" sex role, we suppress our individual identities. We keep ourselves from realizing our full potential. We react, instead of act. We define ourselves through the eyes of male-oriented society, instead of through our own.

The "New" Femininity

Femininity is not a way of looking but a way of being. Notwithstanding the definitions of biologists, social scientists and writers for contemporary women's magazines, the essence of the "new" femininity is:

- Nurturing someone or something.
- Creating empowering relationships.

The "new" femininity is an expression of women's true identity. Since each woman is unique, she will nurture and create empowering relationships in a different way. Reverend Judith Goode, a black Episcopalian priest I interviewed, put it like this, "I do not want to do 'social work,' just to make other people feel good. Helping others is an expression of who I am."

Some women consider motherhood an appropriate way to express their "new" femininity. Lucy is one of them. This is her special story.

Lucy: "Challenges and Children—That's What I Love!"

An 8-year-old boy opens the door of Lucy's brick house. I observe silently that it does have "yukky green" shutters, just as she had told me on the phone. Seated in the living room with a toy on her lap is Lucy. I walk over to her and she gropes for my hand. "So glad that you could come."

But Lucy does not meet my eyes. She is blind. But not helpless! Although she lost her eyesight at the age of 13, she has raised three children of her own, has adopted one and is "shopping" for at least one more.

Lucy gestures toward a chair next to her. "Please sit down. I'd really like to talk to you, but first I have to make sure that the children are all right."

Quickly but deliberately, she makes her way across the room, where an 18-month-old girl is sitting on the floor playing with dolls. "This is my adopted Korean baby, Lo-Ming. She also cannot see. Look how her right eye is completely closed. And she's completely blind in her left one." Lucy gives Lo-Ming a hug and a kiss, and the child responds with a big smile. Lucy smiles back. Perhaps Lucy cannot see Lo-Ming's smile, but she definitely senses that the baby is happy.

Now Lucy walks toward the kitchen, where the other children are eating pizza. "Is everything all right?" she calls out. "Sure, Mom," a boy's voice replies. "We're having a great time!" "I see," she replies, apparently not realizing the irony of her remark. Then she adds gently, "Let me know if you need anything."

After Lucy sits down again, she starts to talk. The words pour out of her mouth:

That's my youngest son, Chris. My two oldest boys are at school. I am babysitting the other two children. Their mother shops and runs errands for me in exchange.

Lucy straightens her shoulders and smooths her white cotton dress. Of course, you want to know how I manage to do all this. I'm sure it sounds very difficult to you, but actually it isn't. What would be terrible would be not having these children to care for—not to be able to make a difference in anyone's life.

I lost my sight in my left eye when I was 6 and became completely blind 7 years later. What an age to go blind. You're already feeling insecure as it is. All my friends totally withdrew from me. It was very painful. But I had to go on living. I had lost my eyesight, but I still had the rest of me. At this moment, I feel as if Lucy has pierced my soul.

She discusses her blindness frankly and matter-of factly, as af it were just one more challenge to be met. Becoming handicapped made me examine my recources—and my dreams—much more carefully than I ordinarily would have. People were so busy telling me that I couldn't do anything that I ended up asking myself, "What actually can I do? What can't I do at all?" Then I started sorting it out. I decided that I definitely couldn't see, but I could still walk, talk, laugh, make other people happy and even read, if I studied Braille. Being blind wasn't going to stop me from living my life. I would do the best I could with what I had. . . .

So I learned Braille, graduated from high school and enrolled at Penn State University. And, miracle of all miracles, I met Ben, an engineering student, who appreciated how many things I could do and understood how much I wanted to be a mother. When Ben told me that he wanted a large family, I immediately thought, "This is the man for me!" Ben and I got married during my senior year, and our first son, Matthew, was born 2 years later. James arrived the following year, and Christopher, the year after that. I was exhilarated. To have children in my life was the fulfillment of my greatest wish. Lucy's resonant voice, flavored with a lilting Puerto Rican accent, is full of exhilaration.

For 5 years, my life consisted mainly of feeding hungry mouths, wiping away tears, changing diapers and doing my best to be a good wife to Ben. I barely had a moment to myself. Then, all of a sudden, Matthew went off to kindergarten and then Jimmy, 1 year later. What would I do when Chris was ready? My husband and I couldn't have any more children of our own. What next? Go to work outside my home? A school would be only place that interested me, because I really do love kids. So I started thinking . . . . "I know how to take care of children, so why not take care of more—that are not my own?" Ben and I talked it over and we decided to adopt, before we forgot what babies were like! Since we already had three sons, we would find a healthy baby girl.

Ben and I were rejected by the three adoption agencies to which we applied. Apparently none of them believed that a blind woman could be a good mother. So we finally found another agency that specialized in placing youngsters with unusual needs. We said that we would be willing to adopt a foreign-born child, because there are more of them available.

Three months later we heard about Lo-Ming. The adoption agency sent us 20 pictures of her, and my husband told me that she was crying in 18 of them. Here was a baby who really needed good, loving care. I could really make a difference in her life. That was a year ago, and we've been happy together ever since. My gaze wanders to the little girl, still playing with her dolls on the floor. How contented she seems.

Lucy puts her hands on her hips. This is only the beginning. We've found an orphanage in Jamaica with children available for adoption. Our home may not be an ideal one for these kids, but right now it's all they've got. We're planning to adopt an 18-month-old girl next month. The child was abandoned at birth. All she knows is the orphanage. Lucy points to a photo next to me on an end table. Ben says she's not smiling in her picture either.

After that, we're thinking of adopting a 4-year-old Jamaican boy, who is also an orphan. Chris wants a playmate, so why not? We're pretty flexible. Challenges and children—that's what I love!

Lucy tells me why motherhood is what femininity means to her:

When we would have discussions in high school about whether women were equal to men, I would bounce the ideas off my parents. They said that women were equal to men, but women were also different from men, because they could have babies.

As a mother, I will dedicate my time to sitting down and having some good, long discussions with my daughter. Will I raise her differently from my sons? Yes. Although I used to be a tomboy, I prize femininity. I think that there are qualities about a woman that are uniquely hers. I will encourage my daughter to cultivate this attitude, "Hey, I'm a woman. That's great!" A primary, and very fulfilling, function in a woman's life is motherhood. Being a mother is something I treasure very highly. It is something I enjoy. My daughter will see that.

I believe that, unless a woman absolutely has to go to work, she should stay home with her children. I saw my parents give up a lot of material things, so that my mother could stay home, and we are doing the same thing. We value our time together as a family. I tell my kids, "I could be working and putting Reeboks on your feet, but I don't choose to. If I'm worn out at the end of the day, it's because I've been making a home for you, not because I've been out making somebody else successful!"

What If You Cannot Bear a Child?

When I was in Dr. Jacqueline Light's office, I asked her this question: "A woman recently said to me, 'I'm not really a woman, because I cannot biologically bear children.' What would you say to her?" Dr. Light replied:

I don't think that mothering is only biological. When a mother interacts with an infant, there's a very intricate response system. It has something to do with reproducing yourself and wanting to see your own characteristics in a child—even if it's just once. If I didn't have at least one child of my own, I would be searching for this child-mother identification.

Any woman who wants a child can find a way to have one—or adopt one. Although you may not have a husband, you don't have to live without a child.

Amy, an employee of a nonprofit association, is a lesbian who is thinking about adopting a child. We had this exchange:

"Amy, if you find a partner, can you envision bringing a child into your life?"

Yes, but I do have some reservations about it—for the child. You know how nasty and mean children can be to each other. I don't think I want to be pregnant. If I ever adopted a child, I would want to have a strong male role model for the child, perhaps my brother-in-law. Since I absolutely adore children, I haven't shut this possibility out. I know that there are many solid lesbian couples "out there" who want to adopt.

If you do not want to raise a child from infancy, you can take in a foster child who desperately needs a good home. Beatrice is a black woman who has decided to express her "new" femininity this way. Here is how she described her experience to me:

"I understand that now you're raising two young children who are not your own. Did you see that these children had a need—that they had to go somewhere?"

"The agency called me and asked me if I could take Pete. He had been on the streets. Josh is distantly related to me. I have had other foster children, too." She turns to her woman friend, sitting across the room. "Remember Lorraine, the 'nympho?' I got her out of a shelter; she didn't have anywhere else to go. When she came here, she was 17 going on 42. Everything was all right, until she got interested in boys. You know, she still calls me."

"What happened to her?"

She's married to someone in law enforcement. Even when I got rid of her, she came back here to live. She said, "Mom, I'm not going to let you say that one of your girls didn't finish high school." So I took her back here. She got on the bus every day until she got her "piece of paper."

"You really were there for Lorraine! What about the two foster children you are raising now?"

I just told Pete, my little "street boy," to get up early, because he's going to have a lesson at 7:00 tomorrow morning. And I bought him a present. Guess what it is? Division flash cards!

"I understand that you work in the public schools?"

Yes. I am a high school hall monitor. I watch out for the kids—keep order and break up fights.

"Has raising Pete and Josh been meaningful to you?"

Yes. I enjoy taking carm of kids. I know that somewhere there ire throw-away kids, sleeping on cardboard boxes downtown. They need someone to give them a hot meal and a place to sleep , to teach them to read and write, to tell them to come in out of the rain—and to make them feel wanted.

I was so deeply moved by what Beatrice said that I added this comment: "I am sure there are many children for whom it would make a huge difference in their lives to be raised by you. It is remarkable that you have raised five children of your own, are now working full-time in a school and still have room in your heart—and in your home—for foster children."

If you do not wish to take full-time care of a child, you can nurture children a few hours a week. This is what Esther, an energetic 45-year-old black woman decided to do, after her own children were grown.

Esther: Touch A Child's Life

I, another lady and a gentleman from my church have "adopted" 23 children from the housing projects. We've done three different activities with them over the summer. The first activity was a cookout at the gentleman's house—he's a minister. For the second activity, we took them to the theater. One of the ushers there was a former student of mine. He asked his boss if we could get 10 kids in free. And the boss said, "Yes." So we took 21 kids in, and we paid for 11. This was something I didn't expect. How could people be so nice?

The third activity we had here at my house. We had a spaghetti dinner for 11 boys and 11 girls, plus my three grandchildren. We had a sleep over in my basement for the 11 girls, who stayed all night. The next morning, the girls woke up, and we fed them. It made me feel so good to see the two oldest girls, who were about 10, combing the younger girls' hair. Each one got her own hair style. I just sat there and smiled, because I was so happy to see how they cared about each other.

This was the last of the summer activities we planned. During the rest of the year, we are going to go to PTA meetings with the kids and just "be there" for them, if they need us.

Church has always been important to me. When I was a child, a lady named Miss Guest used to take me and my brothers and sisters to church by streetcar. (My mother could never go, because she worked.) I think that's why I am so wrapped up in these kids, because I remember how Miss Guest took me to church. It's something you don't forget. She made sure that my brothers and sisters and I got there every Sunday and had seats in the front pew. She didn't just take my family; she took any kids who wanted to go. I thought she was the richest lady in the world, because she always had money for our streetcar fare.

That's why I am doing what I am doing now for the children at my church—because I remember what Miss Guest did for me. When I go into the area where they live, they smile and wave to me. It makes me feel great that I am doing something for them—and it is just a little thing that I am doing.

Every Sunday, I take some children to church. I hope that these kids remember me. I will never know how many of them later on—maybe 20 years from now—will go out and do the same thing. It's like a long chain. All you need to do to start a chain is to touch somebody's life in a good way.

You can also teach children and have an enormous impact on their lives. Wendy, a high school language instructor, has reached out to hundreds of young women. This is how she believes she has influenced their development:

I try to serve as a role model to my students and to give them advice whenever I can. One student of mine recently told me, "I'm not going to go to college; I'm just going to marry well." I replied, "What makes you think anyone is going to want you? What rich man is going to marry an uneducated woman? What are you going to do when you are alone? First you must be educated and then you must have a career—bottom line." I don't know if she understood me or not. But another female student whom I got to know well recently told me, "I'm going to be a realtor, because my mother's a realtor. I need to have a career of my own, because it's going to help me later on."

Nancy, a retired senior citizen, told me what teaching meant to her:

I believe that, of all the work I have done, I have made the greatest difference through teaching. I like "turning on a mind," regardless of the subject matter. It is very satisfying to facilitate a young person's learning, whether it's learning to do something new or simply learning to use one's brain.

Nurturing Is Different from Mothering

To nurture other people does not necessarily mean that you have to be a mother. According to the "new" femininity, you do not have to give birth to, or even raise, a child of your own. Nurturing is promoting the development or growth of someone or something.

If you do not choose to nurture youngsters, you can foster the growth and development of adults—and the world we live in. To Congresswoman Patricia Wynn, nurturing other people is getting laws passed which improve the lives of women.

To run for elected office, you have to not only like people and work hard—but you have to have the motivation. Why are you going to take the leap? Is it ego? Ego is always part of it; it's great when someone pats you on the back and tells you, "My son or brother or whoever thinks you're terrific." Flattery is nice, too, but you also have to have a feeling that you can really do something worthwhile. When I was on the Commission for Women, I testified before the City Council that women should be allowed to be on the local rescue squad. I will never forget the woman who wanted to join. Now I go back and visit the squad. When I see the women working together with the men, I think about that first big trial—the crucible—where we succeeded.

I just read in today's paper that scoliosis screening is now a state requirement in the schools. That was my bill that became law. It happened because a constituent of mine, who had worked on my campaign had a daughter with scoliosis, curvature of the spine. I checked it out and found out that this disease primarily affects women. So I took action. Right now I'm working on a bill for displaced homemakers and making arrangements to appear on a local television show about domestic violence.

Stacey, the 23-year-old newspaper reporter, finds an outlet for nurturing in writing:

When I was in the seventh grade, I began to realize that I had a unique way of looking at things. I knew that I could make a contribution to the world, by giving people an entirely different way of seeing it. I wanted to discover something that no one else knew. I used to see so many closed-minded people; I wanted to shake them and say, "No, no, look at this." Now I can enlighten them by writing. I'm serving a function: I'm helping others. I also take photographs for my articles. It is so fascinating to see something that nobody else sees and show it to them. Old men especially interest me because they haven't been sheltered and repressed they way many old women have been.

Nurturing means many things to many women. To Stacey, it means helping her readers understand the community they live in. To Congresswoman Patricia Wynn, it means working for legislation that will facilitate the full development of women, senior citizens and other adults. To me, it means promoting the growth and development of Planet Earth by volunteering to work for the environmental or animal rights organization of your choice.

Congresswoman Patricia Wynn has gotten laws passed that will improve the lives of millions. Stacey has helped thousands of people see local events in a new and different way. Other women have had a good influence on just a handful of people. Esther told me that she believes that touching even one child's life is meaningful. An empowered woman can nurture a single person—or a multitude.

Nurturing Is Creating Empowering Relationships

You also nurture by creating empowering relationships with everyone around you. An empowering relationship promotes the growth and development of both people in it. If you and your partner, your children, your other relatives, your friends and your co-workers are empowering each other, you have created a center of energy that will spread empowerment to many more people.

Women are more than 50 percent of the population of our power-over society. If each woman had empowering relationships with the important people in her life, our society's values would eventually become more female-oriented. Instead of competing with other people, we would be cooperating with them. Rather than fighting wars, we would be empowering our neighbors.

A Feminine Woman Can Also Achieve

In mutual partnerships, where people are empowered together with each other, each person realizes his or her full potential. A woman in an empowering partnership can not only nurture but also have a productive career. Achievement is compatible with empowerment.

I had this fascinating dialogue with Dr. Jacqueline Light:

"Do you consider your relationships with your children very important?"

Yes. From my perspective, the single most important aspect of femininity is mothering. The gratification of raising a child is extraordinary; it even exceeds the satisfaction of being a wife.

Having children is a "transmogrifying" experience. You don't know what you are going to do until you see that baby and then respond to it. If you have strong maternal instincts, the baby will change everything for you. I have said to many young women, "You think that you're going back to this law firm or that computer corporation? You're not going to want to go." "Oh, yes, I am," they reply. "I'm just going to take 2 weeks off." So they have the baby, take 2 weeks off, don't want to go back to work and become profoundly depressed. If they have bonded to the baby, they just can't leave.

"Do you think that society, the way it is now, values men's 'achieving' more than women's nurturing?"

I don't think men give nurturing less value. I think women do, especially white women entering the competitive job market. They believe that if they pursue a career, they can't be a good mother. When unmarried white women would tell me, "You will have to choose between a career and motherhood," I would ask, "Why?"

"Were you always told that you could do both?"

Yes, always. The white culture has been wedded to the idea that a mother has to stay at home and raise her children. It is the man's role to go into the world and accomplish things for her in her name. The woman's role is to stay home, so her husband doesn't feel "threatened." She can be playing tennis 12 hours a day, but as long as she is "home," everything is fine. This is how the white man has oppressed the white woman.

Actually a certain kind of white male has always wanted his wife to be home for him. He has wanted a "mommy "at home, perhaps because his own mother used to be home. His typical fantasy has been, "She's making brownies" or "She's thinking of me." It felt very good to believe that he was the focus of his wife's attention. He would call his wife up 5 or 6 times a day. Most black women have never been oppressed like this.

White women can learn from their black sisters how to both have a career and be a mother. One trick is to alternate—to get your career to a certain level and then opt for motherhood. You cannot have a $1,000,000-a-year law practice and a little baby. If you like the baby, you are going to want to be with him or her. There's nothing wrong with feeling this way. So you make choices. You may decide to have a $100,000-a-year practice. You may have to practice in a small town, instead of New York. You may decide to take the baby to work with you. There are infinite combinations!

Every woman has her own way of expressing her desires to nurture, to create empowering relationships and to achieve.

Discover Your Own Feminine Identity

To be truly feminine, we have to turn our attention away from men and concentrate first on ourselves.

When talking to radical feminists, I insist, "To blame men for women's suffering is begging the question. Scapegoating is an old escape tactic. While it is important to understand the oppression of women by male-oriented society, dwelling on it allows women to avoid facing how they have contributed to their own oppression by going along with the system. The issue is not whether men are the enemy, but whether women are their own worst enemies."

Free from the grip of men's influence, an empowered woman focuses on her own feminine values. To traditional women I say, "Finding a man or having a husband is not the solution to your frustration, dissatisfaction or emptiness. Your problem—and its solution—is within you. You need to stop paying so much attention to men and start taking a good, hard look at yourself."

If you are straightjacketed by the demands of "being a lady," you need to ask yourself, "What does femininity mean to me? Is femininity just a vague notion that I don't really understand? Or does it have a special significance in my life? Which feminine values, attitudes and behaviors have I adopted over the years? Which ones do I choose to accept now?"

Ask yourself this important question: "Do I seek marriage and children because I want them, or because I think they will make me 'more of a woman?'" Remember, first and foremost, you are a human being. You have the right to make choices about what you believe and what you do. With this perspective, you will be empowered to decide what nurturing and creating empowering relationships mean to you. In truth, there are as many definitions of these terms as there are women. *Yours is the one that is truly comfortable for you.*

Continue your dialogue with yourself: "Do I wear high heels or

lace underwear because I like them or because I think I 'should?' "
Looking attractive is an admirable goal, but conforming to a single,
arbitrary standard of feminine attractiveness is not. There are many
ways to look feminine; no longer is there just one. Consider Cher. She
has broken the conventional rules about how women "should" look.
Instead of frills, she sports a bare navel. On a deeper level, Cher does
not adhere to gender stereotypes either, such as men are "dominant"
or women are "subservient." One can not imagine her playing "second" to her husband in any of her marriages. Yet few of us doubt
Cher's femininity. We even wear her perfume.

When you redefine femininity for yourself, the greatest danger you
face is your fear of being judged. "What will other people think?" you
wonder. Actually, being authentic is the best guarantee you have that
you will really like yourself and that others will genuinely like you,
too. Be yourself, even if experiencing your own empowerment makes
you "unfeminine," according to male-oriented society's current standards.

Femininity and Men

By redefining femininity, you are doing yourself—and men—a
favor. While having a baby is something only a woman can do, nurturing and empowering other people are not. Both men and women
can accept these two feminine values freely and without embarrassment. Imagine how exciting our relationships would be if both men
and women empowered each other! How splendid our earth would
be if everyone nurtured it! How many more children would be cared
for, if both men and women made caring for the next generation a top
priority! Women, in turn, could direct themselves more toward
achievement, a positive male value. Men and women could work together to achieve the social, economic and political goals that now
elude us.

The teachings of a lifetime are not erased overnight. Our challenge
as women is to re-examine our self-defeating attitudes and our stereotyped patterns of thought. An empowered woman is able to think for
herself.

Where Do You Stand?

Who you are affects the world. Each day you live, you have the potential to make a difference in your own life and in the lives of other
people. This does not mean that you have to change the entire fabric
of society. Every empowered woman can make a difference; it is the

quality, not the size, that counts. The question for you is, "What kind of contribution do *I* want to make?"

Women's contributions are special; they do not have to resemble men's. A woman may struggle for years to find who she is and what she wants, a task that men often complete during adolescence. Each day of that struggle, she is making a difference in her own life. A woman's greatest glory may be in helping one person: raising a baby, supporting a woman friend in need or organizing the schedule of a busy executive. It may be benefiting several people, perhaps her clients, if she is a therapist; her patients, if she is a doctor; or the people in her office, if she is an office manager or a secretary.

Sometimes the difference we make is like dropping a stone in a pool of water; it makes circles that get wider and wider, until they are beyond our view. As a receptionist in a women's organization to whom I spoke put it:

What my organization is doing won't benefit me, but it will benefit my teenage daughters when they are adults. I may never see all the results of my work during my lifetime. But the world will be different because I have lived, and that difference is my immortality.

Share whatever resources you have—time, energy or money—with other people, even if it's only a single one.

Spiritual Empowerment

Spiritual empowerment is a vital part of the "new" femininity. Olga, a daughter of two survivors of the Holocaust, describes what spiritual empowerment means to her:

Empowerment is spiritual strength. What do I mean by spiritual? A sense of connectedness to life, other human beings and the planet as a whole. A sense of gratitude, even awe, about the gift of life. A sense of compassion. Whether this is connected to God who you read about in the Bible—you make up your mind. It is certainly not tied to any particular creed or dogma.

As an empowered woman, you connect and relate yourself to the world around you—in ways that affirm your existence and make the world a little better. I don't necessarily mean just sitting around meditating with your friends or even becoming famous. True spiritual empowerment has nothing to do with status. Your contribution may not be anything that is recognized by anyone else or that makes your name a household word. People have contributed wonderful, miraculous things to the world and have never been acclaimed by others. Maybe the most empowered women don't need to be recognized.

Women are very much the bearers of spiritual empowerment. Every woman has a different voice, a unique expression of her empowerment. If we get totally stuck on the male road, we may neglect our own. Feminine spiritual empowerment may very well be what we need most right now in this period of history. We are becoming more aware of our human interdependence, of the critical condition of our planet. A lot of people are waking up.

Having a relationship with God helps you to see yourself within the total perspective of the universe. Reverend Judith Goode relates how she discovered the paradox of our human identity:

I had heard that there was a new, young Episcopalian priest coming to a church in my city. Searching for something, I went in there. It was a "high church"; the incense was so thick that I could not see the altar. Suddenly, within all of the ritual and the liturgy, I found the missing piece I was looking for. Here, at last, was the source of my understanding of who I was.

As I stared at the stained glass windows, I started to think, "I have come to the altar of God as someone in awe of her Creator. I am a person who is both significant and insignificant, at the same time. I am somebody, because I am a child of God. At the same time, next to the awesome mystery of God, I am nothing."

By creating a relationship with God, Reverend Judith Goode reaffirmed her own sense of self, while gaining a sense of connection with the universe.

According to Julia, the self-employed businesswoman, her relationship with God has enabled her to trust, and empower, herself.

While I do not consider myself spiritual in a religious sense, perhaps I am spiritual in an emotional sense. After I get in touch with my resources, I relax and let everything happen. I don't force anything. I believe my mind and body and feelings will take over, so that I will go the right way and become the best that I am. In this sense, I give myself over to a higher Power.

Your spirituality is a critical force in your relationships with others. You cannot create empowering relationships if you are empty within your spiritual core. Loving God enables you to find love in this world. Your deep and abiding love can often overcome a person's resistance to becoming partners with you.

Giving Does Not Mean "Sacrificing"

To give to others is a privilege. Women who say that they "sacrifice" for others really mean that they do not set clear-cut limits as to how much they give. The experience of one woman I interviewed illustrates the difference between giving and "sacrificing." She told me:

Right now I have the opportunity to give to a member of my family. My

16-year-old nephew has been on drugs, and I have taken him to live with me. If I make a small, not necessarily a global, contribution to his life, then I will be satisfied.

"What do you get back from giving?"

The joy of being able to have the opportunity to give, which is totally separate from anything else. I do not think of it as "give and take."

"Would you view yourself as "sacrificing?"

No, because I set limits. Each day, I write down a list of the things he has to do . He has daily responsibilities around the house—and a nightly curfew. If he goes beyond these limits, out of my house he goes!

An Empowered Woman Can Make a Difference

By nurturing someone or something, each one of us can make a difference. Some women find they can make a difference by taking care of children; others do meaningful work outside the home. What all empowered women have in common is that, wherever they are, they create mutual, autonomous and authentic relationships.

Ask yourself, *"How will I leave the world a better place, after I die?"* If you have children, you have a unique opportunity to experience empowerment together with them. If your children are grown, you are able to empower other people besides your family and to care for the world around you.

In your lifetime, at least one opportunity to make an extraordinary difference may be given to you. Will you rise to the challenge? An empowered women does. Consider what happened to Congresswoman Patricia Wynn, just before she decided to run for elective office:

My sister, who was divorced, died of cancer when she was 39. My husband and I took her six children from Massachusetts to live with us. At that time, I was teaching, and I went into politics shortly thereafter. My eldest son was just going into college; my sister's eldest child was in the 11th grade, and she also had twins in 10th grade. My youngest child was in third grade; hers was 1 year older. They were arranged like steps in a ladder. At one time, I visited the teachers of four children, during back-to-school night. We had five in college at one time!

I realize that my husband could have said "No." It is a credit to him that he did not. Instead, he made sure that this very arrangement was in her will before she died. From the beginning, he helped out—in renovating the house and in getting the six children transferred to new schools. After they arrived, he used to go shopping with three grocery carts. Someone would always say to him, "You must be shopping for months." "No, just for 5 days," he would reply. I think we both grew through all of these experiences.

When Congresswoman Wynn decided to double the size of her family, she had no guarantee how everything would turn out. Would she make a big difference in her nieces' and nephews' lives? Would her marriage be endangered? Would her own children suffer? Would she be able to launch her political career? She did not know for sure. Nor can you. So what should you do? Act as if you can make a difference and have faith that what you do will turn out well, in the long run. In order to have an effect on the world, you have to believe you can. Congresswoman Patricia Wynn offers this advice from her own experience:

I went into politics believing that, as an individual, I could make a difference. I had held office in high school and college, and I was elected to the faculty senate at the college where I taught. I was in the State Legislature for 8 years. So I went from community service to elected state office and then into Congress.

In the State Legislature, I was at the forefront of creating an Affirmative Action Plan, getting our state legislature to revise their antiquated code and make it gender-neutral, and coming up with new laws to assist women. I thought, "This can happen; we can do that!" Success breeds success.

To make a difference, you need self-confidence—and the willingness to take chances. Admiral Grace Hopper once said, "A ship in port is safe, but that's not what ships are for." I think you have to take chances. You will never know what can happen, if you don't.

Do not think in extremes. As an empowered woman, you cannot change the world. Nor will make no difference at all. What you can do is add your verse to the poem of the universe. If you have nurtured and created mutual, autonomous and authentic relationships with other people, the world will be a little bit better because you have lived.

Empowerment Exercises

1. Discover Your "Nurturing Self": Start today to nurture something, if you have not done so up to now. Select one living thing and take care of it. You may prefer to start with a simple one, and then work your way up to those that are more difficult. Here are some examples, from the easiest to the hardest one of all:

a. A houseplant
b. A small outdoor garden
c. A goldfish, tropical fish or a turtle
d. A niece, a nephew or a friend's child
e. A baby of your own

Needless to say, the last option is not mandatory!

2. Journal Writing: What Has Femininity Meant to You? In your Empowerment Journal, list the special meanings that femininity has had for you up to now. You may want to spend some time thinking before you write and then return to your list at least one more time, after a week or two. Then look at your list. Does it emphasize nurturing and creating empowering relationships? Or have you defined femininity in superficial—and perhaps destructive—ways? Once you have become aware of your past mind set, you can make a decision how you wish to define yourself as a woman, in the future.

If you prefer, record your responses on a tape recorder and play back the tape.

3. Draw Your "New" Femininity Profile: Reread this chapter. Pay particular attention to the meanings of femininity listed at the beginning. What does femininity mean to you now? Do you think a woman has to give birth to her own child to be truly feminine? Raise her own child? Raise someone else's child? What kind of nurturing experience would be most comfortable for you? Would you prefer to care for people, animals, plants or our whole environment? How?

4. What Kind of Difference Would You Like to Make? Spend some time thinking about what you, as a woman, would like do to make this world a better place. Do you see yourself nurturing or accomplishing or doing both? How do you envision doing something worthwhile? What verse will you write in the universal poem? Does it involve raising children, creating mutual relationships or helping others less fortunate than yourself? Or are you oriented toward male values and so prefer to win victories, control other people and make lots of money?

5. Journal Writing: Making a Feminine Difference Every Day: At the end of the day, it may not seem to you as if you have made a difference, when actually you have. This is because women's contributions of nurturing others and creating empowering relationships receive little recognition in our male-oriented society. So you have to give recognition to yourself.

Find a moment to jot down in your Empowerment Journal at least one feminine way you made another person's life a little bit better. Perhaps you loved a child, made an adult happy or did something to preserve our environment. This exercise can also be done in reverse. Decide each morning to do at least one small thing besides your work that will enhance your relationships with other people and with Nature. Write it down in your Empowerment Journal. Then make sure you do it.

Now that you have re-examined femininity, are you ready to take a good, hard look at feminism and the feminist movement? Believe it or not, the contemporary feminist movement is another obstacle to empowerment. To turn it into a stepping stone, go on to the next chapter.

REALIZE THAT THE FEMINIST MOVEMENT DOES NOT EMPOWER WOMEN

10

"A woman, as a man, has the power to choose, and to make her own heaven or hell."

Betty Friedan
The Feminine Mystique

The feminist movement has been a blessing to modern women. Or has it? When I asked the 200 women I interviewed how they felt about the movement, I was amazed to hear comments like these:

- Feminism may not have hurt me, but it hasn't helped me either. Frankly it's been totally irrelevant to my life.
- I think the feminists have actually harmed women, because of their image. I've never joined a feminist organization, because I don't want anyone to think I'm a lesbian.
- The feminists may have opened up job opportunities for women, but they've given me a headache in the process. Why should I feel guilty because I've decided to stay home full-time and raise my children?

Since its beginnings, today's feminist movement has been a "sacred cow" for women. For the most part, we have been afraid to question its basic beliefs. Few of us have dared to challenge its authority publicly. Like a bad marriage, it may be dragging us down, but it's all we've got.

I think that the feminist movement can benefit from an honest dialogue about its merits and shortcomings. Is the movement empowering the 100 million American women it would like to reach? I don't think so. I believe that the modern feminist movement has cheated us.

At this point, you may be wondering, "Is there such a thing as the feminist movement at all? Has it become so splintered that it is hard to tell who is a feminist and who is not?" No. On one extreme, there are the militants with their roots in the National Organization of Women and some of the splinter groups of the "60s. They cherish their memories of the early New York marches and the publicity about "bra-burning." In the middle, there are the "Gloria-Steinem feminists," who are not really affiliated with any organization, but who embrace many feminist ideals. Then there are the college students for whom feminism is like chlorine in the water. It may have influenced their thinking, but they just don't know it. The feminist movement is all these women.

But what about the vast majority of us, the 100 million who don't even have our names on a single feminist organization's mailing list? We don't have time to ponder the merits of feminism, and many would rather not. To us, Marlo Thomas's announcement at the 1989 Women's March on Washington, "The feminist fringe has become the feminist family" was empty rhetoric. It is a sad fact that many of us don't feel as if we are part of the "family." Some of us feel like black sheep who don't belong at all.

Why? Because the feminist movement unwittingly does a vast disservice to the vast majority of those it strives to serve. It tries to pin a label on women, when our essence lies in our incredible diversity. Not all of us are career persons. Each and every one of us experiences unique struggles, choices, dilemmas and personal transitions that do not fit into any single stereotype. We want to find our own way without being told by anyone, *including the feminists*, what we "should" do.

Now I do not mean to discount the valuable contributions of the modern feminist movement. Due to its efforts, Americans have become aware of the significant problems of women, including inadequate daycare facilities, unequal pay for equal work, poverty, insufficient representation in Congress, rapes and assaults on women and public degradation in pornography. Feminists have encouraged women to fight these abuses by getting together in support groups, setting up shelters for battered women and running for elected office.

But why, 24 years after the formation of NOW, do women still earn 35 percent less than men who do the same jobs? Why are 5 percent of our congresspersons women, when we cast over half of their votes? Why couldn't women get the Equal Rights Amendment passed? Because the feminists have not yet addressed the most important issue of all—our personal empowerment. This is the name of the solution to "the problem that has no name." While feminists have made some gains for women as a group, they have not succeeded in empowering us as individuals. Before we can march to support the ERA, we have to learn to march to the beat of our own drums.

The messages of the contemporary feminist movement are irrelevant to our deepest concerns. Listen to a typical conversation, when women get together. While they compare notes, each one is asking herself, "Shall I choose 'wifehood,' motherhood, a career or some combination of the three? Could I possibly skip one of them? If not, how will I find the time to do everything? When will there be an '8-day week?'" Each woman's personal empowerment begins when she gets down to the basic issue behind all these questions: *"Who am I and what do I really want?"* Then she is ready to decide her priorities, arrange her time accordingly and use her extra energy to work for the goals of all women.

To paraphrase the 18th-century French philosopher Jean Jacques Rousseau, modern women are born free, but they are still everywhere in chains. What is holding us back? Not society's limitations, but our own ingrained habits of thinking. The greatest obstacle to our personal fulfillment is our confusion about what a woman is "supposed to" do, which often keeps us from acting in our own best interests. In order to become empowered, we need to free ourselves from our mental chains.

For example, Sharon, one of the women I interviewed, has been working as an attorney for the past 10 years. She and her husband would like to have a baby, but Sharon fears that taking time off may damage her career—and the image of women in the world of work. Sharon is so "stuck" in feeling guilty and thinking negative thoughts that she may end up depriving herself of what she needs most to become a fulfilled and empowered woman. As she continues to work full-time, she may not advance as quickly as her peers, because of her own feelings of personal powerlessness.

It is a vicious cycle. We will never be able to get the support network of daycare centers, legal protection and government representation we need until, one by one, we start making authentic life-choices. Until then, most of us will just keep running in circles.

The first order of business for modern feminists should not be, "How can women gain more political and economic power?" but "How can we feel empowered within ourselves?" Before women can gain a foothold in society, we have to gain control over our own lives.

Feminists should be telling us, "Find your recipe for personal empowerment. The ingredients are knowing yourself, respecting your right to choose and discovering what you really want—marriage, children, career or some combination of the three. Since each woman is different, your recipe will be unique. And don't worry about whether your empowerment will "threaten" men. If it does, at least you will have your own integrity and self-respect."

Nowhere is it etched in stone that a woman has to have paid employment all of her adult life. Work can include caring for children, the future adults of this planet, and being a volunteer. There is no universal mandate that to be a "real woman," you have to be married, work at a full-time salaried job and have your children—all at the same time. There is nothing wrong with deciding not to marry a man, not to have children, or not to seek a top executive job. As Dr. Jean Baker Miller of Wellesley College's Stone Center has said:

All of us are "real women." Anything to the contrary is based on someone else's beliefs about what they want us to be.

When feminist leaders have addressed women's personal concerns, they have suppressed our individuality by forcing us into a stereotyped sex role:

- *"The personal is the political."* What if you prefer to wear lipstick, perfume, long hair and pantyhose, because that's how you feel (and look) attractive? Why should women conform to a single standard of personal appearance, whether set by men or the feminist movement? What about the woman who opposes abortion because of deep personal convictions? What about a woman who criticizes the National Organization of Women? Should both of these women be condemned by the "movement?" Why do all women have to agree with the feminists?

- *"The personal is the social."* Is your primary responsibility to other women or to yourself? What if you have spent the last 10 years of your life in an executive position where you are miserable? If you decide to quit your job to raise a child instead, are you to be condemned for letting your "sisters" down? Or are you to be praised for fulfilling yourself and so making yourself an empowered woman?

- *"Have it all."* No man alive can manage to take care of a family, work at a demanding job and have time left over for himself. Then why do the feminists think women can do it? Is it fair to a child to drop him or her off at a daycare center 3 weeks after birth? If you are not willing and able to take on the demanding job of being a parent, wouldn't it be better to forgo it, at least for a while?

- *Work like a man."* Is a woman who chooses not to work for either part or all of her adult life a "traitor" to the cause? Is helping your 6-year-old grow up to be a happy, productive adult less "worthwhile" than being a bank clerk? Could the feminists be telling us to imitate men, because men have traditionally been the dominant group in society? Wouldn't it be a better idea for us to get in touch with our own unique feminine values?

- *"Men are the enemy."* Would feminists deny that one-half of the human race can be caring and compassionate? Is there anything wrong with liking men, or even marrying one of them? Rather than attacking or emasculating men, wouldn't it be a good idea to try cooperating with them instead? (Betty Friedan was heavily criticized when she made this suggestion.) Could using male-dominated society as a scapegoat be a convenient device to avoid taking a good, hard look at ourselves? In truth, do we bear at least 50 percent of the responsibility for still allowing men to keep us in a subordinate position?

The feminists have substituted their own stereotypes for the ones created by men. The essence of empowerment is following a path of one's own, not conforming to any single standard of behavior—*including the feminists'*. As a result, many women who don't choose to conform to feminist standards have secretly felt turned off by the movement's unreasonable demands. Not wishing to be openly disloyal to feminism, they have simply ignored it. Other women have been hanging in limbo—confused by the conflicting demands of the feminists, men, and their own inner desires.

Empowered women define their own role and make their own choices. They don't feel that they are living in a prison, built by someone else. For 15 years I myself was "chained up" by words, categories and ways of thinking that were totally irrelevant to me. Rather than thoroughly enjoying that wonderful time I spent raising my three sons, I often felt guilty that I wasn't doing something else more "worthwhile." When I dressed up to go out for the evening, a voice within me whispered, "You're selling out." The inappropriate, confusing, and just plain wrong messages that I received were not from men, but from the feminists.

What does it take to create a movement women want to join, not just observe? Throughout history, an elite has expanded its base when it has had a charismatic leader, has been closely united and has delivered a message in harmony with the desires of the people it represents. On the last point, the feminist movement has failed completely.

Feminist leaders need to take the pulse of those they want to lead. I don't know about you, but I don't want anyone telling me what I should do with my life. I become empowered when I make the choices that are right for me.

When the feminist movement addresses the deepest concern of conteeporary women—personal empowerment—the movement will spread like a brush fire in the dry season. I will be encouraged to follow my own destiny, wherever it leads. Only then will I consider myself a proud member of the "feminist family," not a black sheep. Perhaps you will, too.

A Critique of the Feminist Movement

Most of the women I interviewed were either uninterested in, or highly critical of, the feminist movement. Dr. Jacqueline Light described to me how many black women feel about the feminists:

My older daughter is a feminist, and we have talked a lot about the movement. She agrees with me now that a lot of what the feminist movement is fighting for is largely irrelevant to black women. The problems of the feminist movement are not our problems. Black women have not been oppressed by their men.

I do not think that black women have to be "man-bashers," just because some feminists are bashing men. We have to find out what aspects of feminism really apply to us. Many messages of the feminist movement are directed toward white people. In a global sense, the problem of the black woman is to get her man on a level of parity with her. She can't make an enemy of him. He hasn't oppressed her; the system has oppressed him. For most black women, the feminist rhetoric about male oppression is very much beside the point.

Reverend Judith Goode argued that feminist movement should stop focusing only on sexism. These were her words:

White women suffer from some of the same social stereotypes and limitations as women of color. Yet I have found, much to my sadness, that many white feminists are unwilling to look at their own racism. Sexism is their only priority. As women of color, we have more than one priority. Our agenda is different from white women. We ask, "How can we all be more compassionate? How can we be more righteous? How can we distribute goods and services in a more humane way?"

I believe that it is time for the feminist movement to look at our problems as human problems. The oppression that women suffer, blacks can suffer, and vice versa. We live in a global community: first world, second world and third world. There is no escape, nor should there be.

The white women I interviewed criticized the feminist movement for different reasons. One woman, who was a single parent, said:

I have never identified with the feminists. They have weakened my support system, because they have made me feel I was "copping out," by having children and a husband, and then a male friend, after I got divorced.

Lucy expressed the same feelings, when she described to me her experiences with feminist women at college:

I wanted to get a college degree, so that, if I needed to make it independently someday, I could. But I was also looking for a mate at college; I knew that from the start. When I shared my wish with my female classmates, many of them ridiculed me, because wanting to get married was anti-feminist. But I didn't let it bother me. I didn't hang around with the women who were "hardcore "feminists"— and obnoxious about it. I became more, not less, entrenched in my position. I have always been a fighter.

Sheila expressed an opinion that many women would label "sexist":

When I was younger, I was quite attractive. I met many powerful, interesting men because of the way I looked. I never slept around, but I used "the bait." That's anti-feminist, but it's a part of life. I think the feminists who deny it are the ones who are not very attractive. I'm not very active in the movement. I think that one of the reasons is that, if you succeed without the help of the feminists, you don't think that they are necessary.

One might wonder whether or not Sheila was simply unaware of how the feminist movement had laid the groundwork for her professional success.

Only a handful of my interviewees actually stated that they were feminists. Even fewer had attended feminist group meetings. One woman put it this way:

I have never been involved in the feminist movement, because I am the kind of person who does not do "group" things. Besides I've always been too busy.

Many of the women I interviewed said that they were not really interested in the feminist movement at all. Take Vicki, for instance. When I asked her, "Did the feminist movement have any effect on you?" she replied, "The feminist movement did not affect me at all. Mine has always been a personal struggle. I've never found inspiration from the movement; I've never hooked into it. I've never even read any feminist books." Lucy told me, "I was never aware of the feminist movement in the beginning; it seemed to me just a lot of women burning their bras." More than half the women I spoke with agreed with Vicki and Lucy.

Feminist Ideals Can Be Empowering

While many of us are critical of the feminist movement, we can still support the ideals of feminism. While I was conducting interviews in Boston, I had the occasion to visit a noted spokesperson for feminism. She told me how feminist ideals had empowered her:

"Please go right in; Ms. Martha Dean will be with you in a moment."

My eyes open wide as I step into Martha's spacious office. Every single wall is covered with shelves of neatly arranged books; the only breaks in the pattern are two windows and the door through which I have just entered. As I wait for Martha to enter, I scan the titles: all of them are about women and most are by feminist authors.

Martha glides in a moment later. "I'm so pleased to meet you." Her immaculately clipped shoulder length blonde hair frames her warm smile. "She doesn't look like a typical feminist," I observe to myself. Martha begins:

Feminism is very important to me, in the sense that what I want from my own life is what I want for all people's lives. Feminism is dedicated to creating an environment where men and women can work together in peace, free to be whoever they are. My definition of a feminist is anyone who believes in an equal opportunity and in individual worth.

When I was a senior in college I read *The Feminine Mystique* by Betty Friedan. I said to myself, "This makes sense. This is how I want to live my life." Since then, it has never occurred to me to worry about the future. With feminist ideals to guide me, I am a woman of my own design.

Another very important book for me has been Robin Morgan's *Sisterhood Is Powerful*. It taught me how we must unite with each other to reach our common goals. When I was in graduate school in 1970, everyone was very concerned with getting my husband, Jay, a job, but not with finding one for me. The feeling was, "He is a man; he should get a job." This was not my view. Finally Jay got his "dream job" in Caracas, Venezuela. I followed him there, just as a good wife was supposed to do. Martha sighs a deep sigh.

In Caracas, I needed a purpose. Since I had read about consciousness-raising groups in *Sisterhood Is Powerful,* I said to myself, "Why don't you start one?" So I called up one woman and told her what I wanted to do. She said, "Why do you want to do this?" I replied, "We are all sisters. We need to talk to each other." I was amazed when five women came to the first meeting. After that, my consciousness-raising group took root and spread. At one time there were five separate groups going on in my neighborhood in Caracas. And this was a city where no one had ever heard of "women's lib!" My own group was extremely helpful to me. It helped me make the most important decision I ever made in my life.

Three years later, nothing had changed. Jay's career was going well, but I had no job. I decided that what I wanted to do with my life was to work on women's issues. Then I gave birth to a handicapped baby girl. It soon became clear to me that Angela needed much better medical care than she could get in Caracas. And my marriage was in trouble now. The first 5 years Jay and I had spent together had been very happy. But we were not happy anymore. I was heartbroken.

I had to be very clear about what I would do now, as it would irrevocably affect all three of our lives. I painted the "worst possible case" picture for myself. If I chose to leave Caracas, it would be the end of my marriage. I might never be romantically involved with a man again, and I didn't know if I could endure that. On the other hand, if I stayed, Angela and I would have no future. No career for me, and no rehabilitation for her. Two women's bright promises extinguished like candles' flames. There is a long silence.

Martha stands up in front of the bookcases and points to them, as if she is a teacher talking to a class. Someone once told me, "An educated person has choices. He or she can exercise freedom of mind in all areas of life." So I took time to think through my decision very carefully. Our society is not geared to let women "know" things, so when we "know" something, we have to "catch it," either by writing it down or by telling someone about it. For this reason, I had kept a journal during the past 5 years. No one else ever read what I wrote; it was strictly for myself. When I "knew "something, I would write it down like a crazy woman, so I wouldn't lose it.

My journal became a resource. It helped me to get in touch with what I already "knew." I could go back and see what I wrote 2, 3, 4 and 5 years ago, in order to gain perspective of my life—where I was coming from and where I was going. I spent 6 weeks reading over my journals. Whenever I got a glimpse of the truth, I tried to think it through.

When I made my decision to leave Caracas, at least I "knew" why I had to go. For the sake of two women's self-fulfillment, I had to say "Goodbye." The hardest part was letting go of my nostalgia for the known and my fear of the unknown. I kept saying to myself over and over again, "The worst that can happen is that you can say, 'This time, I've really messed up.'"

Once we were back in the United States, I found excellent medical care for Angela. She is now 16 years old and developing to the best of her potential. After bouncing around from job to job, I am now the director of a feminist organizition—my life's dream. Now my motto is, "If it scares you, do it!"

Martha stares at me very intensely. I have not remarried and don't intend to. It's not that I don't want a man in my life; I've been seeing someone regularly for the past 2 years. As a feminist, I don't want the assumptions that are made about a married woman to be made about me. I have always had the idea that I would get married and end up having three kids, a station wagon and a dog. (My friends still tease me about it by reminding me that all I ever got was a hatchback.) It's still a dilemma for me—wanting these things, but being afraid that they'll catch me in a trap that I can't get out of. Remember I told you that I'm "a woman of my own design?" Feminism is my motif.

In feminism, Martha found inspiration, and a direction for her life. This was also true for Wendy, the high school teacher. She told me that the birth of feminism had changed her whole outlook:

I remember in high school, during the '70s, when women were becoming more politically aware. Feminists are now mainstream people, but then you would have thought they were walking around naked, they seemed so radical. I remember reading articles in the paper about these "flaming liberals" to my father. He would say, "No wonder these women are marching; they are so ugly that no men could want them!" Although his remarks enraged me, I held my tongue. In my heart, I believed that the feminists were making an important contribution to women's lives.

While I was at college, I picked up an early issue of *Ms.* Magazine, and I thought, "This is really interesting; it's a women's magazine, and there are no fashion or cosmetic ads! It has valuable articles, many about the problems of black women and poor women." *Ms.* didn't seem radical to me; it just made sense. It had always seemed to me that, unless you were a feminist, you had to wait until your husband died to realize your potential. Finally, I had found a light in the darkness.

Another woman I interviewed told me how she believes feminism has empowered women:

I think that feminism is wonderful. It has really helped a lot of people. Because of feminism, a lot of women have had to reexamine their lives, which has led to a lot of short-run unrest and tension. But, in the long run, women and men will both benefit, as more and more women realize that they are as valuable as men. For women who want to realize their potential, feminism is an opportunity to validate themselves.

Many women believe that feminism has been empowering, because it has encouraged women to realize their full career potential. Others would go further and say that the feminists have helped women fulfill their *human* potential. Amy, for example, told me that it would have been much more difficult for her to "come out" as a lesbian, if the feminists had not been there to support her. We had this exchange:

"When you 'came out,' you did not have any models. Did you feel that the feminists were helpful to you?"

Yes. Just by existing, they made me feel more comfortable. It was easier; I didn't have to hide so much. Women had already organized and formed support groups for the cause of feminism.

"New groups of women existed, where you could feel perfectly okay?"

"Yes."

To many lesbians, feminism has been a blessing. Dale, the lesbian therapist, actress, and playwright, expressed her gratitude to the feminists in these words:

Eight years ago, I needed total support, which is just what I got from the first feminist theater group I went to. My first therapist was a feminist therapist. She nurtured me, when I sorely needed it. Anything I did on my own had been criticized so much by the people around me that I could not have acknowledged my lesbianism without the support that I received from feminists. I would have to credit them for teaching me that, if we help each other to become empowered, we will become empowered ourselves.

Feminist therapists have empowered many women. The new technique used by most feminist therapists is skilled self-disclosure. A traditional therapist usually remains silent, or says, "Mmm hmm," as he or she listens to a client. A therapist who uses skilled self-disclosure enters into a mutual relationship with the client instead. Miriam Greenspan, a feminist therapist whom I interviewed, elaborates:

I write about skilled self-disclosure in my book, *A New Approach to Women and Therapy*. But it shouldn't be another dogma. A therapist should use this new approach only if she or he feels comfortable with it.

How does a therapist use self-disclosure properly? You need to know who you are. You need to be aware of yourself: your own purposes, intentions and motivations. Many therapists are not very self-aware. Remember, you are serving someone else. You have to be careful not to use the client as a captive audience—not to exploit her for your own needs. Skilled use of self-disclosure does not mean abusing your power as a therapist or losing your boundaries with a client. It certainly does not mean having sexual relations with a client. With this new approach, it is harder to define the therapist-patient boundaries.

Many therapists avoid skilled self-disclosure because it destroys the traditional male model of intimacy. It suggests that you should be able to talk with a client without the cloak of objectivity and neutrality. In general, male therapists have a much tougher time revealing themselves. But women therapists do not have to buy into the male model. They can create their own. They can give themselves permission to be themselves and allow their own personalities to emerge.

A feminist therapist who discloses herself skillfully can be an excellent role model. Miriam Greenspan declared:

Do I act as a role model for my clients? Yes simply because I have a relationship with them. All therapists are role models. But one can intentionally cultivate this kind of a relationship. I do share my life with my clients and I am comfortable doing this.

One woman I interviewed gave me an example of the benefits of feminist therapy from her own experience:

I currently have a feminist therapist who is very empowered and who is also helping me to find and integrate hidden and devalued parts of myself. She has shared some significant facts about her life with me, which has been very helpful. She has been my role model and also my mentor. I have seen my own therapy style change dramatically during the 3 months I have been working with her.

Some of the women I interviewed told me that they had benefited from reading feminist books. As one interviewee put it, "It has been an affirmation of myself to read feminist authors, like Carol Gilligan, author of *In a Different Voice*, who write the truth about women." In her interview, Martha echoed the same theme. While we may not be empowered by the contemporary feminist movement, we may find inspiration—and empowerment—in feminist ideals.

Empowerment Exercises

1. *Focus on Feminist Stereotypes:* Sit down in a quiet place, close your eyes and relax. Think of all that you have read, and heard, about feminism. Visualize, one at a time, each feminist woman you know personally—or have heard of. Do any stereotypes come to your mind? Do you think of feminists as masculine-looking? As aggressive? As dominating? To the extent that you do, your thinking has probably been affected by the media. In reality, all kinds of women call themselves feminists.

2. *Journal Writing: My Thoughts about Feminism:* In your Empowerment Journal, jot down your thoughts about how feminism does or does not empower women. Has the feminist movement affected you? If so, how? Think of examples of women you know, or have heard of, who have been empowered, or held back, by feminism. If nothing still comes to your mind, reread this chapter. Perhaps it will inspire you to take one position or the other.

3. *Create a "New Platform" for Feminism:* Are you satisfied with the priorities of today's feminist movement? Or do you think serious issues are being ignored that should be dealt with? Make a list, either

on paper, on a tape or in your mind, of at least three major concerns of women that their leaders should address. How many of them are being given top priority now?

Skeptical of the old feminist movement, and inspired by the "new" femininity, do you want to fully empower yourself? Are you ready to "take the chance?"

11

LET OTHER WOMEN BE YOUR TEACHERS

Pro-choice, pro-life,
Left-wing, center-wing, and right,
Side by side, we march together
singing a single song:
"We're free, you and me,
To be who we are.
We find our strength within
And through each other."

r. r. j.

What can all the empowered women you have been reading about do for you? Each of them can be your teacher, just like the women with whom you will have empowering relationships in the future. Joy believes that she has become empowered this way.

Joy: Everyone Is My Teacher

"Would you like to interview me in my brand-new hot tub?" Joy asks. "Of course," I reply. After I hang up the telephone, I still can't believe my ears.

Two weeks later, I knock on Joy's front door. My tape recorder over my shoulder, I follow her through her living room and down the stairs. Everywhere I look there are brightly colored hearts, doormats, snack dishes, wall hangings, even pillows on the couch. I wonder why.

The hot tub is even more beautiful than I anticipated. It is outside on a wooden deck, completely surrounded by sky-high trees. Wearing bathing suits, we climb into the 100-degree water, twice as hot as the air outside. Our conversation is interrupted only by the movement of the exquisitely warm liquid surrounding us.

"Why do you have all the hearts in your house?" I begin.

Heart to Heart is the name of the annual festival of the network I founded 10 years ago to bring all the New Age organizations in my city together. Over 700 individuals and groups—all of whom care about creating more peace, joy, love and harmony in the world—now belong to my network. My purpose is to create unity among them, just as I have striven to integrate the different parts of my self.

It is up to me what I get out of my relationships. Some of my most negative relationships have been the most empowering. For example, being involved with my mother, who is mentally ill, has made me much, much stronger. She was schizophrenic, even before I was born. When I was very young, I would watch her burn my clothes and tear up photographs of me. I didn't know that she was sick; I thought that was the way every mother was. Joy strokes her gray shoulder-length hair, which curls softly around her face.

My mother left me when I was 3 years old. I did not see her again until I was 15. As I was sent from foster home to foster home, I always believed that my mother would come back to me. In my fantasy, she was a beautiful woman who was going to be well soon. Then one day I heard that my mother was out of the hospital and was living nearby with my grandmother. So I went to see my mother. Rather than being beautiful, she was an extremely fat woman with no front teeth who talked to herself constantly. I was scared to death of her!

Although my relationship with my mother has been the most difficult one in my life, without it, I would not be as strong as I am today. I have visited her regularly and have taken my daughters along on many occasions. Sometimes my mother would pull up her dress or dance around in the middle of the room. When we would bring her 2 half-gallons of ice cream, she would sit down and eat both of them at the same time! Joy laughs. Although my daughters were afraid to be with her at first, they have learned to love her unconditionally.

Dealing with my mother has been an extraordinary challenge for me. Remembering how she had burned my possessions, and how afraid I had been for my life, it has been very difficult to love her. As I have struggled, I have gone deeper into myself and gotten to know myself much better. Her musical voice, with its lilting Southern accent, has become louder.

From age 3 to age 15, I was in at least a dozen different foster homes. Nevertheless my father always came to see me regularly. Although his visits were very short, he used to take me and my friends out and buy us balloons. He was totally magical—larger than life. Taking my father off his pedestal has been a very important part of my personal growth.

Everyone and everything in my life has been my teacher. The grass is one of my teachers. I make love to the grass. I lie down on it and put my body close to the green blades. Mother Earth is another one of my teachers. As I feel my kinship to the Earth, I commit myself to connecting with God and Nature. Joy gracefully gestures with her arms toward the ground.

Religion has always been very important to me. In one of my foster homes, we went to church, Sunday school, Wednesday night services and Sunday night services. That was four times a week. Plus we had to learn the entire catechism. We weren't allowed to do anything enjoyable on Sunday, not even play canasta or read the comics.

In one church that I went to, there was a Sunday School teacher who was very, very prim and proper. She looked like the epitome of purity; she didn't wear any makeup at all. I decided that, if I was going to be a "good girl," I should be just like this teacher. You see, I was sure that I was a sinner. For a while, I had been thinking about what it would be like to make love and having sexual fantasies. I wanted to wear red lipstick and rouge. When I looked at this teacher, I was sure that she never had any thoughts like this.

When this teacher and I went on a church retreat together, I had a truly enlightening experience. She slept in the bunk under mine. One night, while we were undressing together, I discovered that she had enormous falsies under her bra! Before I had seen her as pure; now I saw her as namby-pamby. Knowing her hypocrisy totally liberated me. I was inspired to be more real—let it all hang out. She taught me something very important, something that had nothing to do with religion at all.

Although I resisted my Christian training, some of what I was exposed to must have penetrated. I believe that God is everywhere and is in everything. Later on, this idea came back to me as an inner teaching.

After prep school and college, I got married to a doctor. Soon afterwards, I noticed that my vision in my right eye was getting weaker and weaker. I was seeing light flashes and black dots; it seemed as if an opaque covering was growing over this eye. I kept telling my husband, and he kept saying not to worry. I was sure that he would know if something was the matter. The possibility that my husband was wrong did not cross my mind. Maybe once in a while it did, but I wanted to believe my husband.

So I kept on thinking everything was fine. Instead my symptoms got worse and worse. Finally, I decided to go to an opthalmologist. He told me that I had a disease in both of my eyes and put me in the hospital immediately. He was not sure whether or not my right eye could be saved. Suddenly I realized that I couldn't always trust my husband to know what was right. After all, he had told me for a long time that nothing was wrong with me. There is a long silence.

When I entered the hospital, everything in my life came to a screeching halt. You see, I hadn't had children yet or even made a head start on my career. My whole world had turned upside down.

For the first time, I took matters into my own hands. I said that I would not have surgery in my hometown; I would seek out a world-famous opthalmologist. On December 30, I went up to John's Hopkins. This doctor operated on me the next night, New Year's Eve. He looked at me and said, "There is a 50-50 chance that I can save your eye. I will give you my very best."

After the surgery, I couldn't see anything. My husband, who was studying to be a psychiatrist, could hardly stay in my hospital room. He could deal with his patients, who were strangers, but he could not listen to me express my emotions because I was his wife. It was too painful for him. At that time, I was totally blind in one eye, and I could barely see light out of the left one. I was feeling so low that I started questioning whether or not there was a God, if this terrible thing was happening to me. I felt 100 percent alone.

Although there were no guarantees, I made the decision to have laser surgery—3 times. It worked. My husband and I divorced. Eventually, I was able to get a job in a child guidance clinic. It was my good fortune that I had a supervisor who adored me. She was my admirer, my friend and my mentor. She gave me lots of space to express myself; she would listen to my every inner feeling. It was an experience I had thirsted for.

Then I started psychoanalysis. It lasted for 8 years, even after I moved to another city. My analyst believed that, because I had lived with so many different people as a child, it would not be a good idea for me to change therapists. So I would lie on the kitchen floor of my new home and have my sessions on the phone.

During my psychoanalysis, I began seeing more and more—with my eyes and in my mind. My analyst encouraged me to be myself, instead of trying to fit myself into a mold. He was able to be with me in a way that was quite profound. I was into meditation and reincarnation experiences, which many analysts want nothing to do with. But he was willing to learn.

I began to realize that a lot of my life I had been preoccupied with superficial, visual things. Since I had been a beauty queen at college, my physical appearance was extremely important to me. Now I realized that what really mattered was to search for truth within, even if it meant being different from the crowd. I began to surrender to my inner voice. I started to ignore what other people told me to do, when it didn't feel right to me.

Now I have a wonderful man in my life. He is there only because I decided to start working on my own personal growth.

I enjoy organizing my annual festivals, with the assistance of volunteers. I know that, as we work on projects together, petty disagreements melt away, and we get to experience our oneness in relationship with each other. I support everyone around me in learning to be with his or her inner self. This is what my job is really about. People are working together with the goal of loving. Under these circumstances, other people are catalysts for inner growth. That's empowerment. Joy's voice is clear and decisive.

"Joy," a deep male voice calls. "It's almost dinner time." "I know," she calls back. Reluctantly we both climb out of the hot tub. As we feel the cold evening air, we shiver simultaneously. After wrapping ourselves in towels, Joy turns to me. "I hope you learned something from me today. For 2 hours, you have been my teacher. After talking to you, I understand myself even better."

Joy and I had formed a mutually empowering relationship. I had gone to see her to find out what she could teach me, and I ended up teaching her.

How Do Women Become Empowered?

The mass media does not empower women. In a male-oriented publishing industry, books about empowered women are rare finds. As one woman I interviewed put it, "There are no resources. How can you possibly know how you are supposed to be?" The largest-circulation women's magazines still push either traditional "femininity" or the trendy "having it all." A traditionally "feminine" woman is portrayed as having a sexy body, a pleasing personality and a husband. A woman who "has it all" (a husband, a career and children), is rarely portrayed as she really is: overworked, underpaid and perpetually exhausted. Either way, a woman is playing a power-under role in a power-over relationship. She is not becoming empowered together with anyone else.

With the rise of the feminist movement, women have been offered a third unliberating option: total devotion to a career. Still, nothing has significantly changed. Women are still being told how they *should* be, rather than being encouraged to make their own choices.

Then why have a few women managed to make a breakthrough? Where has their inspiration come from? Certainly not from reading women's magazines. Armed with my tape recorder, I spent two years asking women this question. As I talked to dozens of them, I kept asking myself, "Why are some of these women empowered and others not?"

The results were fascinating. Almost all the empowered women I interviewed said that they had a female role model: either a mother, a grandmother or an aunt; a friend; or even a woman they did not know, whose life they had read about or heard about. Other women told me that they had a mentor, who had helped them advance in their career. From time to time, I heard about an unforgettable message that one woman had received from another women, which had made a significant difference.

While many women were fortunate enough to have had these opportunities, others did not. At the beginning of my research, I wondered, "If your mother and female relatives were not empowered, are you destined to a life of powerlessness?" "Not necessarily," I concluded. Both my research and my own personal experience reveal that it is possible for an adult woman with no girlhood role models or other "teachers" to educate herself to become empowered. What you need is appropriate personal experience. *You can become empowered now.*

My own adult empowerment experience was the La Jolla Program. After spending 2 weeks in this community, I believed I could do anything. Why? Because my relationships with the other community members had empowered me. They had all been my teachers, especially the women. Each woman had made a unique contribution to my empowerment, and I had made my own contribution to hers.

When I reflected upon the dialogues the women and I had, both spoken and unspoken, I discovered that women become empowered together in 10 different ways. Women usually become empowered by imitating a role model. If they don't happen to have one, they can find one. A woman can also become empowered by observing women who reflect her own personality traits, both good and bad. She can learn from women who give her an important message; create a satisfying career with the assistance of a mentor; and connect with her past through encounters with women who bring back long-hidden memories. Through her sisters, she can experience healing—and empowerment.

The 10 Dynamics of Empowerment

Your empowerment originates in your relationships with other women. You observe them; you talk with them; you argue with them; and you weep with them.

Your mother, your grandmothers, your daughters, your female co-workers and your women friends can be your teachers, if you pay attention to your deepest feelings when you are together. As you get to know these women, you will get to know yourself.

l. Mirrors: Women Who are Like You
Mirrors offer you the gift of self-awareness.

When you find yourself thinking, "This woman is just like me," you have met a mirror. As you watch and listen to her, you see aspects of yourself more clearly. "This is how I really am. This is how life really is for me." Women who mirror your best traits make you feel proud of yourself. You will gravitate toward them. Women who mirror your faults make you feel embarrassed, but let you know how others see you. When you meet a woman who has your worst traits, you may immediately want to run from her. The person you are avoiding is really yourself!

Seeing women who remind you of yourself helps you answer the questions, "Who am I, and where am I now?" If there are many mirrors in your life, you will feel in community with all of them. Knowing that there are other women whose lives, goals or personality traits are similar to yours is empowering.

Your sister, if you have one, is a mirror. She can help you see yourself more clearly. You and your sister are alike in some ways and different in others.

Sometimes parents put labels on sisters to tell them apart. This can keep sisters from understanding themselves and each other. In my family, I was the "brainy" one; my younger sister was the "social" one. Even when I was going out 3 or 4 times a week and my sister was staying home and studying for her Master's degree in social work, the labels still stuck. Now that my parents are no longer alive, I see my sister as she really is. I appreciate that she has intelligence and that I have the capacity to form empowering relationships.

If you have a sister, it may be difficult for you to find out who you really are, especially if she is close to you in age. At first, you identify with her: "I am who my sister is. We both have artistic talent. We both get good grades. We both have brown hair." A young girl who feels that she is exactly the same as her sister is confused. She needs to find out that they are two separate, but similar, people.

Later on, you discover that you are different from her: "I am what my sister is not. She is talkative, and I am quiet. She is smart, and I am athletic. She has lots of friends, and I do not." A teenager who decides simply to be different from her sister, regardless of the consequences, will become someone she is not, rather than who she really is.

Eventually, you realize that you are a complete self—neither a carbon copy of your sister nor a rebellion against her. Your relationships with other women friends evolve the same way.

2. Models: Women You Would Like to Be Like

A model offers you the gift of inspiration: "I can do what she did."

Models who are ahead of you in the struggle for empowerment show you the way. If you listen to them, they will tell you how they did it. As you observe other women who have empowered themselves, you learn what to expect, as you follow the same path.

A feminist therapist with whom I talked sums up how important modeling is in empowering women:

Most depressed women I see have oppressed women in their families. They come into my office saying, "I feel depressed, weak and worthless" and then talk about some woman they are related to who is a "door mat." I can generalize and say that there seems to be a connection between having a strong female family role model and becoming an empowered woman.

Another therapist adds:

One of the three main causes of low-grade depression is having a depressed mother. If your mother was depressed, you have may have modeled yourself after a woman who viewed herself as an inadequate person playing an empty role.

In contrast, many women are fortunate to have mothers, grandmothers and aunts who are positive role models. For example, Vera, a top administrator in the scientific community, told me how her grandmother and mother were examples of feminine empowerment:

My grandmother was an empowered woman. She ran a boarding house, which was exactly what she enjoyed doing, and took care of my grandfather, who was disabled. She also educated all seven of her children. Whoever wanted to go to college was able to go. All but one attended.

Always my grandmother had her mind on her profession. Although she was born during the Civil War when few women were educated, she was a member of the first class of Mississippi College that was open to women in the 1880s. They used to talk about it. Her father got out his horse and cart, saddled the horse, put a bale of cotton in the cart, put my grandmother on the bale of hay and drove her off to college. The bale of cotton served as her tuition piyment! She studied there for 2 years. After that, she was qualified to teach school.

My mother went to teachers college for 4 years in Texas, got an advertising job in New York and had a career in merchandising after that. She was the first president of her local department store labor union. She was the subject of a [upreme Court legal case. They fired her, and she carried it all the way to the top.

During my childhood, my mother was busy with her own projects. She was out most of the time and, when she was in, she was always on the phone. My mother never baked birthday cakes or did things like that. Although she supported me in going to Girl Scout Camp, she didn't get involved in my other activities, like biking and hiking. But she didn't tear me down either. She simply had her own work. I was never told I had to "be a lady," fix my hair, get a manicure or mind my clothes. Not much attention was paid to these things. It was obvious that my mother was unhappy with her marriage, so there was no emphasis on the importance of getting a husband. Marriage was a subject we pretty much avoided.

Reverend Judith Goode said that she was inspired by the examples set by her grandmother and aunt:

My grandmother was a very imposing figure. She was about 6 feet tall and had a voice and a laugh that reminded me of Eleanor Roosevelt. Most important, she had a very strong sense of who she was. As soon as you met her, you knew that she stood for something—and that she was somebody.

Whenever my grandmother came to town, she used to "drag" me to visit all the old and sick people she knew. Some of them had no food, so we brought fruitcakes and other things for them to eat. I used to hate sitting in these people's living rooms—parlors, as they were called then. I was bored to tears. I could not understand why my grandmother visited these people and why she insisted upon taking me along. Now I realize that she wanted to show me something: that my brothers and sisters are whoever I connect with. That's what I learned from my grandmother. She showed compassion to whoever came into her life.

Another strong woman in my family was my Aunt Leila. She was a businesswoman who scrimped and saved until she built a business that was worth almost a million dollars. For a black family in the '50s, this was most unusual! My Aunt Leila used her wealth to buy houses all over the neighborhood for her relatives to live in. Until I was about 5 years old, my family and I lived in one. What I remember most vividly about Aunt Leila is how she never let circumstances overwhelm her. No matter what happened, she just kept going. In my own life, I have done the same thing.

Stacey, the reporter, had a whole family of role models, both male and female.

My dad is a psychiatrist, and I've always respected him. There were many successful men and women, and strong women, in my family. My great-aunt started a big nursing school in Dallas and traveled all over Europe. She used to say, "I don't know why they call me Miss; I ain't Miss Nothing!" Both of my father's parents were psychiatrists. His mother went to Berkeley in the 1920s and was the first woman psychoanalyst in Dallas. She was my idol. I

have a picture of her in medical school—one woman surrounded by 3 dozen men.

Lynda, the editorial writer at one of the nation's leading newspapers, described to me her mother, who was a different kind of role model.

My mother has a graduate degree, a Master's degree in social work, which was very unusual for a woman to have in the '20s. She worked until three of us were born. My father was a doctor. One day a patient of his said to her, "Isn't it too bad that the doctor isn't doing well?" My mother said, "What do you mean?" and the patient replied, 'Well, you're working, aren't you?" My mother was so offended that she quit working, just to preserve my father's reputation, although he had never objected to her having a job. She stayed home with us for a long time, until my youngest brother went to college. At the age of 61, she took the civil service exam all over again and finished first in the city. After that, she had a very rewarding 10-year career. I didn't make the same choices my mother did, but I did work, 3 days a week, while my children were growing up.

A mother can be a positive role model, even if she has neither had a successful career nor enjoys raising children. Vicki, the administrative assistant to a corporation president, told me about what she learned from her mother:

My mother was a very bright, intellectual, multi-talented woman. She loved music, art and languages, especially Latin. She could also draw beautifully. Although she had all these talents, she never managed to forge a career for herself. Perhaps it was beyond her grasp. Although she and her sisters had gone to Bryn Mawr, my mother never got her degree. She dropped out, got married and had eight children. All of her sisters had pursued careers, which was quite unusual for women at that time. One became a physicist; another went to medical school; a third went into the theater.

Believe it or not, my mother totally disdained housework; I never saw her with a broom in my life. I don't think motherhood brought out the best side of her. All of us went to boarding school when we were young; I started when I was 10! She never really did her job as a mother.

When we were children, instead of playing house, we would play "cocktail party." We didn't pretend that we were cooking dinner; we pretended that we were at a party holding cocktail glasses and having conversations. That's how we observed our parents. I never played "house," because my mother never took care of the house. My parents did inspire us to make great friendships, so that's what we imitated.

From her mother's example, Vicki learned to nurture her friends.
You will inevitably encounter women whom you *don't* want to be

like. By being the opposite of who they are, you may become empowered. Sometimes your mother can be this kind of negative model. Julia, the self-employed businesswoman, told me:

Sometimes you are who you are because of negative experiences. As a child, I had a lot of bad feelings toward my mother. I did not want to be like her. My mother depended on other people, particularly my father, who supported her financially, to make her happy. She never accomplished anything special; she did not work for a living. So, when I became a teenager, I wanted to go to college and graduate school, so I could support myself.

Sometimes your mother is a negative model, when you see her in a power-over relationship. One woman I interviewed said:

My family is extremely traditional. My father worked; my mother did not. My mother was a helpless woman, which made me very angry. At a fairly early age, I concluded that I would never get married. I did not see that my mother benefited by being married, and I did not want to be trapped the same way.

This feeling was also expressed by Terri, the high-level military executive:

I came from a very poor family; we had few material goods and certainly no privileges. The work ethic was, "Don't do your homework; do the housework instead. Come straight home from school and take care of your brothers and sisters." To get credentials that I could respect, I had to get away from my family environment and achieve something. I wanted to be a little bit better than average, anything but middle of the road.

I didn't want to be just somebody's wife or somebody's mother. I couldn't imagine myself being a housewife. Why not? I watched my parents' marriage; it wasn't a happy one. My mother was very passive. She did all the work, while my father lost his paychecks at the racetrack. When I saw my father dominate my mother, I thought, "No one is ever going to be able to do this to me!"

Sometimes women who don't have a role model in their family make a conscious decision to find one elsewhere. Jayne, the laboratory scientist, described her experience like this:

I knew that I needed to have my own role models; clearly my mother wouldn't do. So I found a couple of professors, and one good friend, to imitate. Last year, I taught in an elementary after-school science program. I wanted to make sure that these girls would have at least one good role model. They would all be more fortunate than I was.

Jayne deliberately chose to find empowering role models—and then to be one to others.

It is not always necessary to know your model personally. You may want to be like a woman you have heard of or read about. If you don't have the opportunity to meet many empowered women, "long-distance modeling" may be a helpful strategy for you. You may be inspired by a famous woman whom you have never met. Terri, the military executive, told me how she found her role models in library books:

To be true to myself, I had to lead my life the way I thought was best. I had read a lot, every biography in my elementary school library. There was a series about the lives of famous people; I read every single book in it. Amelia Earhart, Clara Barton and Louisa May Alcott stand out in my mind. Later on, when I went to college, I was an English and history major. I read more books about the lives of famous women. The message I got was that, if you are going to be extraordinary, you can't buy into the lifestyle of what women in society are doing at the time.

I read about novelist George Sand and how she would stay up all night writing. She'd get up about 4:00 in the afternoon, visit with her kids, socialize, have dinner, start writing about 8:00 at night and continue until 3 or 4 in the morning. What I concluded was that George Sand was able to write because she maintained a bizarre lifestyle. So when a friend or a member of my family would suggest that I be more "feminine," I would reply, "Yes, that's true, if I want to be like Gidget. But, if I want to be like Amelia Earhart or George Sand, I have to be different. I can't be like most other women."

Dale, the therapist, actress and playwright, was also inspired by famous women whom she read about during her childhood:

I have always read women's biographies. When I was a little girl, I would go to the Easy Reader shelves in the library and read all the books that were there. There were only a few stories about women, mainly Betsy Ross, Elizabeth Blackwell (the first woman physician) and Madame Curie. Because reading was difficult for me, I did not understand the exact details of each woman's contribution. But I would always know the answer to the question, "How did she do what she did?" For example, I didn't know Madame Curie's theory, but I knew about how she fought against the odds. Every woman I read about had something inside her that kept her going while other people were saying, "You can't do this, because you are a woman." All the books I loved were about women who achieved something.

Although Dale did not realize that she was a lesbian until after she grew up, she had selected two lesbian celebrities as role models. Maddeningly, I cannot use their names. In today's society, openly admitting one's lesbianism can be a liability.

Xxx Xxxx and Yyy Yyyy have been big role models for me. From a very early age, I loved Xxx Xxxx's work. When I heard that she was creating with another woman, I was so excited. (Later on I found out that they were lovers.) The combination of Xxx's theatrical ability, Yyy's ability as a writer and their mutual humor is remarkable. Humor is the vehicle that I use in my own plays to make a statement. Of course, I would pick as models two lesbian women who expressed themselves theatrically!

Modeling is not always conscious. You may be modeling yourself after a woman, but be unaware of it. A female district attorney whom I interviewed put it this way:

My mother was in business all her life, even before she graduated from college. She was really ahead of her time. People would call her a "women's lib person" today, although the word hadn't been invented then. During her lifetime, my mother ran three different businesses, all of which were successful. She worked very, very hard.

I did not consciously see my mother as an example. I never did things because I was conscious of doing them or because I wanted to fit in a mold. I just did what I did because it came naturally. I had always seen women work; my mother worked; and there was never any question in my mind that I would work. That's just what women did.

My own experience with models was more complex than the experiences of the women I interviewed. I had no close female relatives who were empowered. As long as my father was alive, my mother followed his every order, even refusing to work when he told her it would make him feel like he had failed as a breadwinner. My mother used to tell me, "A woman is like an empty vessel. She takes the shape of whatever is poured into her. A 'lady' does not lead; she follows."

I wanted to become empowered, but I did not know how. So I began my own search for models, although I was not conscious of it at the time. Three of my college professors, two of them young married women with Ph.D.s—were my first choices. The third, an older, widowed psychology professor, immediately perceived that I was seeking something she had. Dr. Wise was not only my model but also my message-bearer. She sat me down and had some memorable "long talks" with me, one culminating with the memorable message, "If you want to be both attractive and empowered, go wash your hair!"

Upon graduation from college, I put my search for role models on hold. I got married, earned my Ph.D. and had three sons—all within 8 years. But, after my husband left, I was forced to face my own feelings of powerlessness again. I finally managed to find one empowered woman in Miami Beach, my children's elementary school principal. She was an older married woman who also had three sons. I imagined how I might be like her 20 years hence. She told me how she had gotten her B.A. and her Ph.D. when her children were in school, told her husband that she wanted to teach and then climbed the rungs of the school system's ladder. I absorbed her words like a sponge.

When I eventually moved back Washington, D. C., my adopted home, I renewed my ties with my college friends, many of whom were empowered women themselves. One of them became my mirror; another, my mentor. I went into therapy for about 6 months. Slowly I perceived small, but visible, changes in myself. I stopped taking orders from men. My children and I became even more empowered together with each other. I started asking myself, "What do *you* want to do with *your* life, Riki?" My answer startled me. Eventually I concluded, "Empowerment is contagious. Having relationships with empowered women has empowered me."

Choose models who fit you. Although you may admire a woman very much, it may be inappropriate—or uncomfortable—for you to become like her. It is best to select women as models who represent who you want to be, not who you think you "should" be. My Miami Beach elementary school principal was a good fit at the time. For 3 years, I gained great satisfaction from working toward a second bachelor's degree in elementary education, teaching second graders and raising my own three sons.

Sometimes, you may want to get emotionally close to a woman you know who is your model. When you are with her, you may feel extremely inspired. A woman who not only mirrors many of your best traits but also models your ideal self can be a real confidence-builder.

Expect to "look up" to your model. Do not compare yourself with her; you will inevitably become discouraged. Since you have deliberately chosen someone whom you want to imitate, her role is to be ahead of you. When you have achieved all she has achieved, she will no longer be your model!

3. Message-Bearers: Women Who Have Something to Teach You

Message-bearers offer you the gift of an important, relevant message about yourself.

They will share their reactions about how you are acting and what you are saying. "This is how I see you." "This is how I experience you." After they have given you information about yourself, they may also offer you their advice. "This is what I would do, if I were you." Keep in mind that a message-bearer's feedback is influenced by where she is in her own life.

These are the women who care the most about you, because they are telling you how they really feel about you. Their messages are often shared when you least want, or expect, to hear them. At first, you may feel scared, or even threatened, by a message-bearer. Probably, you are resisting what she has to say. Your feelings may be so intense that you even want to run away. Later on you may feel deeply grateful to her.

Four of the women I interviewed were message-bearers to me. Nancy, Stacey and Nora reminded me that, in any situation, there is always a choice, and Isabelle told me to "take more chances." This is what they said:

• Nancy, retired senior citizen:

Early in my life, I made three conscious decisions. Each one has empowered me:

First, I decided to get as much schooling as I could. Having lived through the Depression and seen its effects on people, I realized that money, land, houses and jobs can all go down the drain very fast, if there's an economic bust. Education can't.

Second, when necessary I have changed my occupation. I have gone from accounting to personnel work to teaching and to counseling, as new opportunities have opened up for me.

Third, I decided to be happy, instead of unhappy. I made this decision when I was in my teens. I realized that I could look at things with either a pessimistic or an optimistic outlook. So my motto became, "Make the least of the worst and the most of the best." Throughout my life, I have continued to choose happiness. Underneath my gray hair, there's a lot of vitality!

You know, every second of your life you make a choice . You put your arms and your legs and your heart and your brain somewhere. No one has chains on you. Women often lose track of this.

Whenever you feel "done to" or "pushed," stop and search out the choice points. You may end up doing the same thing, but you will do it because you chose it, not because you think you "should." The feeling is different; it really is. I've tested this out myself. Don't ever give up your right to make choices.

Go through all of the reasons you've been telling yourself you "have to" do it and find out how come you've chosen to do it. When you say, "I should" or "I have to," you're putting in "push" words, where "choice" words ought to be.

• Stacey, 23-year-old newspaper reporter:

I tell my friends, "If you don't like your situation, change it. If you don't want to change it, because it's getting you to where you really want to go, then remember that, and enjoy where you are for what it's worth."

I am empowered because I realize that I can live the way I want to. I don't allow other people to run my life. If they try, I distance myself and nip it in the bud.

Yes, I practice what I preach. At age 19, I got tired of college and dropped out in the middle of a semester. It took me 3 months to realize I needed that degree and I was not in school for my parents. So I went back and graduated on schedule. Then I got a trailer, took my dog and moved to Santa Fe; I didn't like it there, so I left. Why? It's my life, and I can do whatever I want with it.

- Nora, television marketing executive and mother of two:

Sometimes my mother cries, "Why didn't your husband leave you with a dot of money, the way Susie's husband did? Why do you have to struggle?" What she doesn't understand is that my life is not that much of a struggle for me. I don't want Susie's life; I want my life. That's what I've chosen. I have never had a job I didn't like or lived in a place I didn't like. I find opportunities and then make up my mind to get the most from them.

- Isabelle, married free-lance writer, pregnant with her first child:

Take more chances. One of the signs that I have on my desk is, "Ask." Sometimes I find myself saying, "I don't want to call so and so. I'm scared." When this happens, I stop and say to myself, "Don't be afraid to take the risk. The worst thing that can happen is that the other person will say 'No.'" I continually remind myself that, if I want something, I must ask for it.

These four women were message-bearers to me, because I learned something about myself from each of them.

4. Memory-Links: Women Who Stir Up Memories Within You

Memory-links offer you the gift of reminding you of experiences that you have long forgotten.

They will share their own experiences, which are similar to yours in some ways, and different in others. A memory-link tells you, "This is how it is for me now" or "This is how it was for me then."

When Stacey told me about how her father had encouraged her intellectual growth, she became a memory-link to me. Stacey reminded me of how my own father had supported me the same way.

When you are with a memory-link, you may feel nostalgic, sad or joyous, depending upon what is taking place in your life now or what kind of experiences she is making you recall. Getting in touch with your real feelings about what has happened to you in the past is very empowering.

5. Mothers, Sisters, Grandmothers and Aunts: Family Members or Women Who Remind You of Members of Your Family

Mothers, sisters, grandmothers and aunts offer you the gift of connecting with your family heritage. Those in nearby generations you have already gotten to know personally. Others you may have heard family stories about. Both hearsay and personal contact enable you to know yourself better. As Dr. Jacqueline Light puts it:

Like every woman, I was in a generational line with the other women in my family—not just the women I knew but also the women I heard about. There are a lot of stories in families. For example, my great-grandmother, who was the child of a slavemaster, learned to read as a former slave. She was later given formal education and ended up starting her own school. A grandmother of mine decided to split herself off from her husband and his family and move to another city, in order to have control of her own and her children's future. You hear these stories and you use them in your own life.

You know your own mother, and you probably know your grandmother, but you didn't know your grandmother as a young woman. And you definitely didn't know your great-grandmother. You have to take all these women into account, in order to know where your own characteristics come from.

Darlene, Vera's 23-year-old daughter, made this statement to me:

In the past, my mother and grandmother's impressive accomplishments have made me run in the other direction. I have rebelled against everything that they stood for. Yet you cannot live with parents and grandparents and avoid their influence. You cannot be brought up by people without becoming a part of them.

Now I find that, when I am on my own and outside of their sphere of influence, I find myself responding to my friends, "This is something my mother says all the time." When I go shopping, I find myself buying the same vegetables that my mother buys. When I am discussing nuclear energy, I find myself bragging about my grandmother and her anti-nuclear protests. After evaluating her views, I have incorporated them into my own. Yes, I have grown up to be myself. But I also have grown up to be a part of the women who have raised me—a reflection and a legacy.

Some women grow up with a mother who is emotionally distant or who has passed away. They have to receive, and learn about, nurturing from someone else. This was the case with Vicki, the assistant to the president of a large corporation. Although Vicki's mother did not have an empowering relationship with her, Vicki's older sister reached out to fill the void. As she told me:

Having had a fairly distant relationship with her own mother, my mother went on to have seven children. My mother wasn't a "natural" mother, nor did she have someone close to her to serve as a model. My older sister became my mother. She was the one who told me I needed a bra, and what menstruation was.

Because of her older sister's positive influence, Vicki went on to nurture three children of her own, including a daughter.

Charlotte, the high school guidance counselor I interviewed, described her experience with mother substitutes this way:

My mother died when I was 6 months old. After that I had a lot of relationships with mother figures. The one who was paramount in my life was my great-grandmother. She was an old woman, well-respected in the neighborhood. My great-grandmother had great pride in herself. Her husband was dead, but she owned her land—more than a hundred acres. All the people, including the whites, called her "Aunt Emma." We would laugh about how everyone called her "Aunt," instead of "Mrs." But I had genuine respect for Aunt Emma. As a little girl, I always ran around with her.

Then there was my grandmother, whom I dearly loved. I was named after her. I had many other "mothers": aunts, cousins and family friends. I would send cards to all these women, to honor them. By the time I was 30, I finally realized that I didn't need so many "mothers."

Charlotte went on to nurture two children of her own and have a rewarding career working with young men and women.

Mothers, sisters, grandmothers, and aunts may—or may not—play different roles for you now than they did in the past.

- You may still have mutually empowering relationships with them.
- You may once have had empowering relationships with them, which you now miss.
- You may have power-over relationships with these relatives, and now choose to distance yourself from them.

By understanding how your relationships with these different women have evolved, you will understand yourself better.

A woman you meet may become a substitute for a member of your family who has died or who lives far away. At first you may not understand why you yearn to reach out to her. You may even want to hug her. After you get acquainted, you will want to tell your new "mother," "sister," "grandmother" or "aunt" why her friendship means so much to you.

6. Mentors: Women Who Show You The Way

Mentors offer you the gift of realizing your potential.

Behind every accomplished woman is usually a mentor. A mentor teaches you what you need to know about your chosen field of work. Sometimes she actually finds or creates a job for you. She may also extend your network of business contacts.

Charlotte's professional life was vastly enriched, because she had a mentor:

When I went to high school, there was an English teacher-counselor who decided that I was somebody special. She always gave me extra books to read and helped me practice taking tests. She didn't just give me information on scholarships; she took me to the intercollegiate exams. I don't know many women who have fortunate enough to have a mentor like her. Later on, I became a high school counselor, too.

My mentor stayed in my life for many years afterwards. From time to time, she would call long distance and tell me, "Get a pencil and paper." Then she would call out names. "You need to get in touch with these people," she would insist.

Once she said, "Get to know Thelma Thomas Daly," an outstanding black woman who was president of the American Association of Counseling and Development. A few days later, I went to a meeting, and Thelma Thomas Daly walked into the room. Although she was much older than I, we became very good friends. Right before she died, my mentor and I gave a party for her and presented her with a plaque. Thelma Thomas Daly was so delighted—and we were so proud!

No matter what field you are in, you can usually point out at least one woman who might be a mentor for you. At first, you may feel a bit in awe of your mentor and be nervous in her presence. Later on, you will delight in sharing your achievements with her.

7. Messmakers: Women Who Provoke You

A messmaker offers you the gift of confrontation with someone who threatens you.

You probably know at least one hostile, disruptive woman. When she starts arguing or loudly criticizing, other people may express feelings of fear, anger or disgust. You yourself may feel intimidated by her. Because you may not want to hear what she is saying, you will want to shout back at her, or else leave.

Joanne, a student at a black university where I taught political science 20 years ago, was a messmaker in my life. After I had delivered my first lecture, I had given out a reading list of books about the glories of the American political system, all written by white men. After I distributed the lists, Joanne suddenly lost her temper. Standing up next to her desk, she shouted, "All of this talk is nothing but intellectual masturbation. These reading lists are meaningless. We're not connecting with each other at all. We're not talking about political reality, as it exists for black people. We're just talking about the world the way white men see it."

The class was in an uproar. Neelless to say, I was embarrassed and visibly upset. my initial reaction was to run and hide. But, the more I thought about what Joanne had said, the more I realized that Joanne's messmaking had taught me something. I decided to prepare a reading list of books about American politics that included books written by blacks, as well as whites. I resolved to stop lecturing and have class discussions instead. The result was an exciting classroom experience, where my students and I shared our perceptions of American politics openly and honestly.

Don't be put off by a messmaker's aggressive behavior. Many messmakers are actually "movers and shakers," who help women and other minorities break down social barriers. By boldly speaking up for what they believe in, messmakers change the world.

Confronting a messmaker empowers you. As you talk to her and listen to her, you will get in touch with your own strength. You also may find out that what you thought she said was actually not what she was saying at all. Underneath her anger is usually pain.

8. Mavericks: Women Whom You Never Expect to Meet

Mavericks offer you the gift of serendipity.

One of life's joys is its surprises. Chances are that, sometime in your life, you will meet women who are very different from you. They will share feelings and ideas that you may not be able to relate to at all. These women may be in another economic class, of another religion or from a foreign country.

Machi, the Japanese woman I interviewed, was a maverick to me. Although her background and concerns were totally different from mine, by getting to know her, I learned a great deal about Japanese women—and about myself.

At first, you will feel confused, scared or even awed when you hear the stories of maverick women. Listening to them will open up new areas of experience that you can learn about, even if you are not deeply touched.

9. Friends and Neighbors: Women Reaching out for Help

Friends and neighbors offer you the gift of assisting other women less empowered than yourself.

As you observe women who are behind you, as well as ahead of you, in the struggle for empowerment, you will see your own personal growth in a broader perspective. By reaching out to a woman who is behind you, you will enhance your life as well as hers.

You need to become mature, before you can be a teacher to another woman. Samantha, a speech pathologist and editor, describes her own experience like this:

For many years, I used to look up to other women. My friendships, for the most part, were with older women. Now, after many years of growth, I finally feel like a whole person. For the first time, I am becoming friendly with women who are younger than me.

There are many different ways to reach out to your friends and neighbors. You can consciously decide to be a mentor to one or more of them. On an unconscious level, you may also be a mirror, a model, a message bearer, a memory-link, a "mother," a messmaker or a maverick. As you play these roles you will feel more connected to these women—and to womankind.

10. Your Mutual Partner: A Man or Woman Who Grows with You

Your mutual partner benefits, along with you, from what you have learned in your relationships with other women.

As the mirrors, models, message bearers, memory-links, "mothers," mentors, messmakers and mavericks I have described enable you to discover your true identity, your capacity for mutuality will be enhanced. The more you accept yourself, the better you will relate to others.

As Darlene, Vera's 23-year-old daughter, said to me:

My relationships with other people have always been governed by my weight. Whether or not I like myself makes a big difference in how I get along with other people. If I am unhappy with myself, I am unhappy with everybody. If you tell me that you like me, I will not believe you. I think, "How could you like someone like me?" And, if you tell me that you don't like me, I think, "You have every right not to like this fat, awful person."

When I interviewed Darlene, she was striving to resolve this conflict, so that she could eventually enter into a mutual partnership.

Women who validate you, who tell you, "You are not crazy; I feel the same way," will give you the courage to be who you are. Day by day, as you get in touch with what you want, you will become more autonomous. As you start to express your own truths, little by little, you will become more authentic. As you learn to experience a give-and-take relationship with a nonthreatening member of your own sex, you will prepare yourself for a mutual partnership.

As you let other women be your teachers, you will be getting yourself ready to receive your mutual partner. He or she will pick up the torch where others have put it down.

Where Can Women Learn from Each Other?

Mutual empowerment is not an abstract theory, it is a real possibility. If women who are not yet empowered can be brought together in a close and meaningful way with empowered ones, an identification can be made. Through observation, dialogue and friendly support, we can find the inspiration we need to empower ourselves. Empowerment can be a deliberate choice, rather than an accident of birth.

Can a woman who has been raised in a male-oriented society shed her passive, deferential attitudes later in life? Can she discover herself, become autonomous, create mutual relationships and speak authentically? Yes. Although people grow very slowly, with great difficulty, and against great resistance, transformation is possible at any time. *Empowerment will occur whenever women are brought together in a supportive community.*

Empowerment Exercises

1. *Connect with the Empowered Women in This Book:* Go back to Chapter 1 and reread Dr. Jacqueline Light's story. After you reread it, ask yourself:

a. How did I feel after I reread Dr. Light's story?

b. Was she a mirror, model, message-bearer, memory-link, "mother," messmaker or maverick to me? How?

c. Would I like her to be my friend? Why or why not?

Now go back to Chapter 2, reread Vera's story, and ask yourself the same questions. Continue with Alexandra, Annette, Quincy, Wendy, Vicki, Sophie, Margaret, Dale, Lucy, Martha and all the other women who have shared their stories with you in this book.

2. *Take a Look at Your Role Models:* Ask yourself these questions:

a. Who have my female role models been up to now? My mother? My grandmother? Other family members? Female friends? Co-workers? Women I have heard of or read about?

b. Who is my role model now? What traits of hers do I admire? Exactly what does she possess that I would like to have within myself?

3. *Who Are My Mirrors?* Think of the women you know well, one at a time. Start with your grandmother and mother—and sisters and daughters, if you have any. What traits of yours do you see in them? Which of these traits do you like, and which ones embarrass you? Next consider your friends. Do most of them remind you of yourself in some ways? What qualities of yourself do you see in your friends? Or are most of your friends extremely different from you? What have your family members and friends helped you understand about yourself because of their resemblances to you?

Now that you understand how to become empowered, would you like to learn how to empower your daughter? In the next chapter, you will find out how to turn the obstacle of raising a daughter in a male-oriented society into a stepping stone.

RAISE AN
EMPOWERED
DAUGHTER

*"we dare to raise our voices
smash the bottles
learn.
Watch me learn to dare
my arms and legs feel awkward—
we came to ask your help."*

Jean Tepperman
"Going Through Changes"

Mothers and daughters can empower each other. To begin with, motherhood is an extremely empowering experience. From the moment your daughter is born, you have the opportunity to create a mutual, autonomous and authentic relationship with her. Joy, the organizer of a New Age network, told me what she gained from being a mother:

Both of my daughters have empowered me. My first daughter offered me the opportunity to feel like a good mother. She was a marvelous baby, very quiet and very pretty. I probably gave myself credit for her that I didn't deserve. My relationship with my second daughter has been a challenge. She has had limitless energy, and I have often felt very inadequate with her. But I have stuck it out. Now she is an extraordinarily caring, delightful human being.

I breastfed both of my daughters. Many women do not realize how empowering breastfeeding can be—even more than pregnancy. Nursing my daughters was ecstasy; I was so comfortable. I am grateful to my stepmother, whom I came to live with when I was 15. I watched her nurse her two babies and saw how satisfying it was both for her and for them. She was my role model.

Vera, Darlene's mother, had this to add:

I did a lot of things which expanded my abilities because Darlene was there. Having both Darlene and me to take care of, I was forced to manage better and to provide more. When I did something that I didn't particularly want to do, in order to meet her needs, I grew.

For example, last night, I went to the supermarket at 11:00. I didn't want to go. But I went anyway, because Darlene needed orange juice for break-fast. It reminded me of when Darlene was a little girl and she needed favors for her birthday party or she wanted to see Santa Claus. I had to get both of us dressed. I had to put gas in the car. There were so many steps to take, and sometimes I didn't feel like taking them. I regret the times I said to my daughter, "I don't want to do this. This is too much." But often I did do much more than I thought I could.

Before Darlene was born, a therapist said to me, "Children are the best form of personal growth there is." So I looked forward to raising her. I thought it would be like the final hour of a super-heartwarming workshop or a mo-ment when a therapist gives you an incredible insight into yourself. After Dar-lene arrived, I said to myself, "So this is what the therapist meant! It's not at all like I thought it would be; It's hard work!" Raising a child is a forced growth program. Very demanding and very rewarding.

As you both grow older, raising an empowered daughter becomes even more challenging. Most important, you must give your own self a high priority. Your nonverbal messages are, "I understand who I am"; "I know what I want and how to ask for it" and "I am someone without a man" (to paraphrase psychologist-author Penelope Russianoff). As she sees you putting yourself first, she will do as you do.

Although I have never had a daughter, I know what it is like to be one. To write this chapter, I have interviewed mothers who have raised empowered daughters, mother-daughter pairs and therapists who specialize in treating women. Interestingly enough, they all agreed about how little girls grow up to be empowered women.

Although both parents play important roles, it is the mother who is at center stage. Especially when your daughter is young, it is up to you to create the emotional climate for her empowerment. Here are eight steps you can take:

1. Be her role model:
You are the first and most important role model for your daugh-ter. If she respects you, she will want to imitate you. You teach her

by your example. It is not so much what you say, but what you do, that counts. If you are in relationships where you are empowered together with other people, your daughter will be exposed to mutuality. If you have discovered your unique identity and know how to act in your own behalf, your daughter will learn autonomy. If you are "real" with other people—and with her—she will experience authenticity.

Alexandra shares how her mother's example has empowered her:

My mother has always been open to new experiences. She has always been very, very excited about life and very curious about it. My mother used to encourage me to explore all of reality and not to be afraid of other people's differences. Our house was always full of guests; we had many exciting, fulfilling relationships with them.

My mother was also an avid reader. She audited a lot of courses while I was growing up. So I learned, "Use whatever talents you have, and don't be satisfied with the ordinary."

Your daughter is a mirror of your own self. Inevitably, she will be like you in many ways. If you want your daughter to reach for the top, first fulfill your own potential. Lucy, the blind mother of three, describes what her mother did:

It wasn't just Dad who was called to serve God; the calling was also Mom's. Both of my parents were licensed, ordained ministers. They were very active in gang work; they shared the gospel with people on the streets of Harlem. If someone called for help at 2:00 in the morning, say, a woman whose husband was beating her up, one of my parents would respond. They were always there for other people. What mattered was not my parents telling us to do good but that their lives really screamed out loud to us.

Mom was the one who really had the gift in working with the gangs; she never showed a trace of fear. She'd walk into basement tenements that we would never walk into and break up fights. Mom is a very charismatic and energetic person—definitely the driving force in the family. When Dad got an administrative job in the church and began to travel a lot, she would preach at the church. Whenever Mom found a woman in need, either pregnant out of wedlock or on drugs, she would bring the woman home to live with us.

Stacey, the newspaper reporter, says this about her childhood:

I had a wonderful time growing up. We used to get a $5 a week "book allowance" that we had to spend in the bookstore, not anywhere else. Before we were allowed to watch television, we had to make the honor roll. My mother and father never set any other formal academic requirements. But there was an unspoken standard. I used to say to them, "Well, you ask a great deal of yourselves, so I guess you expect no less from us."

If you have qualities you do *not* want your daughter to imitate, or if you make mistakes, let her know. Alexandra told me:

Although my mother is an incredibly empowered woman, she has often been frustrated in her own professional and personal lives. Although she worked outside the home on and off while we were growing up, she never continued in any one career direction. She has also had difficulty in escaping from the shackles of her own past. It is a credit to her that she was honest about her failings.

My mother knew what she did not want to do in raising us. When she did harmful things, she spoke to us about them, so that we knew that they were wrong.

As a mother, you are in a unique position to influence your daughter's behavior. For example, you can demonstrate to her how an empowered woman acts toward men. If you ask men for what you want directly, instead of manipulating them, ("Make him think it's his idea"), you have a head start in raising an empowered daughter. When your daughter grows up, she will probably imitate you.

2. Create a mutually empowering relationship with her.

If your daughter experiences mutuality while she is growing up, she will form satisfying partnerships when she becomes an adult. Even when she is a small child, do not make her feel helpless or dependent; let her experience her own strength. From the time she is a toddler, allow her to participate in the household, even if it's doing something as small as closing a door or putting away a dish. Rather than telling her what to do, make decisions together with her. "Would you rather wear the brown sweater or the blue jacket?" "Would you rather go to the park or to the zoo?"

Dr. Jacqueline Light sums it up this way:

Instead of just saying, "No," parents can help their children to do things. "You want to try to use that knife? Here, let me show you how to do it, and then you try it while I'm standing here." In this way, they don't cut off their children's curiosity.

All of us learn about relationships very early in life. If you grow up in a home where you have no effect on your parents" behavior, you will feel helpless in your relationships later on. If a parent recognizes that a child can—and does—have an important impact on everyone around him, the child will become aware of his or her own strengths.

As your daughter grows older, you can encourage her to make her own choices, rather than simply telling her what to do. Stacey told me how she benefited from this kind of upbringing:

I used to go to my parents and ask them, "What shall I do?" and they used to say, "You'll have to decide for yourself." I used to beg my dad, "You're a psychiatrist. Analyze me. What am I doing wrong? What should I be doing?" His reply was always, "I'm sorry, Stacey, you're going to have to figure that out for yourself." He wouldn't tell me anything. So I would be forced to make my own decisions. I would get a pat on the back for nearly every decision I made. That's how I learned how to take care of myself.

My mother has always said, "I have had one goal—to raise three individual, very independent girls. Unfortunately I was highly successful at it."

Your reward of giving up power over your child is your own enhanced personal growth. Your daughter's reward is learning how to be part of a team—which will empower her in her future relationships, especially with her husband and children. Someday, you may be helping to raise an empowered granddaughter.

3. Value her as much as a son.

Dr. Jacqueline Light describes the way she raised her two daughters:

My husband and I raised all our children alike in many ways. We encouraged both our son and our daughters to participate in physical activities, including competitive sports. We didn't hold the girls back, because they were "too fragile." We flexed the minds of both our son and our daughters, and we encouraged their teachers to do the same. Whenever possible, we have sought out female professionals both as caretakers and as role models for our daughters. For example, our children have always had a female pediatrician.

There are a tremendous number of black parents who raise their daughters and sons alike, up until age seven. Both mothers and fathers are very involved with their children. If anything, there is greater value placed on girls than boys. There has been a lot of debate regarding why. I think it goes back to slavery, when girls were treasured. There was a better chance that you could hold onto them, so that they could take care of you during your old age.

Like Dr. Light, Vicki gave her daughter the message that there was no limit to what she could do. This is an excerpt from our conversation:

"You have two sons and a daughter. Did you do anything different for your daughter to foster her personal growth while you were raising her?"

No. My daughter is as competitive as any of the boys are. She played varsity basketball in high school and got the athlete of the year award. She doesn't think that women are the "weaker sex" in any way whatsoever.

"Did you tell her that?"

Not directly. But she and her brothers were all each other's best friends. It's hard to tell what she observed about me, when I was a struggling young mother.

Vicki is an empowered woman who raised an empowered daughter. Throughout her childhood, Katharine was allowed to discover and develop her own self. Later on, Vicki was rewarded for her efforts. In her words: "Seeing Katharine persevere to make the varsity basketball team, after a lot of hard work, has inspired me. If my daughter can reach her goals, so can I."

Let your daughter be her own person, not a reflection of your own ideas about what women "should" or "shouldn't" be. Old-fashioned stereotypes, such as "Nice girls don't play football" or "Real women get married and have babies" may not fit your daughter at all. Consider what Margaret learned from her own experience with her mother:

When I was in high school, my mother was very distressed that I didn't type well. For some reason, I wasn't typing or taking shorthand at as high a speed as some of the other girls in the class. "How are you going to be a secretary?" she demanded. "That's what a girl is supposed to be." It's this type of outdated message that I don't want my daughters to be exposed to. I want them to be what they want to be—and to have the room to discover it.

From the first day of her life, treat your daughter as a special human being. Let her know that she has many gifts: a fine mind, a strong body and a loving personality. Expose her to all kinds of women: mothers, creative artists, sports figures, office workers and professionals. Encourage her to appreciate their diverse accomplishments. Never hold your daughter back by giving her the outdated message, "This is for boys; girls can't do this."

4. Allow her to explore the full range of her potential.

Most of the empowered women I interviewed were allowed to try everything when they were children. They were not told they couldn't do something because they might make a mess or catch a cold or get lost in the woods. If your daughter is allowed to try a wide variety of activities, she will eventually discover what she can do well.

Whether your daughter finishes first is less important than whether she is on the starting line. If she is only a mediocre swimmer, don't suggest she give up water sports. Let your daughter know that she doesn't have to be win a blue ribbon for everything she does. What is important is that she enjoys herself. As Katharine, Vicki's daughter, puts it: "My mom has always accepted me as I am, not as some ideal person who gets perfect grades and never screws up. No matter what has happened to me, my mom has always been very supportive."

Olga, one of my other interviewees, describes the upbringing that led to her empowerment:

I am the first child of a family of survivors of the Holocaust. I was born in Germany in a displaced persons camp. At age 3 1/2, I came to the United States with my parents.

My mother is the sole survivor of the Holocaust in her entire family. She was born in Poland and spent the war years in a Soviet labor camp. She was in Uzbekistan before winding up in the displaced persons camp, after the war. Although my mother was depressed over the loss of all her family members, I was a very loved child. She always gave me the feeling that I had a lot to contribute, that I was gifted and that I could do anything I wanted to do. She had a lot of expectations that I would accomplish something significant. A great deal of confidence was placed in me. It was assumed that I would have a life of my own and not be anyone's appendage.

A lot of my nurturing came from my father. He was very warm to me when he was home, although he was hardly ever there. He was working all the time, first as a factory employee and then as a manager of his own factory which made caps for children to wear. He gave me the same message as my mother: that I was very capable and would make a valuable contribution in some way.

Fortunately for Olga, she had a nurturing father and a mother who believed in her. Although Olga's mother never had a career, she encouraged Olga to discover her own talents and strengths.

Alexandra's mother also encouraged her to discover—and value—herself:

The most influential person in my life has been my mother. She has really planted the seeds of my empowerment. My mother has encouraged me to value the person who I am—and the person I am becoming. She has showed me that, whenever I have a painful experience, I can use it to expand myself and envision my future possibilities.

Dr. Jacqueline Light echoed these sentiments:

Children need a tremendous amount of free time—to play with other children, to explore, and to do things they may not even tell their parents about. Parents who can afford it, or who can arrange it, should make sure that their children spend time in the woods and on farms and in fields, where they can run and do cartwheels and play with animals. Not organized activities like climbing a mountain, but looking at the water or seeing a sunset. Children need be free. That's the greatest danger for children right now: they are never free.

As a child, I had lots of free time to read, to ride my bicycle and to play with other children. We played organized games, like Germans and Allies. We also played house and pretended to be father, mother or child. It was a satisfying feeling to know that our parents were watching us, while we played. They were in the background, reading the newspaper on the patio, and we were perfectly safe. This gave me a feeling of being valued. So, later on when I hit the bumps, I had a lot of confidence.

I think that most women who feel empowered to accomplish things have this confidence stored inside. Your sense of self has to be strong; you have to feel like you can do something. So many women have had childhoods where their parents ignored them. Their mothers or their fathers or both of their parents put them down and told them they couldn't do this or that. That's hard to overcome. Empowerment comes from within. You say to yourself, "If this way doesn't work, another way is going to work." You keep trying. You don't give up easily.

By exploring the world around her—having fun, experiencing accomplishment and making mistakes—your daughter will get to know herself.

5. Share the "new" femininity with her.

Your daughter will inevitably be exposed to masculine values. Teach your daughter feminine values, as well. Don't focus only on her academic, artistic and athletic achievements. Yes, compliment her if she makes the honor roll or the school orchestra or the varsity basketball team. But tell her just as clearly how proud you are when she takes care of a baby, plants a vegetable garden or finds time to have a heart-to-heart talk with her sister. When she wants to volunteer at a women's center, a hospital or an elementary school, tell her that you value this kind of "accomplishment" as much as "straight A's." Let your daughter know that you love her as the unique human being that she is.

Lucy told me about what she was like when she was growing up:

As a child, I was very much a tomboy. I hated dolls, and I didn't like to play house; I preferred to climb trees. But when it actually came to caring for real babies in the church nursery—I liked that. Since I was a teenager, I have always known that I wanted to be a mother.

Don't be overly concerned with your daughter's appearance. An elaborate hairstyle, colorful makeup or frilly clothes do not necessarily make your daughter feminine. If she is a caring person who is concerned about her relationships with others, then she is a "real woman."

6. Encourage her to be herself.

Your daughter is not an exact mirror image of you. She is a different person. If you want her to become empowered, you must accept this fact. Praise her if she masters a skill you never learned, like horseback riding or algebra, or when she wants to be an oceanographer when you are a successful businesswoman. Let her know *your* moral and intellectual standards; then give her space to discover the world and who *she* is in it. Allow her the space to develop her own unique self. For your daughter to become empowered, she must be allowed to experience herself as a separate and distinct person, not as a "little you."

Your daughter's self is not the same as yours. You may find it hard to accept her differences. Consider this exchange I had with Yoko, a Japanese college student who loved her mother very much, but who wanted to find her own way:

I want to honor and obey my mother, but I also want to respect myself. For many years, it has been impossible for me to do both. When I became a young women, I chose friends who I liked, but not the ones my mother preferred. By following my own path, I made my mother very angry with me. When I would call her, I wanted her to listen to what I had to say about my new friends and my new life, but she would hang up on me instead. I felt so hurt—as if I had betrayed my mother.

What am I to do? In modern Japan, parents and children live in different cultures and have different values. How can I give up mine for my mother's? Since we have been distant for almost 10 years, I don't know how to relate to her anymore. I don't think she knows how to talk to me either. This makes me very sad.

"Time will pass. Perhaps someday, when you get older, your mother will learn to appreciate who you really are and accept your values. In the meantime, you must continue to lead your own life. You cannot be true to yourself if you pretend to be someone you are not."

Family ties in Japan are still very strong. Because her mother is trying to control her, Yoko is finding it difficult to be her own person. How much better it would be for both of them, if Yoko's mother could accept her daughter's new directions.

Have you given up your own self for your daughter? Then you are not helping her to become empowered. Many daughters feel guilty about succeeding professionally when they see their mothers "sacrificing" for them. Some of these guilty daughters eventually starve themselves as a punishment and wind up becoming anorectic. "Self-sacrifice" empowers no one.

A mother who has a fulfilling life of her own does not live vicariously through her children. She empowers her daughter by setting her free and letting her follow her own star. Her daughter's accomplishments—even if they surpass hers—are a joy, not a threat.

7. Allow plenty of space between you, especially during her adolescence and adulthood.

Empowerment is based on self-trust. A mother who trusts her daughter will raise a daughter who trusts herself. When your daughter reaches adolescence, give her lots of privacy. If you have done your job well during her first 12 years, you have little to worry about. Make sure she has appropriate information about sex (especially about birth control and sexually transmitted diseases), and then let her find her own way. Your daughter needs plenty of space, particularly after the age of 13, in order to develop a separate self.

Power-over makes teenage rebellion even worse. A young woman who feels controlled may commit dangerous, or even illegal, acts to prove to herself that she is her own person. Teenagers rebel most against those people whom they perceive as rigid authorities. If you are empowered together with her, chances are her that her adolescence will not be a stormy one.

8. Listen to her and talk to her, not at her.

You may not like what your daughter is saying, but care enough to really listen. When she disagrees with you, accept what she is saying. As your daughter feels that her messages are received, she will experience her own empowerment. As Vicki says:

I don't want my kids to shut me out of their lives. So I have to risk listening to what they tell me. If I can't handle what they say, they are not going to talk to me.

Dr. Jacqueline Light offers this excellent advice:

I have always been extremely interested in what parents can do to strengthen children, so that they can send their teenagers out into the world able to "hit, run and throw." I think that one thing parents can do is to be interested in their children, not in a superficial way, but in depth. Parents should not just read to their children but also listen to them. Parents can teach children without co-opting all of their free time. The secret is to teach without appearing to be teaching.

You need to be somewhat oblivious to other people's opinions. To be oblivious means to be confident—to be really certain that you know what you are doing. Use your common sense. Never mind the books and magazines and newspapers and radio shows and television programs that tell mothers to do all kinds of things. As a mother, you know what is good for your child, for example, not to slap him in the face or to call him names. You don't need to read this in a magazine or hear it on the radio; you feel it in your own gut. It is up to you, when you read or hear something different from what you know to be true, to say to yourself, "This doesn't make sense. I will not do it."

Tune in to your child. What bothers me most right now is that mothers aren't listening to their children. Instead they are projecting a lot of their own needs onto their kids. They expect a child to perform, not for his or her own satisfaction, but to gratify Mother's desires. They overlook what the child wants.

Take time to make friends with your daughter. Tell her what is on your mind. Don't preach or teach; share your life with her. When you talk, ask her to tell you her reactions to what you have said.

Can you receive your daughter's truths, no matter how different they are from your own? Can you tell your daughter the truth about yourself? If so, you will raise an empowered daughter.

How One Grandmother, Mother and Daughter Empowered Each Other

I am curled up on the floor near a comfortable beige couch. Three women, from three different generations, are sitting nearby. Theresa, a bustling, gray-haired woman in her early 60s is in the center of the couch. Theresa's poised, articulate daughter, Liz, is seated in a chair on her right. Debbie, a 22-year-old engineer who is Liz's daughter and Theresa's granddaughter, occupies another chair on Theresa's left. I have already interviewed each of these women individually; now we are talking as a group. I have just asked each one, "How has your relationship with your mother, grandmother, daughter or granddaughter empowered you?" This is what they reply:

Liz (Debbie's mother and Theresa's daughter): There are 2 times, Theresa, that you helped me deal with the next stage of my life.

One time was when I came home from the hospital with Debbie and you came to visit me. I was tired, and I hadn't been the mother of a baby before. I remember feeding Debbie, putting her down and thinking that she would go to sleep. But she didn't; she started crying instead. I didn't know what to do or what she needed. You picked her up, rocked her and calmed her. She really got comforted.

I felt that, in the process of giving to her, you had given something to me—as a role model. For the first time, I felt that it was possible for me to reach out to my child, who was uncomfortable in a way that I didn't understand, and make her comfortable. You showed me what it was like to do this with confidence. I still have a visual image of your sitting in the big chair in our living room rocking Debbie to sleep.

The other time when you empowered me was when I saw you taking care of your mother in the nursing home. When she couldn't talk anymore, you would sing her songs that you had sung to your kindergarten Sunday school kids. Although your mother couldn't even remember your name, she could remember the words of these songs. Both of you would sing these songs together. I thought that this was an amazing way to connect with someone who was "out of touch" by most standards. It was an unforgettable experience for me.

The way you have dealt with the transitions of the past year in both your life and Dad's is an inspiration to me now. When ask myself, 'What's ahead for me?" I think of how you have adjusted to your retirement and taken care of Dad, during his illness. In some ways, this has been your finest hour. You may talk about being on an emotional roller coaster, but I think that you have been very giving to all of us. I feel buoyed up and hopeful that I may be able to do the same someday.

Debbie: In my relationship with you, Mom, I have learned to deal with the enormous intensity and range of our feelings. I have experienced everything from nearly physical violence to immense respect and love—and amazement that anyone could be that good. It has been overwhelming, scary and exciting!

I see a lot of myself in you, and you in me. As a teenager, you have this mythology that you can make yourself into exactly who you want to be, but in reality it doesn't quite work that way. She laughs. You have to accept that your mother is part of who you are. Maybe you want to deny it, but then you look in the mirror, see your face and realize that you are like your mother in many ways. Reconciling yourself is a quite challenge.

I can see why a lot of young people don't want to be around their parents. A lot of painful feelings come up.

Liz: I understand exactly what you mean, Debbie, about seeing your mother in yourself. There are phrases, expressions and tones of voice that I hear in myself that sound exactly like my mother. She glances at Theresa. Now I feel very genial about it. But, early on, it stirred up conflict. You want to think of yourself as unique. Your mother has qualities that you reject. You have spent your whole childhood thinking about how you were not going to be.

When I hear myself using same tone of voice, or reacting the same way, as my mother, I am literally "on the other side." To look at myself honestly is a real turnaround.

Theresa: For a long time, my children have been my consciousness-raising group. Now my grandchildren are coming to me with even newer and fresher points of view. Every time I have an in-depth conversation with one of them, I really get straightened out about what I need to know about their generation. My children and grandchildren give me messages I need to hear.

I feel sorry for people who do not have a daughter or a granddaughter in their lives—to keep *them* straight!

As a mother, you are inevitably a role model for your daughter. Both of you are also mirrors to each other, whether you like it or not. You, your daughter and your granddaughters may also be message-bearers to each other.

What Can Dad Do?

Many women also mentioned the influence of their father, not as a role model, but as a giver of subtle messages. Most of the empowered women remembered their fathers saying to them, "You can do anything you want to do. You can be anyone you want to be." Samantha, the speech pathologist and editor, described how her father had empowered her:

My father was 47 when I was born, so he would talk to me in a very mature way. Sometimes I used to say to him, "I want to be somebody." Later on, when we were together, he would repeat my own words back to me. He would say, "Samantha, you have always told me that you wanted to be somebody." He gave me the feeling that I could do whatever I wanted to do. These conversations with my father led me where I am today. You see, I am somebody now!

Typically, the father of an empowered woman takes his daughter's future seriously. He appreciates her talents, provides her with the resources to develop them and gives her encouragement along the way.

One remarkably empowered 23-year-old woman whom I interviewed related to me an incident that she would always remember. During her freshman year at college, she had told her father how fascinated she was with a course she was taking, "Intellectual History of Modern Europe." He immediately replied, "I've got this book about it that you would just love. Wait right here." Then he ran upstairs and got the book. He gave it to her and said, "When you're finished reading it, Stacey, I'd like you to discuss it with me." Stacey's father delighted in her enthusiasm for ideas, rather than laughing at it or ignoring it.

Lucy described to me how her father's example had instilled in her a love of learning:

Although my father had never gone to college, when I was in the fourth grade, he started taking night courses. He would bring home his college book covers, and I was so proud to put them on my elementary school books.

My dad was always buying books. We were surrounded by bookcases full of encyclopedias and stacks and stacks of volumes for improving our academic skills. Sometimes there was no room for us to sit down! Instead of a television set, Dad bought a stereo. If my parents had extra money, they spent it either on more reading material or on classical music. Doesn't this sound odd in the middle of Harlem?

Because of her father's inspiration, Lucy went on to a 4-year college, where she was the only blind student.

A father who has a power-over relationship with his daughter will stunt her growth. Only when he lets go and allows her to become autonomous will she become empowered. Wendy told me about how her relationship with her father changed from "power-over" to "empowerment together with."

When I was finishing up my junior year at a college abroad, my father and I had a big argument. He told me to do something, and I said, "No." He replied, "Then I'm not going to support you anymore," and I said, "Fine." All I had was about $1,000 that I had saved from working during the summer. But I meant what I said. I returned to the States, worked for a year and took 2 more years to get my degree. Ever since then, my father and I have gotten along well. I earned his respect, because I stood up to him. Then I was strong enough to back up my words with actions.

Now that Wendy is her own person, she and her father both have a more satisfying, and mutually empowering, relationship with each other.

Empowerment is a legacy you can leave your daughter—a gift far more precious than material possessions. Feminine empowerment is a precious treasure, passed down from generation to generation. Each generation makes it a little easier for the next. Debbie, the 22-year-old engineer, summed it up when she talked about the difference her mother had made in her life:

I have grown up taking for granted the freedoms and the options that I have. It never occurred to me that it was a "big deal" for me to want to be an engineer, because I was very good in math. But, as I became more aware, I realized that my mother's generation had gone through the transition that made it possible for me to take my opportunities for granted. So did my grandmother's generation, to a lesser degree.

Yours was the era for change, Mom. I feel as if I have a lot of options now. I don't have to choose to be either a doctor or a mother, the way you had to, Grandma. I can be both. It's not going to be easy for me. But then again, it's not easy for a man to be a doctor, either. The idea that it's easy for anyone is garbage.

I feel grateful to you, Mom, for going through the rocky period. Because of you, I am on the cutting edge. The rest is up to me.

How will you know when you have overcome the obstacles to raising an empowered daughter? Use this checklist to find out:

I am raising an empowered daughter if:

1. I am a role model of an empowered woman.
2. I make decisions together with her, instead of telling her what to do.
3. I give her plenty of privacy.
4. I value her accomplishments, as well as her femininity.
5. I really listen to what she has to say.
6. I share my life with her.
7. I allow her to be herself, rather than a "little me."
8. I encourage her to explore the full range of her potentials.
9. I let her experience the consequences of her actions.
10. I do not try to control her, if she is a young adult.

The more "yes" answers you give, the greater the likelihood that your daughter will grow up to become an empowered woman.

Empowerment Exercises

1. Appreciate a "Girl Child": If you have a daughter, think of all the qualities she has that make her precious to you. If you do not, think of what having a daughter of your own would add to your life. You may wish to write down your thoughts in your Empowerment Journal, or else record them on a tape.

2. An Unsent Letter to My Mother: Sit down with a pencil and paper in a quiet place. Write a letter to your mother, which you do not intend to send. Tell her how she empowered you as a child; then detail the things she did that held you back. You may also want to write a similar unsent letter to your father.

3. A Dialogue with My Daughter, Mother or Grandmother: Would you like to have a dialogue like Debbie, Liz and Theresa had in this chapter? It is not as difficult as it seems. At an appropriate time, ask your daughter, mother or grandmother to tell you how you have empowered her. Then let her know how she has empowered you. The dialogue will kindle precious memories, as each of you remembers experiences that you had together long ago.

Rather than asking the questions spontaneously, you may wish to make an appointment for a conversation and include more than one other person. A tape recording would make a unique Christmas present—and a priceless family heirloom!

Raising an empowered daughter is one way to make a difference in another woman's life. But there are other ways, too. Would you like to know what they are?

MAKE A "NEW" CONNECTION

In a swirling sea of faces,
We share a life raft;
In a single, silent second
Your eyes and ears meet mine.
Who are you anyway?
I'd like to know.
As we talk and listen closely,
Will I finally meet myself?

r. r. j.

How did the women I interviewed become empowered? In their stories, they have told you. All of them first experienced empowerment together with someone else in these two ways:

1. By observing, or creating, mutually empowering relationships with other people they knew.

Reverend Judith Goode and Vera had empowered grandmothers whom they modeled themselves after. Alexandra, Esther, Lynda and Amy had empowered mothers to imitate. Julia, on the other hand, became empowered by doing exactly the opposite of what her mother did. Samantha, Stacey and Olga all had supportive fathers.

Although Terri and Dale had no flesh-and-blood models at all, they became empowered by reading about famous women. Although some of these far-away heroines were mavericks, whose experience was remote and exotic, they were all teachers to Terri and Dale.

Dr. Jacqueline Light, Charlotte, Quincy and Denise all created partnership marriages. Each of them was fortunate enough to have had a chance to observe their parents' marriage, which was a model of mutuality. Vera became empowered as she transformed her own power-over marriage into one where she became empowered together with her partner.

Vicki, Lucy and I created empowered relationships with our children. Since our babies were born with a "clean slate," we were able to be models of mutuality, autonomy and authenticity—and then reap the benefits. Theresa created empowered relationships with her grandchildren as well. She was wise enough to realize that they, too, could be message-bearers.

Remember Alexandra, who told us her story in Chapter 2? She managed to recover from her incredible trauma because of the support she received from the other people around her. As she said to me:

After the trauma, I was surrounded by sympathetic people who could tolerate my pain. My family, friends, and community were all there for me, even during the trial. I have an extremely large network of friends, who protected me—actually created a cocoon for me. I had to work hard to climb out of their cocoon after my assailant was sent to prison.

I never could have healed without my sister and my brother. No matter what has happened to me, my sister has always given me a safe place to go. Even though she left home when I was 11, she has always loved me totally and accepted me unconditionally. During the past several years, there have been times when I have felt that I had no one else to turn to. So I was able to be authentic with her, and my brother, throughout the terrible aftermath of the crime.

When you allow yourself to be vulnerable—not from a place of weakness but from a place of strength—you are truly authentic and empowered. After the trauma, I found the courage to go on by acknowledging my needs and then clearly asking others for what I wanted. It was only with the support of other people that I recovered. That's been a huge lesson for me.

Within her "cocoon" of caring family and friends, Alexandra could not only be autonomous but also authentic.

Alexandra was not the only woman who created empowering mutual friendships. Amy's friendships with homosexual men empowered her to accept her lesbianism. Joy found a friend in her mentor, who really listened to her and allowed her to fully express herself. During the last 3 years, Paula and I have both become empowered in our mutually supportive friendship.

Several women I interviewed had created empowering relationships with their therapists. In this kind of one-to-one connection, there can be empowered communication. Annette took a leap and shared her tale of abuse with a therapist. He listened to her and accepted what she said. Then he helped her realize that what she was feeling was valid, not "crazy." In therapy, Sophie also found an outlet where she could share her true self with someone else. Both Annette and Sophie went on to create other empowering relationships, particularly with their children.

Joy found that she could be authentic and autonomous with her psychoanalyst. He gave her a place to be real and supported her, as she discovered herself through meditation. Other women I interviewed told me that their therapists were memory-links and, if they were female, also mirrors. But therapy has its downside. In a power-over relationship with a therapist, a woman does not become empowered. When Vicki found herself in this situation, she was wise enough to flee.

2. By meeting new people in a support group, seminar or empowerment community.

If there are no men or women in your life who can be your teachers, then you can meet new ones. A support group, seminar or empowerment community offers you the opportunity to make many new empowering connections within a short period of time.

Women instinctively know that they empower themselves just by being together. During the past 3 centuries, American women have gained strength by sharing experiences in sewing circles, quilting bees and coffee klatches.

More than half of the empowered women I interviewed for this book told me that they had belonged to a women's group at some time in their lives. With support from members of their group, they were able to survive divorce, bereavement and countless other tribulations.

The CR (consciousness-raising) groups of the '60s and '70s were a first step toward the development of communities. Modern women realized that they could find out what was wrong with their lives by having conversations with other women whom they had never met before. When these women stopped focusing exclusively on men, they freed themselves to look inward. The "Women Who Love Too Much" groups of the '80s, which developed from the book with the same name written by Robin Norwood, showed codependent women how they could deal with their problem by supporting each other. CR groups, women's support groups and "Women Who Love Too Much" groups all gave women opportunities to reach out to other women.

In Chapter 3, Wendy told us how the women's support group that she started empowered her:

I became connected to one of the women in it. Not physically, but emotionally. I realized that I would care if something happened to her, and that she would care if something happened to me. I said to myself, "Yes, you can do things by yourself. Just because you're single doesn't mean you can't still enjoy life." . . . Now I have developed a sense of self. I realize that I am responsible for the quality of my life. It is up to me to find out what I want.

Wendy discovered her personal identity in a women's support group. She also formed a mutually empowering, caring, nonsexual relationship with another woman in it.

Martha became autonomous through the consciousness-raising group that she formed. Remember what she said in Chapter 10?

In Caracas, I needed a purpose. Since I had read about consciousness-raising groups in *Sisterhood Is Powerful,* I said to myself, "Why don't you start one?" So I called up one woman and told her what I wanted to do. She said, "Why do you want to do this?" I replied, "We are all sisters. We need to talk to each other."

The other women in Martha's consciousness-raising group supported her courageous decision to find her own self. Afterwards, Martha decided to pursue her calling and give her handicapped daughter the professional help she desperately needed.

Dale became authentic first by participating in a women's theater group and then by attending a women's camp. Do you recall what she told us in Chapter 8?

I was asked to co-direct a women's camping week where there would be a series of workshops. I was a "straight" woman; the co-director was a lesbian. There would be something for everyone. I accepted. For the first time I would be completely on my own, away from my parents, my husband and my children.

In the women's camp, Dale found models and mirrors of lesbianism, her authentic sexuality. By observing other women who had already found the courage to "come out," Dale was inspired to do the same.

A weekend seminar can be very empowering. After Denise and Dan attended a relationships seminar, they were enabled to create a partnership marriage. For the first time, they had the opportunity to observe partnership models—couples who related to each other in a mutual, autonomous and authentic way.

In communities, mutual support becomes even deeper. Women discover themselves in empowering relationships with other women. Once women are in touch with their identities, they are free to develop their full potentials.

How a Community Empowered Margaret

Remember Margaret in Chapter 7 who found her calling? Her breakthrough occurred in an empowerment community. Several members of her community were message-bearers who told Margaret to "wake up." In our interview, she described to me what happened:

A week ago when I arrived at this community meeting, I was so ill with my ulcers and colitis and migraines that my doctor did not want me to make the trip. But I said to him, "I am going. I need the time and the space for myself. I need to figure out whether or not I can handle my job any longer."

After talking about my problem with the community, I realized that the reasons for staying, which were very clear to me, sounded silly when I shared them with other people. I couldn't even cry about how I was hurting—about my loss of friendship with my boss and my lack of self-confidence. I was not even angry; I was just empty. All my energy had been drained from me by my job.

The reactions of the community members surprised me. One woman said to me, "You look so beaten." I didn't really think of myself as beaten, but I guess I appeared that way. Another woman told me, "You don't really want help, and so there's nothing I can do for you." A third woman said, "I don't want to invest time and energy in an empty person like you. When you put something into an empty person, it is just absorbed; nothing is given back. You don't have any good feelings to share with us."

I started asking myself, "Do I really want to continue being an empty person? I'm not getting any energy from working at my job; I just keep losing it. I feel so trapped—by my boss, my husband, my kids, my friends—and most of all by myself. Sometimes the pains in my stomach and my head are so bad that I can hardly stand them. Why should I continue sacrificing my health, my peace of mind, my energy, my self-respect and my ambition?"

Then Margaret came face to face with a person who had almost her exact problem. This mirror enabled Margaret to see herself as she really was.

In the community, there was a very well-educated, highly successful professional woman who had the very same problem as mine. She was being strangled by office politics; she was depressed; and she had no vitality. Sitting across from her, I could see her crying. I thought, "What is she doing? I don't want to be like her. She's divorced; her children have left home. She has so few satisfying relationships, because she hasn't got the energy to establish any."

Seeing a mirror image of myself made me realize, "It's not going to get any better. No one is going to save you. The members of the community may wipe away your tears when you are ready to cry, pat you on the back or put their arms around you, but when you go back home, you may never see them again. After this community meeting is over, you are on your own. No one is going to help you out of this but you."

When I went to another community meeting later on, the woman who is the mirror image of me was talking about how she had just lost her job. She was weeping and saying, "I fear for myself, for my spouse and for my children." I found myself telling her, "People who want to work, work. You may not do exactly what you want to do, or make exactly the salary you want to have, but you will work again. The next job you get may not be exactly the one that you want, but maybe the one after that will." Neither of us has any job prospects now, but we view our lives very differently.

According to Margaret, the community was the catalyst for her empowerment.

This community experience has been very intense—and very valuable to me. Since I have started attending these meetings, my priorities have changed. I appreciate that I already have what is most important to me: my family, a nice house and all the food we need. If I quit my job, I may not have a lot of spending money, but that's okay. My family and I are not going to starve.

I could not have gotten in touch with my own strengths just sitting on my patio by myself. I needed someone to say to me, "I can't help you the way you are now. You really don't want to get well. I'm not going to carry your burden for you." Until now, I thought that someone else would come along and make everything "all better" for me.

While Margaret might have benefited from a women's support group, she experienced her empowerment most dramatically in an empowerment community. In the meetings she attended, Margaret met a mirror, and message-bearers, who helped her see what she had been doing. Aware of their value, she saw herself clearly for the first time. In the community, she decided to find her calling.

It is possible to for you find models, mirrors, message-bearers and other teachers in a support group or a seminar. But it is not only the people who attend but also the climate that makes an empowerment community especially effective.

For example, in her spiritual meditation community, Alexandra found a safe space where she could be authentic. Since no one in the community had power over anyone else, everyone in it was empowered to communicate honestly. Alexandra could comfortably share her trauma without fear of being ridiculed or ignored. As she put it:

In my spiritual meditation community, I found safety. Since the trauma, I have allowed myself to go to the depths of my vulnerability with the members of this group. Until then, I was dabbling here and there—without any focus.

Why a Community Is More Empowering Than a Group

For many years, I myself avoided groups completely. I believed that their pressure to conform would threaten my own individuality.

As a teenager, I had seen a majority "gang up" on a few group members who were different. In college I had learned that, in a mass, people lose their identities. They all become followers, seeking truth outside themselves—in a leader and in his or her ideas.

The turning point in my attitude toward groups was the est training, a national seminar series created by Werner Erhard. No, I did not attend willingly. A friend of mine insisted that est would be "life-changing" and dragged me there screaming and kicking. She was right; est did change my life. I spent 2 weekends and 2 evenings in a hotel room with 300 other people—most of whom were revealing their innermost feelings. Although I did not yet have the courage to speak a single word, I experienced the first stirrings of personal empowerment, as I listened. While group members were expected to conform to external standards, to wear name tags, sit in chairs and stay in the room, they were free to share whatever was inside them.

At different times, I felt embarrassed, inspired, nostalgic, bored and angry. I observed people who reminded me of myself. I communicated with people whom I admired and wanted to be like. A few reminded me of members of my family. Some women told stories I couldn't relate to at all. Others, particularly the timid women and the domineering men, made me furious, although I didn't know why.

Est, however, was not a community. Each seminar had a leader who set strict rules for the participants. Conformity to the norms of the group, rather than expressing one's individuality, was emphasized during the seminars. There was a definite agenda of topics that had to be covered, and "processes" that had to be completed. Nevertheless, people managed to create empowering relationships with each other.

After having several more group experiences, including Focusing workshops and an Intensive Journal™ writing seminar, I began to realize their value. You can learn more with other people than you can by yourself.

If empowerment takes place in relationships, then a community—a special kind of group—offers an ideal opportunity for creating empowering connections within a short period of time. While the members of a community are encouraged to take into account the needs of the other community members, they think for themselves and act by themselves.

In the La Jolla Program, originally supervised by the late psychologist Dr. Carl Rogers, I experienced a community where a person was encouraged to maintain his or her individuality. People who disagreed with the group, no matter how few, were listened to. Their opinions, no matter how unconventional, were respected. Although there were 30 men and women in our community, each looked for truth within himself.

In a Women's Empowerment (WE) Community, women are most empowered to learn from each other. These communities are organized by women, according to feminine values. Empowerment takes place as women communicate together with each other. Instead of a leader, there is a facilitator. Instead of strict rules, there are flexible standards. Instead of group conformity, there is self-expression. Instead of a predetermined agenda, the conversation flows wherever it goes.

You Are a Unique Individual;
You Are Also Part of the Universe

Appreciating our uniqueness can make us feel special; it can also make us feel lonely, separate and distant from other people. In a WE Community, we realize that, as human beings and as women, we are all one. We share human characteristics, and we share female traits. Yet each one of us has a different body, a different personality and a different way of experiencing reality. By connecting with other women who are similar to and different from us, we see ourselves more clearly. We also experience an exhilarating feeling of being part of a greater universe.

Each of us is unique. Yet, at the same time, we are part of a network of all women. We learn who we are in relationship to other women by finding out how we are similar and how we are different. In my opinion, a WE Community is the most effective vehicle for self-discovery. It is possible to get to know yourself in one-on-one encounters with female friends, but this is very time-consuming and often frustrating. How much easier it is to find out who you really are while you are surrounded by a bevy of supportive women!

There are other ways to begin to create empowering relationships, but they are less effective, and sometimes more expensive. Talking to family members and old friends can be valuable, but they are often too close to you to see your problem in a broad context. More frequently, people who love you may tell you what you want to hear, rather than honestly confronting you. WE Community members, who do not have ongoing close relationships with you, have less at stake.

While individual psychotherapy has its value, it is usually expensive and time-consuming. An experience with a therapist is often passive, rather than interactive, and so less likely to be empowering. Unlike WE Community members who give you a great deal of feedback, a therapist mainly listens to you. Sharing with one individual, however well-trained he or she may be, is a more limited experience than interaction with many people.

Although women's support groups are valuable, they generally focus on a specific problem, such as codependency. The women who attend are not usually aware of their roles as mirrors, models and message-bearers. There is a hidden pressure to conform to the group's values, which are sometimes feminist ones. This keeps many women from being themselves. If one woman dominates the discussion, the others may find themselves playing a power-under role, which does not empower them.

For women dissatisfied with their relationships, the WE Community experience can be a cradle of empowerment.

The WE Community Experience

Have you avoided women's groups in the past? A WE Community is not like them. Because there is no leader, no agenda and few rules, the atmosphere is free and unstructured. All the members are encouraged to be their own persons. They remain autonomous and authentic in the mutual relationships they form.

In a WE Community, you have a unique opportunity to make many empowering connections with other women and men for the first time. In an open and responsive environment, you discover yourself.

In what other ways is a WE Community different?

1. In a WE Community, no one has power over anybody else. You have the opportunity to experience mutuality, perhaps for the first time. In an atmosphere of mutuality, you are best enabled to learn from models, mentors, message-bearers and other women and men who can empower you.

2. Each member is aware that other women can be her teachers. Like everyone else, you have come there prepared to tune in to the other members. You have modeling, mirroring and other empowering experiences more frequently and more intensely.

3. There is empowered communication, not "talking at" each other. You experience other people deeply, not superficially. As you talk, and listen to each community member, you ask yourself, "How am I when I am with this person?" Then you express your feelings honestly to her or him. When other people share their feelings with you, you receive what they have to say.

4. There is no fixed topic for discussion. Members ask each other, "Tell me about your significant relationships—and your important projects." Your answers flow from the past, as well as the present. You share your life stories, as well as your current concerns.

5. You are empowered to act, not just to keep on talking. You leave the WE Community with positive relationship experiences and renewed energy to interact differently with your family members, co-workers and friends.

It helps to decide in advance of the WE Community meeting which concerns you want to work on and what you expect from the other members. Your answers to these questions will affect how you will behave in the group and what you will get out of participating. Although the group has a definite, but hidden, direction, you will create your own experience.

In the WE Community, you will meet women and men at different levels of empowerment. Being in their presence can help you learn about parts of you, and feelings you have, that you may not yet be aware of.

You will also have many opportunities to experience empowering communication. After you talk to someone, you will ask yourself, "When I am with this person, how do I feel? Happy? Sad? Relaxed? What expands in me? Joy? Grief? Inner peace?" As this person, in turn, reflects your thoughts and understands your vision, she or he will empower you to act. When someone talks to you, you will listen carefully and then tell her in your own words what you think she or he is saying. As you share your feelings with other people in the community, you will get to know yourself better.

The benefits of a WE Community are not only learning from the other members but also giving of yourself to them. Once you recognize your potential as a mirror, model or mentor, you will start making a difference within the group. As you share what you know with someone else, you will become more aware of your own strengths.

Your First Step Toward Empowerment

By going to a WE Community meeting, you have taken the first step toward empowerment. No one with power over you has kept you from going. Something happened in your mind that made you decide to go. You have chosen to use some of your time and energy to attend a WE Community meeting, rather than wash the floors or go to a movie.

A WE Community meeting is an ideal setting for you to experience empowerment. You are free to say what you want to say, remain silent if you choose and leave whenever you want to.

It is your WE Community; you get as much—or as little—out of it as you put into it. At any moment, you can talk about yourself or else pull back and let the other people talk. You can make contact with all the community members, some of them or none of them. You can either monitor what you say or say whatever you feel, regardless of the reactions of the other community members. You can wear a facade or you can totally be yourself. You can strive to "fit in" with the community or you can struggle to find your own unique voice.

There is always a lot of tension at the first WE Community meeting. This is because the community members are afraid to risk opening up right away. Although a few are eager to get to know the other women who are there, most of them feel sad or lonely, even though they are in a room full of people. Although the initial silence is painful, it is inevitable. Everyone needs time before she or he can trust the other community members.

A New Way to Make a Big Difference

One way you can make a big difference in the lives of other people, as well as your own, is to organize a WE Community. You may decide either to start from scratch or to reorganize an existing consciousness-raising or "Women Who Love Too Much" group.

If you decide to become a WE Community organizer, follow these guidelines:

1. Hold the WE Community meeting at the same location every week. It may be either in a public meeting room, a church or temple, your home, or another member's home. Make sure that there is a restroom and a telephone for the members to use. See that someone not attending the meeting, or an answering machine, is available to handle incoming telephone calls. Parents may bring their children, if the children are properly supervised.

2. At least 1 month before the first WE Community meeting, put a notice:

- in the calendar or classified section of your local newspaper,
- in the newsletters of organizations you belong to, and
- in any other appropriate publications you are familiar with.

Exactly how you word the notice is up to you. Here is a suggestion:

ATTENTION: Would you like to create satisfying relationships, fully develop your inner potential and meet other women and men who will support you? A Women's Empowerment (WE) Community is forming in your neighborhood. Call (your first name) at (your telephone number) for details.

After you have placed the notice, go through your telephone book and invite every woman and man in it who might be interested in attending.

3. Leave a package of blank name labels and a marker on a table near the door. Each person who attends may wear one if she or he chooses. If possible, put at least two copies of this book on the table for community members to borrow.

4. Make up a WE Community Resource List. This is what the top of one looks like:

Your Name	Your Address	Your Telephone Number	Your Significant Relationships	Your Skills and Talents	Your Special Interests and Projects

Place it, along with a pen, on the table near the door next to the name labels and the books. Each person should have an opportunity to write down her or his name, address, telephone number, significant relationships, skills, talents, special interests and projects on it.

5. At the beginning of each meeting, state the mutual understandings of the members. These are not "rules," but suggestions to make the sessions run smoothly:

- Meetings will take place at least once a month. Three or more members of the community may organize additional meetings.
- Everyone can sit wherever she or he wants—on the floor, on a chair or on a pillow.
- Although the meetings will start and stop at prearranged times, people will be allowed to arrive and leave at their convenience. Normally each meeting will last 2 or 3 hours.
- Each person may bring her or his own food, if she or he wishes. A hostess may also serve food, if she or he chooses.
- Drinking juice or soft drinks, knitting, embroidering, sewing and writing are permitted during the community meeting. Smoking, drinking alcohol or taking drugs are not.
- Everything said in the meeting is strictly confidential and not to be shared with others outside the community.
- No one talks more than 5 minutes at a time. You will be told when your time is up.
- No one has to speak.
- Say whatever you are moved to say. Any polite response is acceptable.
- Women and men can linger and socialize at least 15 minutes after the meeting is over.

- WE Community members are strongly urged to bring a friend to at least every other meeting.
- Members are invited to share their knowledge about meditation, yoga, body awareness or any other similar discipline during the meeting, or to invite a guest who will do this.
- The next meeting is on (day of week and date) from (starting time) to (ending time) at (address). This is how to get there . . . .(Give brief, clear directions.)

6. The following topics are recommended for discussion:

- With whom do you have a significant relationship at the present time? Is your relationship satisfying? How can members of the community assist you in making this relationship more mutual, autonomous and authentic? How can they assist you in creating new relationships?
- What are you working on in your life right now? What would you like to work on? How can community members assist you in moving your project forward?

7. Bring a stopwatch or clock with a second hand, and keep it with you. Use your stopwatch or clock to keep track of the time. If necessary, tell a person who speaks when her or his 5 minutes are up.

8. At least once during the meeting, go around the room and invite everyone to say how she or he felt when each person spoke. Be prepared for some people to express anger; others, sadness or boredom. Do not try to contradict their feelings; let them be.

9. Do not allow any person to bully, intimidate or coerce the community or any member of it. If her or his behavior persists, ask her or him to remain silent for the rest of the evening. Invite the members of the community to share their reactions about what this person is saying and doing. Are they feeling controlled?

10. Any person who smokes, drinks alcohol or takes drugs in the meeting room is to be warned once and then asked to leave. Let the community support you in dealing with her or him.

11. Allow yourself to speak, and react to the speakers, just like the other community members. Remember, you are an organizer, not a "leader."

12. At the end of the m ing, have a "sound-off" time when people can share their feelings about the community meeting itself. "Sound-off" should last between 15 and 30 minutes.

13. Keep a list of local emergency facilities, such as Twelve Step programs (for example, Alcoholic Anonymous, Al-Anon and

Codependents Anonymous) and rape crisis centers, on hand, which you can use to refer any person with a problem that requires immediate attention.

14. At least once during each meeting, ask if anyone else wants to be an organizer. Allow anyone who says "Yes," to take over your job at least once.

15. Once a month, duplicate the WE Community Resource List and give a copy to each person at the meeting.

If you want further guidance, I recommend that you attend my **Empowered Woman** ™ Seminar, when it comes to your area. Write to me at the address at the back of this book for specific details.

If you do not have the time to organize a WE Community, then join one. If you decide to become a WE Community member:

1. Do your best to come on time.

2. Although you do not have to read this whole book, you should read Chapters 4, 11 and 13. Either buy it, or borrow it from someone else.

3. Talk about yourself, your relationships and your projects openly and honestly.

4. Give your full attention to whoever is speaking. Receive what each person says, no matter how uncomfortable it makes you feel.

5. If you have had an experience similar to one that is being described, share it.

6. When another person's words stir intense feelings within you, let her or him know.

7. Allow other people to give you emotional support. Support each person in whatever way is comfortable for you.

8. If someone does not want to talk at all, respect that person's silence.

9. If someone is monopolizing the conversation in your opinion, then say so.

10. If you are delighted, bored, angry or frustrated with the community meeting, speak up especially during the "sound off" period at the end.

11. When you have to arrive late, go to the bathroom, make a telephone call or leave early, please do so quietly.

12. If there is a particular person you would like to get to know, find an opportunity to talk with her or him outside the meeting room, during or after the meeting. Ask the WE Community organizer to introduce you, if you prefer.

13. After you leave the meeting, spend at least 15 minutes reviewing what happened. Which stories moved you deeply? Do you know

why? Did you find a mirror, model, message bearer or another person who might empower you?

14. Bring a friend, or a guest who is knowledgeable about yoga, body work, dance therapy or another similar discipline, to at least every other meeting.

15. When you receive a WE Community Resource List, identify any person whom you would like to get to know. Call or write to this person, or ask the WE Community organizer to introduce the two of you at the next meeting.

In WE Communities, Men Are Welcome

In contrast with CR groups, WE Communities welcome men. Why? Now that women are aware of our subordination, we are asking, "Where do we go from here?" The answer is, "We need each other—and we need men—to reach our goals and achieve satisfaction in our lives. We cannot do it alone."

Instead of criticizing or excluding men, WE Communities welcome them as partners in a common cause, the empowerment of women. In WE Communities, we have the opportunity to share our unique relationship skills with men. Women and men can work together to design relationships based on empowerment, not power.

Why will men attend? Patriarchy, sexism and injustice in the workplace are costly to men as well as to women. The purpose of WE Communities is to facilitate women and men working together in partnership. In mutually empowering relationships, women use their newly discovered talents and energies to benefit both themselves and men.

In a WE Community, You Learn Partnership Skills

How do you experience mutuality if you don't know what it feels like? What do you do if your parents and grandparents had power-over relationships, and you want something different?

If your parents had a mutual partnership, you have a head start in creating your own. They were your models. A woman in a partnership has usually observed someone else's, usually her parents' or grandparents'. By watching how they became empowered together with each other, she learned how to do the same. As Quincy, the woman who had an exciting mutual partnership with her late husband, observed:

If adults repeat childhood patterns, then partnership in marriage was a very natural pattern for us. Like all children, we both had a list of qualities we didn't like about our parents. But we both chose to replicate the style of our parents' marriages. Although our ethnic backgrounds were very different, each of us came from a very solid marriage where both parents were partners.

Quincy and her husband Joe not only learned about mutuality at an early age but also received support for their partnership later on from both sets of parents. Denise and Dan had neither experience. Nevertheless, they managed to create a strong partnership marriage. They both said that they had learned new relationship skills in the relationships seminar they had attended. I asked them to tell me about their experience. We began:

"What was your parents' marriage like, Denise?"

Denise: They loved each other, but they were a bit too "picky" for my taste. There was always an undercurrent of critical feeling between them.

"Dan, tell me about your parents' marriage."

Dan: "My father's and mother's marriage was very much like our own marriage during the first 7 years. It was very happy on the surface, but there were underlying tensions, which were not being dealt with.

"Did you both make a conscious decision that, if you were going to have a relationship later on, it was going to be different from your parents'?"

Denise: Yes. We played it out, but it didn't work very well. I wanted a harmonious atmosphere, and so did Dan. We didn't want to fight about anything. As a result, there were a lot of unresolved issues, because we thought it was not okay to have arguments.

"Can you be much more honest and open with each other now?"

Denise: Yes. We are honest all the time. We don't hold anything back. And it's okay, because we don't "drag in the kitchen sink" and get to play all the old games we didn't realize we were playing. Now we call each other on them.

"Did you get all of this from the relationships seminar you attended?"

Denise: I would like to say that we worked it out ourselves, but the relationships seminar was really incredibly important to us. For me, it was an opportunity to experience how I felt in certain situations and then to have extremely honest feedback from the people around me.

The relationships seminar was not like going to the marriage counselor, who would say, "You do this" or "You do that." In the seminar, when I would avoid dealing with my feelings, I would remember other times in the past when I did exactly the same thing with Dan. I realized that I was acting the same way in the relationships seminar as I did in real life. So I had to confront what I was doing, and that what I was doing wasn't working.

Dan: In my parents' marriage, it was not okay to argue. It wasn't okay in Denise's parents' marriage either. So when both of us came to a point where we needed to fight, we didn't know the rules. A fight was a threat to our marriage.

One of the things we learned in the relationships seminar was how to fight fairly. Now we know that, when we fight, we don't give up until the issue is resolved. Each of us knows that the other person has the strength to "hang in there." If you are afraid that the other person is going to walk out, then you won't have the confidence to follow the disagreement to its conclusion.

"To many people, your mutual partnership is an unheard-of possibility."

Denise: Early on, it was for us, too. We did not get any preparation—

Dan: —any training for our marriage. We didn't have any models; we didn't know any ground rules; we didn't understand how to express what we were really feeling to each other.

Denise: The minister gave us a few suggestions like, "Just before dinner is a tough time. Help each other out with the kids." But none of his advice really related to where we were then. We were struggling to work out a two-career marriage, and we had no idea that other couples were facing the same problem.

"You were leading your lives almost in a vacuum. You couldn't really knock on your neighbors' doors and ask them, 'How is it for you?'"

Denise: Until we attended the relationships seminar, the only models we had ever had were our parents. We had observed our friends, but only on the surface.

With over 100 people in the room, I started to realize, "A lot of people feel the same way I do." By hearing intimate details about other people's lives. I found myself thinking of new and different possibilities. I would never have thought of solving problems in these ways.

"None of us are presented with more than our parents' lives."

Like most of us, Denise and Dan did not have parents who showed them by example what a partnership marriage was like. Until they took a relationships seminar, they knew only what they saw.

For those people who have not been privileged to observe a mutual partnership, a WE Community offers this opportunity. You will benefit from it if you are ready to let other people show you how to be real, how to listen deeply and how to create mutuality.

If you are in a relationship with someone else, invite her or him to accompany you to a WE Community meeting. Both of you will:

* find out how you really behave in relationships,

- discover what kind of a relationship you really want, and
- learn how couples who are empowered together with each other communicate.

If you and your friend already have a mutual partnership, both of you can share your skills with others. You will be amazed how you can grow—and then show other people the way—once you see the possibilities!

What is "NEW?"

If you are a woman who cares about empowerment, you are invited to join the national Network of Empowered Women (NEW). Its purpose is to educate women about how to maximize their potentials and to facilitate members' sharing their skills, talents, special interests and ongoing projects with each other.

NEW is different from traditional feminist organizations, because its purpose is the well-being of all people. NEW welcomes men, as well as women. NEW welcomes mothers, housepersons, and salaried workers, as well as upwardly mobile career women. Both "men's work" and "women's work," parenting, nurturing and creating warm, loving environments, are celebrated.

As a member of NEW, you will get on the NEW Regional Resource List. A copy of the list will also be mailed to you. It will contain the names, addresses and telephone numbers, along with the professional skills, talents, interests and special projects, of members in your region.

The list can be very useful to you, particularly when you have discovered your calling. For example, if you are starting a women's art gallery, or a mail order business, you want to benefit from the experience of people who have already done it. Your source of assistance is just a letter, or a phone call, away. With modern fax machines, Federal Express and low weekend telephone rates, geography is a technicality when you are seeking information.

By belonging to NEW, you will be able to connect with people in your region who have common professional skills and interests. Your membership in NEW will be your instant introduction to a new teacher. Aware of the dynamics of empowerment, both of you will strive to create a mutual, autonomous and authentic relationship with each other.

Local WE Community Resource Lists are for the use of the members of that WE Community only. If you want to give and receive the benefits of sharing your resources with a regional network, you should join national NEW directly. Your membership in the Network of Empowered Women will be a giant stepping stone toward empowerment.

Empowerment Exercises

1. Join—or Form—a Local Women's Empowerment Community: Now that you have almost finished this book, you know that there is a brand-new way that you, as a woman, can make a difference. Participate in a WE Community. Let other women be your teachers. Be a mentor, model or message-bearer to someone else. You may never know the full extent of your impact.

During the WE Community meeting, observe how people in mutually empowering relationships interact. If you are in a partnership, both of you can make a difference in the lives of others by sharing what you have learned. You can be the models its members were never privileged to have. If you partner is willing, join an existing WE Community. Better yet, set up your own.

2. Become a Member of the National Network of Empowered Women: Join NEW and add your name to its Regional Women's Resource Lists. It is your chance to find a mentor—or to be one.

In infinite ways, an empowered woman can make a difference.

What Lies Ahead?

Empowerment never ends. In our male-oriented society, where we are continually confronting obstacles, we must learn how to turn these obstacles into stepping stones. In this book, I have told you how the empowered women I interviewed have succeeded. As you travel your own unique path, refer to each of the 13 chapters you have just read. Be sure to share this book with a friend. The more we know about empowerment, the better our lives will be.

By creating empowering relationships, can we, as women, change the world? Yes. Empowerment is not just for women alone. Men can become empowered in their relationships when they are willing to accept our values. Members of different ethnic groups can be each other's teachers. Nations, as well as individuals, can be partners. All humankind can live in harmony with Nature.

Women have a mission not only to become empowered but also to see that empowerment spreads throughout the Earth. As Reverend Judith Goode said to me during our interview:

Though things go wrong and injustices continue, women cannot afford to sit back and not act. We must stand up and sing our song.

Stand up with strength. Stand up with compassion. Sing a song that unites all of us in a chorus of human understanding.

If our Planet is to have a future, women's vision of the world—"empowerment together with" instead of "power-over"—must become a reality.

A FINAL NOTE

Just by buying and reading this book, you have crossed a giant stepping stone. I would like to support you in becoming more empowered. If you want to attend my **Empowered Woman**™ Seminar, join the national Network of Empowered Women, organize a local WE Community or share your own personal empowerment story, please write to me c/o the Network of Empowered Women, P. O. Box 22213, Alexandria, Virginia 22304.

I look forward to hearing from you.

POSTCRIPT

Nine days after I finished writing this book, my beautiful, gifted eldest son took his own life. Although I was consumed with shock and grief, I found wisps and shreds of the 200 stories of the empowered women I had interviewed floating through my brain. I particularly remembered the story of Esther, who had also lost her eldest son. During my first free moment, I went back to my notebook to recall exactly what she had told me:

When my son died, I thought that I would just fall apart. I cried a lot, but my mother gave me strength. She said, "Bo's gone. But I know we're going to see him again. He's just waiting for us to come find him."

The day of the funeral, the church was so crowded. You should have seen the people that were there for him. Everybody was just coming and coming and coming. It made me feel stronger to know that Bo had so many friends. Still, I just knew that I was going to act up—you know what I mean? But I didn't. You see, if I had been terrible, everyone around me would not have been able to hold up. I had to be strong for them. My mother was strong for me, so I had to be strong for her—and for my husband and for my children. I really surprised myself! (Her voice gets much louder and higher.) You just don't know what you can do—do you know that? The lows and the highs—you can survive both.

Now, not a day goes by that I don't think about Bo. Every time I look at his picture—or at my granddaughter—I see his face and feel his spirit. For me, Bo's still alive.

Rereading Esther's words gave me enormous comfort. Remembering how Alexandra survived the aftermath of her trauma also inspired me. I became acutely aware of how my family and friends were reaching out to me, just as Esther's and Alexandra's had reached out to them. Every letter, every phone call and every visit that I received gave me renewed strength.

My memories of Bill also empowered me. My relationship with him was the first mutually empowering one I had ever had. Each day of our lives we gave each other joy, friendship and courage. "You can do it, Mom!" was one of Bill's favorite expressions. We shared our love of fruits and vegetables, of good books, of good music and of good friends. But most important, we shared our belief that, by working together, men and women can create kindness, understanding and peace.

Bill is dead now, but his memory will live on forever. Empowered by our deep and abiding mutual love, I will go on with my life's work—to create the more compassionate world that was Bill's greatest dream.

SUGGESTED
READINGS

These books, papers and articles were most helpful to me in my research on feminine empowerment. Most of the books can be bought at your local bookstore. If you do not find what you are looking for, check the latest edition of *Books in Print*. If the book is listed, you may order it either through a full-service bookstore or from the publisher. If the book is not listed, you can probably find it at your local, or university, library. The papers can be purchased through the mail.

1. Empowerment and Power:

The Psychology of Self-Esteem by psychologist Nathaniel Branden (New York, Bantam Books, 1969) is an important book for all women who seek empowerment. Relying on his own personal and clinical experience, he explains in simple language how to respect and believe in yourself. Dr. Branden has also created a set of audiotapes, *The Psychology of High Self-Esteem*. They can be ordered from Nightingale-Conant Corporation, 7300 North Lehigh Avenue, Chicago, Illinois 60648.

In her book, *In a Different Voice* (Cambridge, Massachusetts, Harvard University Press, 1982), psychologist Carol Gilligan explores the different views men and women have about relationships.

Brian Lanker's *I Dream a World: Portraits of Black Women Who Changed America* (New York, Stewart, Tabori & Chang, 1989) is a beautiful, inspiring book of photographs and one-page biographies of empowered black women. All the photographs are worth viewing; read the biographies of the women you find particularly fascinating.

If you want to further understand the difference between male-oriented society and women's view of the world, read *Women's Reality* by psychotherapist Anne Wilson Schaef (New York, Harper & Row, 1981). Although Ms. Schaef uses the terms White Male System and Female System instead, her insights are relevant.

2. Mutuality, Autonomy and Authenticity:

The theory of empowerment through relationships has been developed by psychiatrist Dr. Jean Baker Miller and her colleagues at the Stone Center for Developmental Services and Studies of Wellesley College. Dr. Miller's pioneering book, *Toward a New Psychology of Women*, (second edition, Boston, Beacon Press, 1986) describes in detail how power-over relationships are destructive to women. Her paper, "Women and Power" (Wellesley College, Wellesley, Massachusetts, Stone Center Paper No. 82-01, 1982), further develops the theme of the importance of mutuality.

"The Development of Women's Sense of Self," also written by Dr. Miller (Wellesley College, Wellesley, Massachusetts, Stone Center Paper No. 12, 1984) tells how women are kept from becoming autonomous in relationships because of the demands of male-oriented society to be "independent." In "The Construction of Anger in Women and Men" (Wellesley College, Wellesley, Massachusetts, Stone Center Paper No. 83-01, 1983), Dr. Miller discusses why it is important to express anger authentically.

Dr. Janet Surrey's paper, "Relationship and Empowerment" (Wellesley College, Wellesley, Massachusetts, Stone Center Paper No. 30, 1987) lays the foundation for an alternative way of relating to each other, becoming empowered together with someone else. Her description of a Women's Action for Nuclear Disarmament (WAND) workshop in which she was involved illustrates how a proper balance between autonomy and mutuality develops in relationships

While these papers are written in scholarly language, they are worth plowing through. You can purchase them by mail. Write to the Stone Center for Developmental Services and Studies, Wellesley College, Wellesley Massachusetts 02181, for further information.

3. Empowering Partnerships:

Warren Farrell's *Why Men Are the Way They Are: The Male-Female Dynamic* (New York, McGraw-Hill, 1986) is *the* book on how to get beyond conventional male and female sex roles. Learn how to stop viewing men as "success objects" and start being real with them. If you would prefer to listen to Dr. Farrell talk about his ideas, there is also an audiotape, *Why Men Are the Way They Are.*

Creative Divorce by psychologist Dr. Mel Krantzler (New York, New American Library, 1973) takes the approach that divorce can be a positive, and even an empowering, experience. If you are divorced from your husband, or are thinking about getting a divorce, you should read this book.

Erica Jong's article, "The Perfect Man" (*Playboy*, December 1982, p. 184) is written with tongue in cheek. But it contains an eloquent quote from Nancy Friday and a few interesting insights from the author. Skip the cover and go straight to page 184.

In "What Do We Mean by Relationships?" (Wellesley College, Wellesley, Massachusetts, Stone Center Paper No. 22, 1986), Dr. Jean Baker Miller presents her concept of mutuality in relationships.

Melody Beattie's book, *Codependent No More* (New York, Harper & Row, 1987), and Robin Norwood's book, *Women Who Love Too Much* (New York, Pocket Books, 1985), are the best works on codependency that I have read. Ms. Beattie and Ms. Norwood don't just describe the problem; they present practical ways for women to solve it. If you think that you may be in a codependent, power-over relationship, both of these books are "musts."

Maggie Scarf is a sensitive writer who uses a psychoanalytic approach. In *Intimate Partners: Patterns in Love and Marriage* (New York, Ballantine Books, 1988), she probes deeply into the reasons why some relationships are mutually satisfying, and some are not.

4. Empowering Communication:

Dr. Jean Baker Miller's paper, "What Do We Mean by Relationships?" (Wellesley College, Wellesley, Massachusetts, Stone Center Paper No. 22, 1986) vividly describes what empowering communication is like. Her excellent study of Anne and Beth illustrates her theory.

The late psychologist Dr. Carl Rogers is really the "father" of empowering communication. Read Chapter 17 of his book, *On Becoming a Person* (Boston, Houghton Mifflin, 1961), very carefully.

5. Old Myths and New Realities:

If you want to check out a few of the old myths, read Colette Dowling's *Perfect Women* (New York, Simon and Schuster, 1988) and *The Cinderella Complex* (New York, Pocket Books, 1981). Also take a look at psychologist Penelope Russianoff's *When Am I Going to Be Happy?* (New York, Bantam Books, 1988) and *Why Do I Think I Am Nothing Without a Man?* (New York, Bantam Books, 1983).

In her article, "Careers and Kids" (*Ms.* Magazine, May 1988, p. 62), Edith Fierst advocates taking time out to have a family and working part-time while the children are growing up. Ms. Fierst documents her position with material she gathered from a questionnaire she circulated. Her article is definitely worth reading.

Mary C. Hickey's article, "Mothers in Law: The Dilemma of 'Having It All'" (*The Washington Lawyer*, Volume 2, Number 5, May/June 1988, p. 38), describes how women lawyers who try to "have it all" end up having nothing. Although her reporting is definitely biased, she makes a strong case.

If you still believe in trying to "have it all," read Carol Orsborn's book, *Enough Is Enough; You Don't Have to Be Perfect* (New York, Pocket Books, 1986). It should cure you, once and for all. She speaks from the heart—and from experience—because she's "been there."

6. Self-Discovery:

Robert Fritz's book, *The Path of Least Resistance: Learning to Be the Creative Force in Your Own Life* (New York, Fawcett Columbine, 1989), tells you how to stop "solving problems" and start looking at yourself at a deeper level. The author offers his own fascinating insights about how you can create a song, a work of art, a business or the life you want.

In *Focusing* (second edition, New York, Bantam Books, 1981), psychologist Dr. Eugene T. Gendlin goes beyond the mind to the body as the source of our most important information about ourselves. The focusing technique is explained simply, and in minute detail. By reading this book, you can learn to understand the messages that your body sends you.

You Can Heal Your Life by Louise Hay (Santa Monica, California, Hay House, 1984) is one of those rare books that actually delivers what it promises. Under Ms. Hay's expert guidance, you confront the forces that keep you from fulfilling yourself and then make positive affirmations to move forward in your chosen direction. If you want to go even further, there are other books, audiotapes and a workbook by Louise Hay that you can order directly from Hay House, P. O. Box 2212, Santa Monica, California 90406.

Henrik Ibsen's classic play "A Doll's House," which can be found in *Ibsen: Four Major Plays*, Volume I, translated by Rolf Fjelde (New York, New American Library, 1965) describes the struggle of a 19th-century Norwegian woman to find herself. As you read it, see if you identify with Nora.

Dr. Ira Progoff's *At a Journal Workshop* (New York, Dialogue House Library, 1975) is the classic book about journal writing as a tool for discovering your self. His Intensive Journal™ method of self-analysis is very helpful, particularly during a time of transition. To purchase the book, or to participate in a journal-writing workshop, write to Dialogue House, 80 East Eleventh Street, New York, New York 10002.

Virginia Satir's *Self-Esteem* (Berkeley, California, Celestial Arts, 1975) is a beautifully illustrated long poem about what it means to a woman to have a self.

Be sure to take a look at *Passages,* by Gail Sheehy (New York, Bantam Books, 1977). This best-selling book describes how a woman's identity unfolds during the different stages of her life. How fascinating it is to see yourself in the perspective of time!

Wishcraft by Barbara Sher (New York, Ballantine Books, 1979) tells you how to get what you want, after you know what it is.

In their paper, "From Depression to Sadness in Women's Psychotherapy" (Wellesley College, Wellesley, Massachusetts, The Stone Center, Paper No. 36, 1988), Dr. Irene P. Stiver and Dr. Jean Baker Miller write about how depression is a barrier to self-discovery. They also offer their own suggestions about how depression can be overcome.

7. Empowerment in the Workplace:

Dr. Matina S. Horner, former President of Harvard's Radcliffe College, has written a pioneering article, "Toward an Understanding of Achievement-Related Conflicts in Women," (*Journal of Social Issues,* Volume 28, 1972, p. 157). It is the definitive work on why women don't achieve in our male-oriented society. Although Dr. Horner focuses primarily on academic achievement, her article is still worth reading.

In her controversial article, "Management Women and the New Facts of Life," (*Harvard Business Review,* Volume 67, January-February 1989, p. 65) Felice N. Schwartz presents the notion of two job paths for women: the Total Career Track and the "Mommy Track." Look at the article and then come to your own conclusion.

To find out more about why, and how, to find your calling, read Marsha Sinetar's book, *Do What You Love; The Money Will Follow: Discovering Your Right Livelihood* (New York, Paulist Press, 1987). It gave me the inspiration to press on with writing this book.

Further reading is sparse. There are many books on power in the workplace, but not many on empowerment. Hopefully, there will be soon.

8. Sexual Empowerment:

Whether you are heterosexual, bisexual or lesbian, you will find valuable information in *For Each Other: Sharing Sexual Intimacy* (New

York, New American Library, 1982). The author, Dr. Lonnie Barbach, is a sex therapist.

In *Man Sharing: Dilemma or Choice?* (New York, William Morrow, 1986), Audrey B. Chapman gives you an idea of just how far a sexually empowered woman can go. Her book may shock you—or delight you. In any case, it is worth reading.

Woman and Love: A Cultural Revolution in Progress, by Shere Hite (New York, Alfred A. Knopf, 1986) is an encyclopedic study of the relationship between sex and love for women. You don't have to read the whole thing, just the parts that interest you.

An empowered woman is usually sensuous. Read *The Sensuous Woman* by "J" (New York, Dell Publishing Company, 1971) to find out what it means to be a sensuous woman and how you can become one.

9. The "New" Femininity:

Because the "new" femininity is new, there is not much literature on it. For comparison, you might read Dr. Toni Grant's *Being a Woman: Fulfilling Your Femininity and Finding Love* (New York, Random House, 1988), to learn what femininity is not.

10. Feminism and Empowerment:

The Sisterhood by Marcia Cohen (New York, Simon and Schuster, 1988) tells the stories of four very different leaders of the modern feminist movement: Betty Friedan, Gloria Steinem, Germaine Greer and Kate Millett. Although the book reads like a novel, it is actually a history.

Betty Friedan's classic, *The Feminine Mystique,* (Middlesex, England, Penguin Books, 1963) is considered by many to be the "bible" of the modern feminist movement. In this well-researched study, Ms. Friedan shows you how feminism can help you discover yourself.

Robin Morgan's *Sisterhood is Powerful: An Anthology of Writings from the Women's Liberation Movement* (New York, Random House, 1970) is the most eloquent collection of feminist essays and poems I have ever read. Even if you are not a feminist, you cannot help but gain a deeper appreciation of these women's beliefs and struggles when you read this book.

11. Modeling, Mirroring and Others Ways to Become Empowered:

A New Approach to Women and Therapy (New York, McGraw-Hill, 1983) is a fascinating book written by feminist therapist, Miriam

Greenspan. It focuses on how women can benefit from a therapist who uses skilled self-disclosure rather than hiding herself.

In *Giving Away Success: Why Women "Get Stuck" and What to Do about It* (New York, McGraw-Hill, 1984), Susan Schenkel presents a practical program for women to empower themselves based on behaviorist psychology. Hers is different from mine; you may want to compare the two.

As of now, there are few other quality books for the lay reader on this subject.

12. Empowering a Daughter:

Kim Chernin's *The Hungry Self: Women, Eating, and Identity* (New York, Times Books, 1985) is an excellently written book. If you or your daughter has an eating problem, this book can help you understand its causes—and what you can do about it.

While you may not agree with everything that Letty Cottin Pogrebin writes in *Growing Up Free* (New York, Bantam Books, 1981), you should definitely glance through it. Like a cookbook, it contains many recipes. Choose the ones that will work for you and your daughter.

13. Women's Empowerment (WE) Communities:

Although there is not yet any literature on Women's Empowerment Communities besides this book. Carl Rogers has laid their foundation. His book, *Carl Rogers on Personal Power* (New York, Delacorte Press, 1977), describes the benefits of empowerment communities for both men and women.

For information about The La Jolla Program, a 2-week empowerment community for both men and women, write to: Dr. Bruce Meador, Director, The La Jolla Program, Center for Studies of the Person, 1125 Torrey Pines Road, La Jolla, California 92037. The La Jolla Program is administered by the Center for Studies of the Person, an organization that was founded by Dr. Rogers.

INDEX